Education, the Anthropocene, and Deleuze/Guattari

Researching Environmental Learning

Series Editor

David B. Zandvliet (*Simon Fraser University, Canada*)

VOLUME 5

The titles published in this series are listed at *brill.com/rele*

Education, the Anthropocene, and Deleuze/Guattari

By

David R. Cole

Foreword by Will Steffen

BRILL

LEIDEN | BOSTON

Cover illustration: Image by Tatiana Plakhova (complexitygraphics.com)

All chapters in this book have undergone peer review.

The Library of Congress Cataloging-in-Publication Data is available online at https://catalog.loc.gov

Typeface for the Latin, Greek, and Cyrillic scripts: "Brill". See and download: brill.com/brill-typeface.

ISSN 2542-9639
ISBN 978-90-04-50595-7 (paperback)
ISBN 978-90-04-50596-4 (hardback)
ISBN 978-90-04-50597-1 (e-book)

Copyright 2022 by Koninklijke Brill NV, Leiden, The Netherlands.
Koninklijke Brill NV incorporates the imprints Brill, Brill Nijhoff, Brill Hotei, Brill Schöningh, Brill Fink, Brill mentis, Vandenhoeck & Ruprecht, Böhlau Verlag and V&R Unipress.
All rights reserved. No part of this publication may be reproduced, translated, stored in a retrieval system, or transmitted in any form or by any means, electronic, mechanical, photocopying, recording or otherwise, without prior written permission from the publisher. Requests for re-use and/or translations must be addressed to Koninklijke Brill NV via brill.com or copyright.com.

This book is printed on acid-free paper and produced in a sustainable manner.

Advance Praise for
Education, the Anthropocene, and Deleuze/Guattari

"Anyone still in doubt about the political and ethical significance of environmental education needs to read David R. Cole's exceptional *Education, the Anthropocene, and Deleuze/Guattari*. Cole demonstrates with perfect clarity and keen detail how a radical rethinking about the environment rests with also rethinking educational praxis by understanding unconscious drives and desires that perpetuate the Anthropocene and which complicate traditional educational efforts. This is a remarkable and incisive book, that captures the contemporary moment eloquently, and also provides readers with an outstanding website full of contributions and resources from interdisciplinary researchers engaged in rethinking the Anthropocentric moment."
– **P. Taylor Webb, Associate Professor, Faculty of Education, The University of British Columbia**

"David R. Cole's new book provides a critical reading of education, through the matrix of Deleuze/Guattari theory, examining the problem of the future and how we might escape the Anthropocene, to find what Guattari called 'the joy of living'. An optimistic and positive view based on the idea that we can change."
– **Michael A. Peters, Distinguished Professor, Faculty of Education, Beijing Normal University**

"While collective human-more-than-human earthly entities are paused in a temporal limbo of precarity; education needs room to breathe. The speculative and gestural possibilities for living within a new mode of humanity depend on it. The planet deserves it. This book by David R. Cole finds new spaces, a place to inhale, as he invites a host of others onto a stage we humans thought we occupied alone."
– **Karen Malone, Professor of Education, Director of Research, Swinburne University, Melbourne**

"Cole's original and unique book directly speaks to those educators seeking to escape the nightmare of the Anthropocene. It offers an incisive, Deleuze-Guattarian analysis of dominant, yet barely acknowledged drivers of the Anthropocene, and follows these through to stimulating expositions of new ways of learning, teaching and doing pedagogy. In doing so, it offers alternative understandings of how we could practice education that can provide escape routes from the Anthropocene that are not about escapism. It does this in a no-nonsense, hard-hitting style that is entirely appropriate to the urgency of the overwhelming planetary crisis. The book is thus also a demonstration of how

to produce original and significant knowledge in ways that can help rejuvenate and re-imagine transformative practices for education. It is a must-read for anyone interested in combining contemporary theory, research and educational practice in ways that can usher in utopian futures."
– **Esther Priyadharshini, Associate Professor in Education, University of East Anglia, UK**

"A brilliant and incredibly timely book. Cole not only provides an original analysis of the trends that have led to our contemporary crises, but more importantly, he shows how Deleuze and Guattari's work can provide a model for 'thinking and learning differently' in the Anthropocene."
– **Daniel W. Smith, Professor of Philosophy, Department of Philosophy, Purdue University, USA**

"In this erudite and carefully crafted conceptual book, with many entry and exit points, David R. Cole challenges the reader to think how education and educational practice can enact a feasible way out from the effects of end-of-world narratives and provide an escape from the entrapment of the Anthropocene."
– **Juan Francisco Salazar Sutil, Professor of Anthropology, Institute of Culture and Society, Western Sydney University**

"Congratulations to David R. Cole for producing a much needed and timely contribution in response to a key question of our time: What does it mean to be learning in the Anthropocene? While reading this book, I was reminded of an assertion by Albert Einstein in a letter, dated 21 March 1955, written four weeks before his death, that 'the separation between past, present and future has only the importance of an admittedly tenacious illusion'. The past is still with us and the future is within us, but we live in the now. We cannot undo the past through linear extrapolation from what went wrong to an idealized future that will save us from perishing in the sixth mass extinction. What we can and must do – and keep doing – is, according to Cole, 'to try and figure out the patterns, tendencies, rhythms, repetitions, forces, and drives that have ... gone to make up the present'. Non-linear analysis of the drives that throughout human history have brought us the Anthropocene allows us to continually reinvent the now as an expanded time dimension and elucidate practices and opportunities for learning in the Anthropocene. One seldom comes across a book that, right from the beginning, is at the same time intoxicating to read but also impossible to put down as soon as one has started reading. With every page one reads and – if not immediately grasped, rereads – one becomes more and more convinced that there is a treasure hidden within, but that it takes hard work to dig it up."
– **Jan Visser, President & Sr. Researcher, Learning Development Institute, Professor Extraordinary, University of Stellenbosch, South Africa**

Contents

Foreword IX
Will Steffen
Preface XI
Acknowledgements XII
List of Figures and Tables XIII

1 **Overview: The Problem of the Future** 1
   1   Introduction 1
   2   What Is the Position of the Future? 2
   3   Why 'Deleuze/Guattari'? – An Analysis 7
   4   Education, Social Change, and the Future 12
   5   The Future of the Anthropocene 16

2 **Tool-Enhancement** 21
   1   Introduction 21
   2   Prehistory 22
   3   The Beginnings of Civilisation: Agriculture 24
   4   Metallurgy 27
   5   Global Trade 31
   6   World Machine 37

3 **Carbon Trail** 41
   1   Introduction 41
   2   The Discovery of Fire 42
   3   Fire, Light, and Society 44
   4   The 'Energy-Life' Threshold 47
   5   Furnaces, Mining, and Individual Energy Exchange 49
   6   Steam Engines 52
   7   Fossil Fuel Capitalism 56

4 **The Phallocene** 61
   1   Introduction 61
   2   The Phallic God-Heads 62
   3   One Phallus-God 64
   4   Establishment of Phallus-Worship 67
   5   The Working Phallic-Week 71
   6   Digital Phallic-Endeavour 75

5 Atomic-Time 82
1. Introduction 82
2. A Universe of Atoms 83
3. Atomic Theory 87
4. Electricity 90
5. Quantum Mechanics 93
6. The Atomic Bomb 96

6 Teaching and Learning Differently in the Anthropocene 103
1. Introduction 103
2. Attending to the 'Forces of Control' at the Local Level 104
3. A Global Thinking Matrix 109
4. What Is Pedagogy of/in the Anthropocene? 118

7 Incremental Movements towards a New Society 121
1. Introduction 121
2. The Great Leap Forward – A Green Utopia? 123
3. Changing Society at the Micro-Level 127
4. How Can the Minor Societal Changes Be Augmented? 132

8 Conclusion: The Double Bind 138
1. Introduction 138
2. What Is the Double Bind? 139
3. The Double Bind of the Future 142
4. The Role of Politics in the Double Bind 144
5. Realism and 'Fabulation'... 147
6. This Is the End of the 'End-Times' 150

References 155
Index 178

Foreword

There is already a vast amount of literature on the Anthropocene, and more is being written every day. But this book by David R. Cole – *Education, the Anthropocene and Deleuze/Guattari* – takes a very fresh and innovative look into the concept and the reality of the Anthropocene, challenging us to think more deeply about what the Anthropocene really means and how we might respond to it. The work definitely breaks new ground, arguing strongly for the central role of education in dealing with this unprecedented challenge to humanity.

The book is a deep dive into what it will take to change the course of the Anthropocene. To meet this challenge, we must first understand what the Anthropocene actually is. To those scholars in the natural sciences, the Anthropocene is both a proposed new epoch in the 4.5 billion year Geologic Time Scale that charts the course of the planet's history, and it is also defined as a new state of the Earth System, arising from vast and rapid changes to the structure and functioning of the contemporary planetary life support system. But Cole has more innovative ways of conceptualising what the Anthropocene is.

Perhaps the most confronting of these new conceptualisations is the Anthropocene as a 'singularity'. That is, the Anthropocene bends the space-time relationship by fusing the future with the present and past. That is, the Anthropocene is simultaneously a product of the many forces and contingencies of our past but, at the same time, an accelerating rush into a very risky and potentially catastrophic future. It crushes time – past and future – into a very dynamic present that poses massive challenges for humanity in the here and now.

Despite the many different interpretations of the Anthropocene in the literature, a few common threads are also present in this work. This new epoch challenges deep-seated beliefs and current political and economic systems to the core, exposing the types of thinking and acting that are accelerating the current course of the Anthropocene towards a possible collapse of contemporary society. This work also deals with the fundamental drivers of this new, dangerous epoch and takes a systems-oriented approach to dealing with them.

Like many analyses of the Anthropocene, this book has fossil fuels and capitalism clearly in its sights. However, in contrast to the large number of analyses that propose changes in technologies and governance systems as the key to surviving the Anthropocene, David R. Cole focuses more deeply on what we think, value and believe, with education at the centre of the approach, describing education as an 'escape route' out of the trap that the Anthropocene represents.

This new form of education must deal with a time in which the future is wildly unpredictable and is rapidly closing in on the present – the so-called 'Great Acceleration'. What should such a form of education look like? This book takes us on a tour through this new educational approach. It is about what we want our future to be – how can we navigate and steer the Anthropocene into a future in which our children can not only survive but thrive. This requires new ways of thinking and doing, and a major overhaul of our education system.

In short, this book is a stimulating journey into the possible trajectories of the Anthropocene, and the critical choices that we must make to steer the trajectory to a safe landing. To quote the introductory chapter, the book attacks the Anthropocene challenge with a synthesis "... wherein the future ruptures the present, time is manipulated to create an enlarged 'now' that provokes potential co-evolution as education and social change."

In the 21st century, the Anthropocene has become a prominent narrative, not only in academia but in societies around the globe. This book provides a unique and thought-provoking view into the Anthropocene, and promotes the role of education in tackling the most fundamental question that humanity now faces: where on Earth are we going?

Will Steffen
Emeritus Professor, The Australian National University, Canberra

Preface

This book came about as an intersection between two events. The first was a public gathering that I organised called 'Dark Horizons' in April 2017 with Andrew Culp and Bogna M. Konior at the New School in New York. I wrote a paper for this evening called: 'Black Sun: The singularity at the heart of the Anthropocene'. In this piece, I envisaged the architecture and structure of this book, without filling out the evidence and relations to education and social change that we find in these pages. Further, in May 2017, as a guest of the Center for Values in Medicine, Science and Technology, in the University of Texas at Dallas, I listened to a speech by the author Kim Stanley Robinson, who spoke about the Anthropocene, and inspired me to initiate the Institute for Interdisciplinary Research into the Anthropocene (https://iiraorg.com/).

Since that time, the web site has acted as a means to enable interdisciplinary research with respect to the Anthropocene. This book presents the research and findings of the Institute, as one combined argument. This argument is a step towards the new art of living as suggested below by Félix Guattari:

> We cannot conceive of solutions to the poisoning of the atmosphere and to global warming due to the greenhouse effect, or to the problem of population control, without a mutation of mentality, without promoting a new art of living in society. (Guattari, 1992/1995, 2)

Acknowledgements

At the outset of thinking about this book, I was part of a research centre, the Centre for Educational Research at Western Sydney, led by Professor Margaret Somerville. Margaret encouraged us to think broadly about contemporary educational issues, and to achieve this, we were organised under the themes of equity, globalisation and sustainability. As such, this book owes much to the thought and research processes that transpired as part of the Centre for Educational Research, Western Sydney University, 2012–2016.

I would like to thank Jan Visser of the Learning Development Institute (LDI) for discussing important issues regarding education and the Anthropocene. I have also been inspired by David Christian of the Big History Institute at Macquarie University and his approach to the Anthropocene. Additionally, I had initial communication with Alain Gras of the Sorbonne and Karen Malone of Swinburne University, Melbourne, at the beginning of organising the: Institute of Interdisciplinary Research into the Anthropocene.

> **Special Note**
>
> This book does not tell you what to do. Rather, it provides an original analysis, from which pedagogy, teaching and learning, and powerful units of work may be built. The purpose of this method is to move environmental education from the periphery to the centre of the curriculum. This book follows a Deleuze/Guattari (1984, 1988) heterodox method, that evolves educational action from an analysis of the unconscious drives of the Anthropocene. User end, context-based, educational episodes may be viewed through contributions hosted at https://iiraorg.com/education-the-anthropocene-and-deleuze-guattari/

Figures and Tables

Figures

1.1 Graphical representation of an OODA cycle in autopoietic cognition (© Hall 2011, used with permission). 4
1.2 The 4-zone material cloud analysis of the Anthropocene. First presented at 'Dark Horizons' the New School (New York) on 20/4/2017 (© Cole 2020). 15
4.1 From deterritorialisation to fossilisation (from Falb 2020, used with permission). 80
5.1 The view of Earth with electrical lights. Source: Wikimedia Commons licence: https://commons.wikimedia.org/wiki/File:Earth%27s_City_Lights_by_DMSP,_1994-1995_(large).jpg. 92
5.2 Illustration of the atomic bomb taken from manga comic Akira (1993). Source: AKIRA / アキラ by Katsuhiro Otomo. 100
6.1 Global thinking in the Anthropocene: 'Citizen, economy, technology, environment and flow' (© Cole 2020). 110
6.2 Global thinking in the Anthropocene: 'Citizen', 'economy', 'technology', 'environment' and 'flow', as a plane superimposed on: 'Tool-enhancement', 'Carbon trail', 'the phallocene' and 'Atomic-time' as four conical spirals (© Cole and Baghi 2021). 111

Tables

2.1 The pedagogy of tool-enhancement. 40
3.1 The pedagogy of the carbon trail. 60
4.1 The pedagogy of the phallocene. 81
5.1 The pedagogy of atomic time. 102

CHAPTER 1

Overview: The Problem of the Future

> I am all the names of history.
> NIETZSCHE (1889)

∴

1   Introduction

As I write these words, one might say without fear of contradiction, that 2020 has already been a calamitous year. At the start of January, Australia saw the worst bushfires in its history, raging through 18 million hectares of forest, killing over a billion animals, 33 humans directly, and 450 other people since that time, due to the effects of smoke inhalation (Pickrell 2020). After this disaster, caused by global warming, the COVID-19 pandemic has created new, turbulent, and unpredictable conditions for humans to survive and sustain. As I begin this introduction to the book in June 2020, the US is experiencing an implosion of civil unrest, sparked by the murder of George Floyd, mass unemployment, and the continued spread and death of the virus COVID-19. In sum, I would like to bracket all such events, and stipulate that they are happening in the Anthropocene, a new geological era heralded in by the action of humans on the planet Earth (Crutzen 2002). Clearly, the Anthropocene designates a time of significant change, brought on by previous historic tendencies, movements, and human actions that are flowing through us, in and as the Anthropocene, and whose drives will be analysed in detail in Chapters 2 to 5. This book stipulates that the only feasible way out from the effects of these drives is through education, and even though a dedicated chapter has been designed to further explicate these escape routes (Chapter 6), the whole of this book, and every word or figure in it, aims towards this escape from the entrapment of the Anthropocene (Clark 2015). As such, this is not a positivist approach to education; i.e., that simply expounds on pedagogy with evidence, but progressively builds a conceptual framework through the chapters that follow, into which real teaching and learning events flow through engagement with the ideas. In sum, this book: (1) Equates the future with the Anthropocene to create a new time dimension, or expanded 'now' (N), into which educational practice may be built (Chapter 1); (2) Analyses the four drives of the Anthropocene through a nonlinear history to create opportunities for pedagogy that subverts these drives, Nx (Chapters 2–5); (3) Explicates these opportunities (Nx) at the local level, and works globally through a thinking matrix (Figure 6.2) (Chapter 6); (4) Applies the resulting educational practice to social change (Chapter 7) and the double bind (Chapter 8).

We are born into history, at a certain date, and with a specific lifespan. However, this statement immediately ties up time with its measurement. In contrast, the problem of the future (and hence of the Anthropocene) concerns the nature of time itself, and not only how we measure it (Smith 2019). One could state that time is more complex and inter-laced than the potentially segmented and regular measurement of time. Hence, the problem of the future is a function of understanding these complexities, and, of separating the measurement of time from time itself. We cannot simply measure future time, all that we can do is to try and figure out the patterns, tendencies, rhythms, repetitions, forces, and drives that have through history gone to make up the present, and work out which of these waves are more likely to continue and/or amplify, and which of these will cease and/or diminish. This is what this book will attempt to do with respect to the Anthropocene, and how education can make a difference given this scenario (Le Grange 2019). Pertinently, the past is over, the mistakes and travesties of history are finished, and even though, for example, one might object to the environmental and ecological damage that has been furnished by the people on the Earth through time (cf., Wakefield 2018); tellingly, this sentiment does not change the reality in which we find ourselves. The intent of this book is to move beyond such sentiment, to deal with the real drives and forces that have created the Anthropocene, and to look for potential escape routes and ways out of the certainty of mutually assured destruction, named as 'the sixth great extinction event'. These escape routes, understood as education (beyond any limiting designation), are to be found in the continual reinvention of the 'now' (N) in this text, and, as such, is positioned to take hold of how the future assails us as the Anthropocene, and has been created by the human drives through history (Nx).

2   What Is the Position of the Future?

This book takes into account a substantial time range in Chapters 2 to 5, by presenting over two million years of hominin 'tool-enhancement', and on top of this tool evolution, builds the 'carbon trail', 'phallocene', and 'atomic-time' (these concepts will be explained further in their respective chapters). The point of this construction is to understand how to escape these drives through education as a continually recreated time dimension of 'now' (N). For most of this time span, humans have had an ability to apprehend time, and have consequently lived almost entirely in time, by observing the patterns and rhythms that pass through time, and by acting according to them. One might say that it is only in approximately the last 3500 years that humans have had the means to measure time, and since the specific invention of the sundial in Egypt and Babylon (Rohr 2012). It is the contention of this book that even though the measurement of time, and a mechanised view of time have come to dominate consciousness, due to the associations between time, labour, capital and power, there are deeper rhythms and cycles in time, that bring us closer to the nature of time itself, and that can untangle us from a straightforward and regulated view of 'clock time', that is unhelpful with respect to understanding the future of the Anthropocene, and how to escape it via education. One way to begin this untangling of time from its measurement is to posit the OODA cycle, which is stands for: Observation, Orientation, Decision, Action, as theorised by Boyd (1996), see Figure 1.1. The OODA cycle shows how a cognitive function may start in the past and carry forward into the future as a wave pattern, and that can be repeated as such in the future. The average or middle value of the OODA cycle is the expected future (X), but in Anthropocenic times of non-linear climate change, positive feedback loops, and temporal convergences and divergences (Figure 1.1); the certainty of the expected future is in doubt. Indeed, one would anticipate a stochastic future (Figure 1.1), as climate change ramps up, with many divergences from any projected present mount up, and these futures are more likely to occur the deeper we proceed into the Anthropocene, as the non-linear and feedback effects of the human-made epoch become apparent. As Figure 1.1 shows, calendar time will continue, yet at the same time, the future will become more unpredictable, as the Anthropocene unfolds, and the influence of human-produced divergence as global warming intensifies (the result of the four entwined human drives, Chapters 2–5).

As we can see through this diagram (Figure 1.1), the future is knowable, but open to contingency, perturbation and divergence, depending upon factors that will change what we expect with respect to tomorrow today (this is the learning complex of now, N, in time, that this book attempts to create). In the specific terms of the Anthropocene, one of the most prominent factors in this stochastic future, and hence motor of change of divergent futures, is the ubiquitous release of carbon dioxide due to the burning of fossil fuels, along with multiple other human produced pollutants, as has been recorded and labelled as the 'great acceleration' since 1945 (Steffen et al. 2015). One might suggest that the 'great acceleration' since the end of the Second World War,

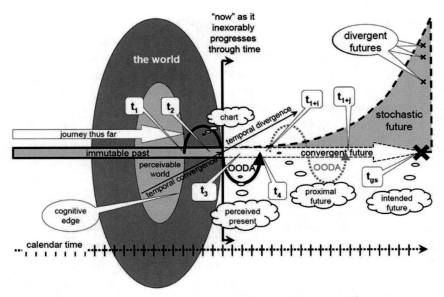

FIGURE 1.1   Graphical representation of an OODA cycle in autopoietic cognition (© Hall 2011, used with permission)[1]

has seen an unprecedented meshing and enhanced functioning of integrated world machines, driven by commerce and powerful concerns, as will be seen in particular in Chapters 2, 3 and 5. As these actions and connections have taken place, our relationships with the future have been progressively brought forward and buckled, as the future is at once closer to us through our enhanced technologies and machines, and yet productive of more potentially divergent futures, as suggested by Figure 1.1. In sum, the great acceleration could be seen as a mode of 'heating up' of the world through the combinations of world machines, or thermodynamics, that brings into play an early statement by Nick Land (1995: 133) about commentaries on Deleuze/Guattari:

> Since the history of thermodynamics is the history of technicizing commerce – of modernising machines – any account that autonomizes science inevitably moralises social change (into political theatre), or allows moralization to persist unperturbed, and this is a trap to which most writers are at least sometimes snared

Hence, following this quote, the fundamental problem of the future, and that this book addresses with respect to the Anthropocene and education, concerns this moralisation of the future, into, and as a projection of what we want the world to be, and would like it to become according to our human wishes and desires (cf., Chapter 7). Most of us can imagine a better future, one in which humans have paid heed to the warnings of science, and have used current and innovative technological solutions to arrest climate change, to stabilise the environment to a liveable median, through which we can survive and flourish, as happened for much of the Holocene (cf., Gupta 2004). Such a median point is represented in Figure 1.1 by the intended future, and the cross (X). However, to reach this median point in the future of a stabilised climate, the words, figures and facts of science have to be translated into social action and behaviours with global impacts, and, significantly, without the frequently negative mediations of politics, human nature (e.g., greed, lies and ego), and the consequent societal values and needs that currently drive, and have primarily driven human society and social change throughout history (Chakrabarty 2009); for example, having the desire to live an advanced, consumptive, and high-energy lifestyle. At the present time, it could be objectively stated that we are more likely to head towards the stochastic future of Figure 1.1, and the enhancement of climate chaos, than the median point, that most of us would most likely wish to achieve, yet may wonder how we can get there, given the facts of history and our shared human nature and drives (Chapters 2–5). In sum, this book veers from giving a moralistic or schadenfreude account of this differential between what we want, and what is likely to happen in the Anthropocene, but genuinely attempts to realign the drives and creation of climate chaos through education (N) and consequently as social change (Chapters 6 and 7, and through the dates of Chapters 2–5, as breakout points or plateaux (Nx)). Clearly, this resolution is a necessarily complex and many layered business, but, as is speculated in this book, it is collectively our best chance of success.

This writing presents a many layered analysis, – we live 'with' the future, as an ever present and changing reality, that has been named (by us) as the Anthropocene (Rigby 2009), and that is based on the science of climate change, and the movements in human history that have produced it, for example, accelerated, global, carbon dioxide emitting technological-social development. The future is unresolved, yet the drives that have created it have produced non-linear and comprehensible patterns and rhythms through history, and that shall be specifically explored in Chapters 2–5, and, in total, may be understood as an educational complex of now (N), to be changed (by us) through teaching and learning. The issue of the future as determinate or otherwise, comes to us in and as the Anthropocene, resolves itself or presents (partial and momentary solutions), disappears, and then comes back, like so many other rhythms, patterns, ideas, flows and projections that we will attend to in the unfolding of this book like multiple, inter-linked OODA cycles (Figure 1.1). The point here is that even though the immutable past gives rise to the thought-projection that the future of climate change as catastrophe is unavoidable, and includes a myriad of highly disruptive and chaos-inducing planetary fluctuations, such as widespread fires, increased drought, hurricanes, typhoons, cyclones and severe floods; the set up and analysis of this book, is that the future is exactly constituted by these fluctuations and perturbations, and not their diminishing through a normative, moralistic or human-only-centred foci (Haraway 2015). In other words, the future is already with us through these rhythms and fluctuations, the problem lies in recognising these patterns, and adjusting our drives accordingly as a reinvented education (N).

In brief, the speculative and analytic thought posited by this book, and the empirical reality that we live in, have to be aligned and superimposed, with respect to imagining how to achieve a mode of multiple emergence, or escape routes from the current state of convergence between climate change, human activity, and disaster: as education. To illustrate this point, two of the most prominent thinkers in the field take alternative paths out of the Anthropocene, that require different thinking mechanisms and apparatuses to be successful. Bernard Stiegler (2018) envisages the Anthropocene as the 'Neganthropocene', a deliberately dark and provocative description of this human produced environmental reality. Stiegler (2018) concentrates on the convergence in technics and control that are present in one world capitalism, in terms of which, for example, we are becoming more and more likely to be bound up and dissected through our relations with digital technologies, that are programmed to be increasingly invasive and productive of submissive, consumerist, pro-capitalist identities. Stiegler (2018) supposes that we have to break out from these subjectively induced worldviews, that are increasingly augmented and targeted by and through technology, to make any difference in the Anthropocene. In contrast, Bruno Latour (2017) figures a connection between the gamut of different sciences that are recording and examining the effects of the Anthropocene, such as environmental science, oceanography, geology, biology, chemistry and physics, with the politics and governance of the situation. In recognising that the permissible level of carbon dioxide to be released into the atmosphere was passed in 1990, it could be said that we have been hopelessly scrambling to limit emissions ever since, through numerous failed international climate agreements (cf., National Research Council [NRC] 2010). Latour (2017) imagines stronger, and more environmentally attuned political governance, that will put in place measures that will effectively deal with climate change, and return the path of humanity to a sustainable route. He imagines enhanced collective political agency, that properly takes into account the science of climate change, and that destabilises humanity's sense of entitlement and domination of natural systems. In a sense, both Stiegler (2018) and Latour (2017) imagine political and social revolution in the light of climate catastrophe, with Stiegler in line with Marxist calls to attend to the general capitalist economy, its control functions, and the way it is maintained and produced through technology to effect change in the Anthropocene, whilst Latour envisages a naturalisation of consciousness, whereby we adjust our lives to the ecological patterns and forces of the Earth. Regarding this book, the specific position with respect to the future is a Deleuze/Guattari (1972/1984, 1980/1988) philosophical nexus, and from this synthesis, wherein the future ruptures the present, time is manipulated to create an enlarged now (Nx), that provokes potential eco-revolution as education and social change (Chapters 6 and 7).

3   Why 'Deleuze/Guattari'? – An Analysis

Deleuze was a philosopher, dedicated to producing a minor philosophy (Deleuze and Guattari 1975/1986), that attends to the gaps, false starts, and irruption points in western philosophy. His aim was not to oppose western philosophy in a dialectical fashion, but to fashion another philosophy from within, that brings us closer to a 'new science of thought', that is unhinged and separate from the prejudices, assumptions, and ways in which thought can be pinned down, controlled, and turned into a manufactured and complicit propaganda machine by dominating powers and interested parties (cf., Patton 2000). Guattari was a militant, practicing anti-psychiatrist at La Borde institute outside of Paris, that became a hub for radical and expressive thought from the 1950s onwards (Guattari 1995/2009). Guattari was concerned with the practical and real outcomes of thought, and wanted to put his ideas into action to help change the world, and move society towards revolution. As a combined writing/author team, Deleuze/Guattari (as used in this work) produced a 'cause célèbre' in the book *Anti-Oedipus* that was published in 1972, but was associated with the May '68 student uprising in Paris (cf., Starr 1995). They followed the publication of *Anti-Oedipus* with the second volume of Capitalism and Schizophrenia called *1000 Plateaus*, that was less well received, but gives them a formidable oeuvre to work with. These two books are not directly about the environment, or ecology (even though *1000 Plateaus* includes the significant influence of Gregory Bateson's (1972/2000) *Steps to an Ecology of the Mind*). The question remains as to why base a book about the Anthropocene and education on their philosophy, given the wealth of other material in the field?

The answer is that their philosophy presents a unique and unorthodox means to escape the unconscious conditioning of the Anthropocene, in, as, and through education because: *it opens up time to learning* (Nx). This is why a non-linear analysis of the drives in history has been executed (Chapters 2–5), that is entirely underpinned by the philosophy of Deleuze/Guattari (1984, 1988). This analysis follows on from the notion that the philosophy of Deleuze/ Guattari is pragmatic, and works to create escape routes from entrapment at strategic points or plateaux, but will not enhance the traps as a new overlay of metaphysics (Chapters 2–5). The metaphysics that the Deleuze/Guattari (1984, 1988) analysis denotes lays parallel to the formation of the plateaux as escape routes from the unconscious drives as they are excavated. The Deleuze/Guattari (1984, 1988) analysis of the four unconscious drives of the Anthropocene is also heavily influenced by Deleuze's (1962/2006), engagement with the philosophy of Nietzsche, as this is where the theory of the drives comes from. In contrast to these points, other books about the Anthropocene and its escape routes, hypothesise about what to do with respect to its origins, and, as such, look for ways out of its overwhelming, terrifying influence (e.g., Bonneuil and Fressoz 2016). Some examine the scientific evidence for exponential human influence on the planetary systems, and hence date the Anthropocene after the Second World War, and the swelling of global, industrialised human societies and their multiple (often toxic) outputs. Further, 1945 marks the dropping of the two atomic bombs on Japan, and, hence for many, designates a turning point in human influence on the environment (e.g., Monastersky 2015) in terms of the dispersal of radioisotopes such as strontium-90 and plutonium-239. Others point to the 18th and 19th century developments in steam engines, the harnessing of their mechanical power to drive machines and factories, and it concomitant reliance on the burning of fossil fuels such as coal (Jonsson 2012), to explain the origins of the Anthropocene. Others still point to the development of standardised production processes, and the sale of products in global markets, to emphasise the destruction of specific biomes and the loss of biodiversity in general due to planetary human expansion (Tsing 2015). In contrast, analysts go back to the beginnings of sedentary human life, and organised agriculture taking place in proximity and in the sway of settled cities, after 10,000 BC (Smith and Zeder 2013), to express the foundations for the Anthropocene, and how humans have come to dominate the environment. This book, following a Deleuze/Guattari (1984, 1988) philosophical overview of the situation, goes further back than any of these speculative origins of the Anthropocene, to link the current geology of humankind and the state of the planet, with the evolution of hominin drives in general, more than two million years, and specifically examines the drives of: 'tool-enhancement'; 'carbon trail'; 'the phallocene', and; 'atomic-time', to create an expanded or immanent base for now (N), and to present escape routes through education as specific dates in these trajectories or plateaux (Nx).

The Anthropocene has been renamed as the 'Capitalocene' (Moore 2016), as the 'Chthulucene' (Haraway 2015), the 'Anthropomeme' (Macfarlane 2016), and a multiplicity of different terms such as the 'Anthrop-obscene' (Parikka 2015), but also the 'Plasticene', 'Plantationocene' (Tsing 2015) and 'Mis-anthropocene', and, of course, there are many other (90+) variations on the 'ocene' theme (cf., Chwałczyk 2020). Again, these designations, parallel to differences in the speculative origins of the Anthropocene, serve alternate rhetorical, theoretical, and ideological models, that suggest variable ways to construct and apply the concept of the Anthropocene to the current situation, and, hence, to the future and how to escape it as now (N). In contrast, this book remains with the overall designation of the Anthropocene, but clarifies the influence of the phallic-same in Chapter 4 as the 'phallocene'. Further, this book, working from a Deleuze/Guattari (1984, 1988) intellectual perspective, that could be understood as immanent materialist (Cole 2013, 2014), speculates that the Anthropocene is a singularity, in that it is an absolute convergence in the space/time continuum, wherein, for the first time on the planet Earth, a species (humans) has engineered the conditions for its own extinction (Moynihan 2020): *and is conscious of this fact*. The singularity of the Anthropocene is simultaneously a naturally occurring phenomenon (a black hole), and something that has been constructed through the combinatory forces of the human drives in evolutionary history (Chapters 2–5), and hence transgresses the human/nature divide. Further, it is specifically out of (linear) time, in that it suggests a recursively produced and repeated end to human history (cf., Chapter 8), yet it is simultaneously a point in time that is evacuating, sucking and bending time, as we advance through the event horizon on which the Anthropocene is located, and, the as yet unimaginable dislocations and disruptions that it will and is causing (the sixth great extinction event). Combined, this reading of the Anthropocene as a singularity, enhances the sense of a complex educative figure, and a new, darker, resulting pedagogy or –N (cf., Thacker 2011).

I am influenced in my reading of the Anthropocene as a singularity by the technological singularity, and the 1990s uptake of this perspective on the singularity by Nick Land and others at the University of Warwick (cf., Land 2018). More specifically, I was part of a group called the CCRU (Cybernetic Culture Research Unit), that took the technological singularity as a means to combine theory with fiction, to produce alternate narratives and methods with respect to the general computerisation of everything (including thought/life/education). It seemed to me that this move captured the desire and madness inherent in technological culture, and very pointedly depicted how society was changing and rupturing (from within) during the 1990s, under the influence of, for example, capital and globalisation, combined with the ubiquitous computer products of big tech companies such as Microsoft and Apple. The CCRU took a cyberpunk approach to these developments, and evolved a specific mode of 'theory-fiction' that reshaped and played with the technological singularity, until it became unrecognisable from any previous renderings and, indeed, its origins (CCRU 2018); and hence provides a blueprint for the educative practice suggested here through the rupturing points (Nx). The focus of the naming of the Anthropocene as a singularity is to imagine something similar (through writing and thinking/teaching and learning), and in so doing, to release the creative, mad and desirous 'affects' of the Anthropocene, without falling into cliché. Deleuze/Guattari (1984, 1988) give us the conceptual tools to achieve this, for example, the assemblage, schizoanalysis, rhizomatics, but only if handled appropriately (not as normatively agreed or reductive practises), and applied within the scope of rendering the Anthropocene as a complete singularity, to rupture the present as N.

The analytical framing of the unconscious drives in history in this book comes from a thorough engagement with the philosophy of Deleuze/Guattari (1984, 1988) over many years. In their first combined work, *Anti Oedipus*, a displaced, material, Kantian synthesis of capitalism and the unconscious is induced, that centres on the critique of pure desire, and that offers an escape route through the practice of schizoanalysis. In *1000 Plateaus*, the universal history from *Anti-Oedipus* is broken up into dated, non-sequential plateaux, and hence the escape route of schizoanalysis is offered as multiple (rhizomatics), and as stemming from each plateau as assemblages or planes of immanence (after the philosophies of Husserl & Spinoza). The strategy of multiple escape routes from *1000 Plateaus* is followed here, and thus the historical analysis of the Anthropocene as unconscious drives is broken up as dated plateaux in each chapter (two-five) as yNx (y = chapter, N = now/education, x = date). Chapters 6 and 7 continue with the multiplicities of escape routes as rendered in Chapters 2–5, and show how that following a Deleuze/Guattari (1984, 1988) analytic does not lead to one solution to climate change. Indeed, the escape routes from the Anthropocene are multiple, but what stops action is the entrapment of its reality through self-reciprocating desire as and through capitalism. In this book, the question of what to do about climate change is deliberately non-prescriptive, and left open for educators to innovate and create their own solutions in response to the plateaux. Of course, there are many other consequences to basing the historical framing of the analysis of the Anthropocene on Deleuze/Guattari (1984, 1988), such as a combined and unified rational human self (agency/activism) will not be posited to save the world (as it is already fractured); many of these consequences can be read imperceptibly throughout this whole text.

The move to base this book on the philosophy of Deleuze/Guattari (1984, 1988), at once recognises that we have entered an important new epoch and territorial, planetary zone, called the Anthropocene, that is irreversible, and that doing anything significant about it is a complex and multiply layered process, which has many escape routes (Hamilton 2017). Hence, this book deploys a mode of 'ecological accelerationism' with respect to the Anthropocene, in that its greatest and most damaging extent is imagined and posited as real, yet its forces, that are often hidden, unconscious, subverted, transformed and made subterranean in general thought/life/practice – are exposed and discussed here through the Deleuze/Guattari analysis of history (Chapters 2–5); alongside the more noticeable effects and changes in the environment that we are witnessing due to global human activity (Clarke 2014). This book moves beyond simply applying the conceptual terminology of Deleuze/Guattari to the Anthropocene and education, but works to produce a genuine synthesis of both through historical analysis and escape as education (this is one of the many reasons for choosing Deleuze/Guattari as the intellectual frame from which to operate). The result is a material approach to the history of the Anthropocene as drives, and its unravelling through, in, and as education, that looks to circumvent idealism, in that an ideal point, direct mental extraction, or oppositional escape routes from the singularity of the Anthropocene (however ingenious sounding and loaded with potential), are not posited, but, indeed, are resisted. This book does not explicate the historical analysis of Deleuze/Guattari (1984, 1988), but purposefully demonstrates its use, through the creation of the plateaux in Chapters 2–5, and the difference these plateaux can make in terms of education and social change (Chapters 6 and 7).

Consequently, the educational escape routes depicted here are necessarily complex, entwined, multiple, non-designations (because they have to be taken up and acted upon by others), and inter-laced as series of plateaux or Nx. Most noticeably, techno-solutions to the Anthropocene, such as geoengineering or carbon sequestration (cf., Demos 2018), are not held up as 'humanity's salvation', nor are United Nations mandates, such as the Sustainable Development Goals (SDGs), or the Education for Sustainable Development (ESD) programs, as these initiatives are tied up within and function as power-structures, in effect, they are influential markers of money flows, that are subject to and part of the many ways in which global capitalism currently works (cf., Fedosejeva et al. 2018), and that is fundamentally responsible for creating the problem of climate change in the first place, as they are connected to the manipulation of its solutions to enhance capital flow (cf., Chapter 8). Rather, the ecological and green revolution that this book incites as education, actually comes from within the material structures and processes that it analyses in history, through the non-linear, unconscious realities of the drives, that Chapters 2–5 present, and the irruptions in education and social change that this analysis suggests (Chapters 6 and 7), as their combined plane of immanence (N).

The philosophy of Deleuze/Guattari (1984, 1988) makes sense when taken as whole, and applied to matter flows and complex arrangements, such as the production of the Anthropocene and its loosening through education. Deleuze/Guattari present an immanent materialist analysis (Cole 2013, 2014) of the situation, that penetrates the desires that humans afford capitalism as now, yet recognises that on this plane of production and variant ecological destruction of the world, is the only possible way out of this process, as its potential realignment as teaching and learning in the present (N). This book wishes to change the future, away from inevitable eco-collapse due to global warming, to produce a means to survive the forces that have been unleashed by humans (i.e., by capital). Yet to in anyway circumvent the impact of the singularity of the Anthropocene, we need to move beyond the 'rhetoric of the ecological sublime', and address the real, deeply set, unconscious forces that have produced and are producing the Anthropocene, and this book does this by combining historical analysis from Deleuze/Guattari, education, and social change.

4   Education, Social Change, and the Future

The problem of the future which this chapter addresses is compounded and exemplified through the education and consequent social change that we may extract as 'now' (N), due to and through teaching and learning (Cole 2011). The Anthropocene is a 'future present' in that it is a new epoch that we have moved into due to human telluric influence. Co-existent with this 'future present' are different generations of humans, who have been born at variant stages and levels of realisation of the Anthropocene. In 2019, the charismatic figure of Greta Thunberg helped to spur on a global 'school strike' movement (Fridays for Freedom), that wished to pressurise governments to act on climate change, and to purposefully manage the impacts of the Anthropocene. These demonstrations drew enormous crowds of supporters around the world, mobilised by the clarity of the message, and the simplicity of the solution, i.e., that if enough young people (and connected others) gather in these marches, and show that they care enough about the state of the environment, politicians (in democratic nations at least) will be forced to act, and pass legislation that, for example, restricts the emissions of carbon dioxide. Many organisations have used the popularity and outreach of Greta Thunberg and the spread of her message to bolster efforts, for example, to enable teachers and students to study climate change issues in the classroom in a cross-disciplinary fashion (e.g., Devine-Wright 2013). As such, the general theory behind this approach is that education provides the means to change the minds of the next generation, who will, after becoming knowledgeable, emboldened, and passionate about climate change, effect social and ecological transformations through their actions.

Of course, no-one should deny the potential of this educative plan of action for the environment. However, the general problem with this straightforward vision of the future (i.e., climate activism through climate education), is that even though it is possible to demonstrate real gains in terms of student's knowledge about the environmental impacts of climate change, and, further, one can improve a teacher's efficiency and effectiveness with respect to delivering cross-curricula units on climate change, the question remains with respect to being able to critically analyse if anything changes overall given these initiatives (Hamilton 2011). For example, as part of doing research for this section, I watched a video of a climate change curriculum that had been implemented in Dubai hosted by *The Guardian* (Sprenger et al. 2019). The video was inspiring, as it showed very young children talking passionately and articulately about climate change. At one point, the video features the class enthusiastically planting trees in the desert, just outside the perimeters of the school. Afterwards, young girls stood up in front of the school, with a flashy multi-media projection of nature behind them, the girls imitating Thunberg's powerful rhetoric about climate change. A journalist from *The Guardian*, who had come along for the ride to visit the school with the CEO of the climate change education curriculum provider, asked if any of this display of climate care really made any difference, in this fossil fuel capital of Dubai? The CEO immediately shot back that we should seriously look at ourselves, and our own sustainability, before we criticise others, for at least doing something (Ibid.).

This anecdote demonstrates part of the problem with respect to designating education as a genuine but straightforward change agent for and in the Anthropocene (cf., Cohen, Hillis Miller and Colebrook 2016), – and that contrasts the approach of this book, that creates education through a transformation of now (N) after a historical analysis of the drives from Deleuze/Guattari (1984, 1988). Even though future generations are continually passing through educational institutions, their participation in genuine rebellions against the status quo (as action on climate change necessarily has to be), is managed and frequently co-opted by the capital forces that fund and run the institutions where the students learn (Hoffman 2005). In the case of the school in Dubai, even though the children were making genuine attempts with respect to articulating positive environmental messages, the whole infrastructure in which they were formulating those messages was at that very moment, responsible for enormous, global fossil fuel emissions, through the international sale and use of oil (Angus 2016). Pointedly, I doubt whether the school would be funded at all without this substantial and ongoing global fossil fuel monetary exchange. I noticed that the children did not mention the geopolitics of oil in their speeches. Coincidentally, the school assembly where the children demonstrated their environmental credentials, was attended by an official from the Dubai government. Hence, of course, the children could not state overtly controversial opinions, or say anything revolutionary, political, or that might raise the ire of this important attendee. I concurrently wondered how long the tress that the children had planted in the desert would survive. In sum, even though our hearts might be touched by children marching for climate change, or talking positively about taking real steps to help the environment, it does not take very much critical thinking to dispel these 'shows' as so many illusions. Worse still, they are 'shows' that are precisely designed to hide the reality in which we presently live, in which climate change is being augmented with little signs of abatement (Keys et al. 2019).

Thus, the educational provision and subsequent social change that this book presents moves carefully, so as not to be caught up in the superficial gloss that can refigure young people as climate activists, without attending to real change. Firstly, an in depth, nonlinear analysis inspired by the philosophy of Deleuze/Guattari (1984, 1988) is required to enable understanding of how we have come to produce the Anthropocene through its drives (Chapters 2–5), all of which is specifically educational through the dated escape routes (Nx). I was sparked to design and articulate this historical-educative analysis by Félix Guattari's four zones of the unconscious diagram (1989/2013), in which he suggests that the zones of Territory (T), Ideas of the Universe (U), Social Flux (F), and Machinic Phylum (Φ) constitute a schizoanalytic take on the unconscious. In this book (Chapters 2–5), Guattari's (2013) 4-zones are refigured by applying Deleuze/Guattari's philosophy (1984, 1988) to the Anthropocene as 'Tool-enhancement', 'Carbon trail', the 'Phallocene', and 'Atomic-time', that lead to the black hole or singularity of the Anthropocene, in a non-linear material cloud analysis (Figure 1.2).

As one can see in Figure 1.2, each zone presents a flight path with dates that is being dragged into the black hole of the Anthropocene singularity. These dates suggest plateaux through and in which phase changes have occurred that have precipitated the contemporary Anthropocene as unconscious behaviours, and their consequent escape, that leads to an expanded now (N), new learning, and as a rupturing from the future. In the darkness of the singularity, the different stochastic futures are mixed up and blended, in a vision of

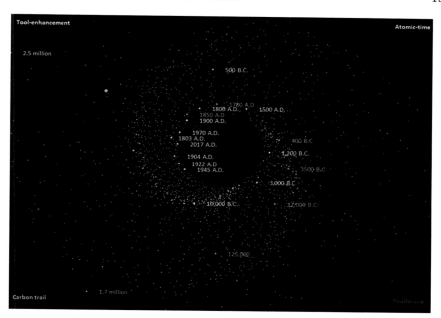

FIGURE 1.2   The 4-zone material cloud analysis of the Anthropocene. First presented at 'Dark Horizons' the New School (New York) on 20/4/2017 (© Cole 2020)

the future that is contrasted by the perfect idealism of the young children, who have been coached to repeat ecological harmony and local climate solutions, through their cross-curricula climate change education (Læssøe et al. 2009). The difference that this book makes to the Anthropocene debate, and the precise separation from education becoming a vehicle for climate change illusion (and hence continued fossil fuel capital domination), is that it enables the challenging of deep seated drives, beliefs, and material formations, through Nx, that have produced the exact conditions for the sixth great extinction event, and will be revealed in this book by applying a Deleuze/Guattari (1984, 1988) analysis of the drives of history to the Anthropocene. This challenging and analysis (Chapters 2–5) leads to a reformulation of education on different grounds other than merely feeding children with pro-environmental messages, that they repeat uncritically (Chapter 6 + Nx). Further, the social change that this book designates (Chapter 7) is precisely designed to question the status quo of the fossil fuel capitalist present and its subsequent futures.[2]

The question remains, does the strategy and tactics that this book puts forward with respect to climate change, education and Deleuze/Guattari have any chance of success? The problem for academics working in this field, is that we are most frequently too spread out, institutionally and disciplinarily categorised, and hence muted from speaking out collectively about the fossil fuel capitalist present in advance (cf., Clark and York 2005). Further, most academics are too worried about their job security or chances for promotion, to speak vigorously about these topics, because their research must ultimately challenge the reliance on capital flows from fossil fuel industries, if it is to provide a genuine way out of the current situation. I have found in the synthesis of Deleuze/Guattari (1984, 1988) to be a powerful and potentially uniting approach to the Anthropocene, that has the ability to cut through the divisions and ways in we are potentially nullified and reduced to miserably egoistic, individualised intellectual work, primarily subject to the market for success. Rather, the Deleuze/Guattari (1984, 1988) emphasis on material unconscious forces, and the manners in which they have passed through history and society, here retraced to produce an analysis of the thought patterns and power in the Anthropocene, gives us at least a chance for success as (Nx). This analysis is, admittedly, at times challenging work (Chapters 2–5), and subsequently doing anything meaningful about the Anthropocene can be equally provocative (Nx, Chapters 6 and 7), yet if we don't at least try, we will certainly leave the unremitting legacy of the sixth great extinction event for our descendants. In sum, this book is an attempt to furnish the groundwork for an eco-revolution in the future as an expanded now (N), in and through education, for others and ourselves to collectively enact. This groundwork leads to at least three interrelated paths, on which the Anthropocene will unfold.

5   The Future of the Anthropocene

> The new planetary consciousness will have to rethink machinism. We frequently continue to oppose the machine to the human spirit. Certain philosophies hold that modern technology has blocked access to our ontological foundations, to primordial being. And what if, on the contrary, a revival of spirit and human values could be attendant upon a new alliance with machines? (Guattari 1996a: 267)

The Anthropocene is designated as a singularity in this book to fully realise its time-warping and world destroying potential (the first path). This singularity is a machine, and it is the intention of this writing that this machine is fully realised and acted upon in education. However, if nothing or little is done to curb the path on which we are currently headed, everything that has been exhaustively written about will happen in terms of climate change disasters over the next few years (e.g., Steffen et al. 2015), and these events will be exponentially increased due to positive feedback, for example: through augmented wild or bush fires, higher sea levels, greater atmospheric temperatures, more hurricanes, typhoons and cyclones, the potential for severe drought, unpredictable food harvests leading to widespread starvation, potential flooding due to intense precipitation, and changes in the sea chemistry because of escalating carbon dioxide absorption (acidification), and the global die off of coral reefs (Hughes et al. 2017). Taken cumulatively, the full effects of climate change mean annihilation for the continuing human inhabitation of the planet Earth, and the full onset of the sixth great extinction event, of which we are the overwhelming player (Ceballos, Ehrlich and Barnosky 2015). This book is designed to work against this path, and to attempt to alter the course on which we tread, not through force feeding children with environmental messages in education to regurgitate, but that will never be enacted, or to invent new global, environmental 'salvation' technologies, such as geoengineering solutions, enhanced high tech renewables, carbon capture, or making everything we consume sustainable; but by attending to the inherent drives that are forming the Anthropocene (cf., Hamilton and Grinevald 2015), and trying to escape them through education as the time dimension N_x. In other words, this book looks to enact an edu-critical approach to the Anthropocene, one that enables deep questioning with respect to the formation of its drives, and their continuing progress in the world, as multiple educational escape routes through and as an expanded thinking time dimension.

The second path that the Anthropocene will take in the future, implements some measures to curb the augmentation of climate change in the Anthropocene, but does not revolutionise the fossil fuel situation (cf., Malm and Hornborg 2015), and hence does not enable the move to 'eco-revolution'. This is the path advocated, for example, by mainstream politicians suggesting a New Green Deal (NGD), or by green pressure groups, who lobby governments to take greater care of the environment, and steer policy away from following the tenets of runaway market economics, and the domination of one world capitalism (Guattari 1989/1996b), but, the economies remains neoliberal in nature. In short, this path looks to enact a 'greener' capitalism, often through legislative measures, and by blocking highly polluting industries and activities, whilst leaving the basic fossil fuel infrastructure and their capital flows intact. Some have called this path 'atopian' (cf., Walker 2003), or as a future that is as good as can be expected, given the current settings for human society, and the runaway capitalist option that seems to have been frequently chosen. However, given the amount of carbon dioxide that has already been emitted into the atmosphere, and the irreversible nature of these emissions, it can be surmised that it is almost certain that this option will not be enough to reverse the tide of global warming, and return us to Holocene conditions for life in Earth anytime soon. Further, given the often wildly differing estimations of future Anthropocene atmospheric calculations, and, for example, how perplexing it is to understand precisely how the positive feedback loops will work once climate change steeply takes off (Steffen et al. 2018); the first two future options for the Anthropocene almost entirely merge into one another, in, and as the wholesale die off of the sixth great extinction event. In short, it may be stated with assurance that it is only the third option for the future of the Anthropocene, that humanity has any real chance of surviving and flourishing into the future.

The third option is to take account of the unconscious drives that have produced the Anthropocene, as an historical analysis from Deleuze/Guattari (1984, 1988) and its escape routes (Chapters 2–5), and purposefully act upon them through new regimes of education and social change (Chapters 6 and 7): and as an expanded time dimension now (N). In Chapter 7, I suggest that a Green Utopia is a necessary designation to help deal with the unconscious drives that have led to and produced the Anthropocene. This Green Utopia should not be read as an idealism, or unrealizable point through and by which we may be duped into believing an impossible green dream is possible, or that we should buy into, in terms of every latest green gadget set to miraculously solve climate change (Galaz 2014). Rather, the Green Utopia is a foil for the imaginary through and by which the necessarily complex and multiply layered social transformations can be formulated and reimagined in and as education/(N). Specifically, in Chapter 7, I discuss 'degrowth', consciousness raising, and a critically immanent approach to understanding how capitalism cynically manipulates and transforms green messages and initiatives to its profit-driven advantage, and through its very processes. Deleuze/Guattari (1988, 1991/1994) created the concept of 'geophilosophy', which is useful at this juncture when understanding how I am suggesting we move to break free from the stranglehold of capitalism in the Anthropocene as education. In *1000 Plateaus*, 'geophilosophy' corresponds to the plateau of 10,000 BC, a date which signifies the start of the Holocene, the retreat of the last ice age, and the beginning of favourable conditions for human society to thrive and prosper. The plateau asks the absurd question: "Who does the Earth think it is?" which is the introduction to locating thoughts from below, from within, and from the usually neglected stratum of the Earth, on top of which we have constructed our civilisations in the unfolding of the Holocene since 10,000 BC.

In contrast, the book: *What is Philosophy?* by Deleuze/Guattari (1994) includes a chapter called 'geophilosophy', which is about how Greek philosophy became a territorial and colonising force in world history as state sanctioned western philosophy, for example, as can be seen through developments in modern western phenomenology (e.g., Heidegger 2010). Hence, there is an implicit eco-politics to 'geophilosophy', in that the powers of the Earth may be captured and used by dominating forces to control and subjugate others, including non-humans. Significantly, there are two senses to geophilosophy, one of the bottom-up, chaotic, natural forces, that have been progressively shut down and compromised by human civilisation in the Holocene, and as the power to harness these forces, as demonstrated by western philosophy, and through its enabling, for example, as models of the Greek state or polis. This book looks to render a geophilosophy in Chapters 2–5 that adds to notions of interdisciplinary education (Gough 2006) by capturing the immanence of the Anthropocene, both in terms of its power, and its destiny (in time), and that enables us to do something about the analysis, as and in teaching and learning (Nx) as escape routes (cf., Mcphie and Clarke 2015). This immanent capturing is a material geophilosophy, that has as its unravelling the positing of future eco-revolution in and through enhanced and transformed pedagogy, that results in the momentum of social change (Nx + Chapters 6 and 7); frequently as hard fought battles, and that does not underestimate the powers that have been unleashed by capital, or the abilities of capitalists to maintain and reformulate themselves, and to potentially reassert their dominion over nature, even as its depletion closes in (see Chapter 8 – the double bind). In sum, this book as a whole may be understood as a new ontological and epistemological approach to the Anthropocene based on the work of Deleuze/Guattari (1984, 1988), and that looks to evolve educational practises for its dissolution through an expanded time dimension as now (Nx).

Special Note

The following chapters (Chapters 2–5) are designed to evolve user end, context-sensitive pedagogy, teaching and learning episodes and units of work, in addition to their discussion in Chapters 6 and 7.[3] The strategy consists of: after reading these historical analyses, educators will be enabled to create new teaching and learning encounters to be deployed, shared, and commented upon on the IIRA web site (see tables of pedagogy at the end of each Chapter 2 to 5). These chapters do not present a linear narrative of emergence from a state of nature to (Western) civilisation, but present an account of the drives of the Anthropocene. Every date in the following analyses is a plateau, or 'plane of immanence' upon which pedagogy and learning can be constructed. Overall, each date adds to the plane of immanence that this book produces as: (yNx) where y = the chapter designation (2–5), N is expanded now/education, and x is the specific date under analysis.

Notes

1. For an animation of this graphic see: http://tinyurl.com/3cxnw3
2. See ongoing results of this experiment on https://iiraorg.com/
3. These pedagogic resources will be housed at https://iiraorg.com/education-the-anthropocene-and-deleuze-guattari/

CHAPTER 2

Tool-Enhancement

1 Introduction

Tools are an everyday part of our lives. We use them unthinkingly, as a means to enact all sorts of tasks. The level of automatic non-thinking involved with tool use, creates the sense that our use of tools works on the unconscious and preconscious levels, or as a tendency/enhancement (even though there are conscious, cognitive, and logical processes also vitally involved with tool use). It will be argued in this chapter that tool use is entirely locked in with our evolutionary pathways, and is the first inter-linked line of flight (Figure 1.2), relating to the human domination of the environment, that we now call the Anthropocene (Lewis and Maslin 2015), along with the other three lines or curved lineages, that will be described in this matter cloud analysis of the Anthropocene (Chapters 3–5). The Deleuze/Guattari philosophical analysis of (1984, 1988) tool use, is one of 'tool-enhancement', wherein the idea of the tool usages runs alongside the actual use, not as any original technics (Stiegler 1998), or as something particularly and solely human (Hobbs and Angela 2000); but as a two-way, interchangeable, explanatory, and experimental mechanism, that examines how and why tools and human behaviours have changed over time. The Deleuze/Guattari historical analysis of tools presented here is designed to uncover the ways in which tool-use has resolved into an unconscious drive, and how that drive is a force present in the Anthropocene. Of particular concern to this book and this chapter, is how human tool use has morphed from an aspect of subsistence survival mechanisms, to a means to universally exploit and dominate nature, with, it seems, no clear resolution in sight. The Deleuze/Guattari (1984, 1988) approach is hopeful in that differential change is the primary focus of the analysis, and hence a revolution in the ways that we currently use tools is possible, indeed, their contemporary adaptation is one of the main aims of the thinking that will take place in this chapter. However, the change thesis of this chapter comes with a caveat, in that the analysis of the fluctuating conditions for and about change, uncovers the deep lineages and evolutionary aspects of these variations, and these factors explain why it can be frustrating to implement new tool uses, alongside, and within the ubiquity of change. It is straightforward to posit the cliché that 'everything must change', which is certainly the case with respect to the Anthropocene, in terms of behaviour, tools and climate change, but this repeated message can become an idealism, deflected from material implementation, by deeply engrained habits, beliefs, and potentially false consciousness. The purpose of this chapter is to challenge the instincts and automatic functioning of tool usage through education (tNx), that coincides with the most damaging effects of the Anthropocene, such as climate change, to excavate a path to a genuinely new agenda for tools, through education and society.

2 Prehistory

Homo sapiens and tool use have evolved due to mammalian expansion after the age of the dinosaurs and the KT extinction event (Rose 2006), 65 million years ago. Evidence for hominins using tools comes from sites in southern and eastern Africa, with the first definite, substantial use of tools, as collections of crudely shaped stones, pertaining to the species *Homo habilis*, and dates back approximately two million years (Mithen 2007), whilst there are claims of an earlier species in the hominin family, *Australopithecus garhi* using tools at about the same time or even earlier (tN1), perhaps two and a half million years ago (Asfaw et al. 1999). Further, there is evidence to suggest that the use of tools goes back to three and a third million years in the extended hominin family in Ethiopia, Africa (McPherron et al. 2010) through archaeological records found around dwelling sites. Of course, one can observe other creatures today, for example, monkeys, crows, even fish using tools to enhance and change their forms, and to do simple jobs, such as the prising of food like grubs from holes in logs (Shumaker, Walkup and Beck 2011). Hence, the drive of and to tool-enhancement is not uniquely human, but for the purposes of understanding how we have got to the point of the Anthropocene, and potentially creating the conditions of our demise through the sixth great extinction event, we need to comprehend how and why the drive of tool-enhancement is so thoroughly embedded in our deep, instinctual functioning.

The specific use of tools by *Homo sapiens* could be said to have come from the various hominins who evolved from hominid primates in what we now know as southern and eastern Africa (Wood and Harrison 2011). One can speculate that the conditions for hominin evolution were optimal where we find high concentrations of the remains of the early hominins and their often piled, discarded tool use. Admittedly, the archaeological records are only of stone and bone tools, as any wooden sticks or other implements made of perishable materials will have long since vanished. In the middens of archaeological sites, shaped and flaked stones, reworked bones, and shells used for different purposes have been found in various hominin sites (cf., Toth 1987). The significant for this chapter and book, is that the intensity of the tool usage and subsequent enhancement seems to proliferate and grow once the hominins leave their ancestral homes, and start to travel and adapt to new environments, firstly across Africa, and into the flat, savannah lands. Some have suggested that the trigger to use tools in a directed and focused way was climate change, and the push to search for food beyond the specific range of the tropical forests and the immediate, lush environments, where the hominins began their descent from primate hominids living and climbing in the trees (Raichlen et al. 2010), to becoming walkers.

However, this chapter, in line with Deleuze/Guattari (1984, 1988) does not establish definite reasons, causes, or origins for these changes in behaviour, and thus explain 'tool-enhancement' as an enclosed nexus, but looks to the complex and entangled through-lines and emergences from the hominin cradle of development to the present day Anthropocene (Chapters 2–5). Certainly, specific usages of tools and the tools themselves would have been adapted and changed along with the hominins, as they pushed across Africa, and eventually spread out to colonise the rest of the Earth's landmass (Lambeck et al. 2011). Evidence from the archaeological and fossil records points to the development of more complicated, lightweight, and better crafted tools, with different uses and body adaptations, as hominins moved and relocated (Marzke 2013). Movement in groups fundamentally requires different types of behaviours and tools to enhance these behaviours, in contrast to sedentary ways of living through and by which species occupy the same territories; and the nomad/sedentary difference is one of the pivotal modes of analysis of this chapter and book. Whilst the hominins are well fed, and stay in the same places, tools are not essential parts of their enhancement, but serve to gain the hominins extra food, and work as a supplementary means to exploit food sources, and to perform other repetitive tasks. The tools will be generally piled up and stored close to where the hominins live (d'Errico and Backwell 2009). However, once the hominins leave these safe places, the tools that they deploy become essential and bonded parts of their lives, and their purposes quickly multiply, as the hominins encounter new environments such as extended grasslands, cold weather, mountain ranges and desert, and food sources and jobs to perform potentially diversify or halt.

This prehistory analysis of tool-enhancement does not attempt to '(re)centre' a narrative of human emergence in the hominin groups that have evolved from primates and great apes, or ignore the complex inter-relatedness of the hominins with a changing environment (and themselves), other animals and available tools, shelter and food, as they made their way across and out of Africa (cf., Ellis and Ramankutty 2008). Nor does it look to make the route to the contemporary Anthropocene purely functionally; i.e., as another tool that (re)produces everything in the evolutionary past, to make it seem useful and in/of a direct continuity to today. Rather, this Deleuze/Guattari (1984, 1988) analysis of enhancement through time, attempts to present the full scope of complex tool development, by connecting it to the carbon trail, the phallocene and atomic-time (Chapters 3–5) through nonlinear emergence; and thus showing how these fluctuating relations are deeply rooted, reciprocating extensions, habits and beliefs from and about the body, nature, feelings, and thoughts, that have led to collective and individual actions in the world. Tool-enhancement to and of the evolving hominin form changed in flux-like waves for approximately two and half million years, and mainly involved using stone and other at-hand implements, such as sticks and bones to directly work with and in the world in a nomadic fashion when the groups were moving (cf., Brain 1989), and in a sedentary manner when the groups of hominins stayed in the same place over a period of time to establish limited early settlements, for example, in caves, or on plains with simple shelters made from organic materials, or in the relative shelter of forests.

Hominin tool-enhancement (Roux and Bril 2005), of this extensive prehistoric era, that is present in our DNA, instinctual body memories and movements, was used to perform tasks such as kill food to eat (meat), build temporary shelters, chop wood, collect berries and fruit, make clothes as the hominins pushed to colder climates, or to practice shamanistic ritual and art to stimulate the imagination, language and story-telling. In summary, the tool-enhancement of the hominins transformed over time from predominantly working with large rocks as crushing tools, to sharpening, chipping and shaping rocks more carefully and finely, e.g., as flint axe heads (cf., McHenry and Coffing 2000). As different species of hominin hunter and gatherers and subsistence early farmers became extinct over the course of two and half million years, to leave *Homo sapiens* alone in the hominin family amid nature, the focus of the tool-enhancement began to transform in time from nomadic survival, limited subsistence communities and shamanic worship, to sedentary power, control of the environment, and eventually being directed to the production of surplus value in the present day global capitalism of the Anthropocene. The next section will take this analysis of tool-enhancement forward, in term of this interrelated developmental and evolutionary trajectory as agriculture.

3 The Beginnings of Civilisation: Agriculture

The first significant shift in the focus of the drive to and from tool-enhancement by hominins comes from 10,000 years BC (tN2), even though data for the evolution of *Homo sapiens* and the beginnings of modern human cognitive abilities dates back 200,000 years, and includes some small scale, fixed settlements, for example, in caves, rainforests or in temporary shelters. Evidence shows that large scale, permanent settlement, organised agriculture, and the rearing of livestock, did not predominantly occur for 188,000 of these years (cf., Anderson 1999), making the shift in tool-enhancement from nomadic and subsistence life, to sedentary city-building purposes, a recent change, and that has occurred uniquely in terms of communities of *Homo sapiens*. Agriculture and settled, hierarchical society, gradually developed in different parts of the world at approximately the same time after 10,000 BC, as the last ice age receded, and as humans moved into the environmental and climate stability of the Holocene, in places such as the Mesopotamia, East China, the Ganges and Indus catchments, the Nile, West Africa and in the Meso and Andean Americas (Mazoyer and Rouda 2006). In these places, the conditions were right after 10,000 BC in the Neolithic age, for tools, e.g., pottery, to enhance the human form in terms of helping to create and maintain larger, more permanent settlements through agriculture, and eventually to support the structured societies that these settlements imply (though this did not happen quickly, or at the same pace/manner in every civilisation, cf., Manning 2004).

This analysis of tool-enhancement does not concentrate on the reasons or origins of this change, from largely living in and as part of nature, to the beginnings of dominating and permanently transforming nature through agriculture and settlement, but attempts to unravel the knots and tendencies through which we have arrived at the destiny of the contemporary Anthropocene (cf., Whitehead 2014). The beginnings of agriculture at 10,000 BC for *Homo sapiens*, means that the fundamental energy-resource equation between *Homo sapiens* as part of nature, and *Homo sapiens* as an exploiter of nature was beginning to change. If we compare up-to-date, globalised, capitalist society with societies still living in the pre-agricultural 10,000 BC era, e.g., some remote Indigenous Amazonian tribes, and Aboriginal Australians that exist outside of the white mainstream, and that have maintained their oral traditions and culture; one may immediate note that these societies and their members have a much greater and more specific working knowledge of and contact with nature (e.g., Wright 2017). Therefore, one can suggest that the beginnings of widespread agriculture serving a sedentary population is the birth of specialisation, and particular knowledges becoming sedimented in the roles of certain groups of people, whose skills can determine the wellbeing of that society through a consistent food supply and, for example, the skill of pottery making using tools. Hence, a thoroughgoing, sensitised, and well-grounded knowledge of and in nature for everybody, gradually becomes secondary to knowing one's place in society, and obeying the rules by and through which a particular society operates. In sum, one can say that the planning and execution of agriculture, and all that this entails through understanding and working with the rhythmic cycles of the seasons in a specific place, is the foundation for a rule-living and mechanistic, place situated culture, based on a 'agriculture-tools-human' societal structure (and is hence suggestive of its escape routes, tN2).

However, it is incorrect to suggest that nomadic and subsistence tool-enhancement completely died out after 10,000 BC, or that sedentary, agriculture-based, city-building tool enhancement is better or more advanced that nomadic and/or subsistence tool-enhancement, or that it subsequently took over as the preferred means to exist (Barkai and Yerkes 2008). What happened according to this Deleuze/Guattari (1984, 1988) analysis after 10,000 BC, is that the energy differentials, and the forces between tools and their work in and by the populace, was starting to be gradually altered. In the predominantly nomadic or limited settlement, subsistence, pre-agriculture age (which existed for several million years); the energy expended making, using and maintaining the tool was approximately equal to the energy received from its use. For example, in nomadic, hunter gatherer, and pre-agriculture societies, sharpened axe heads made from flint and fixed to thick branches through vine, would have been valuable weapons and tools, carried and treasured by their makers, as a vital means for survival (cf., Khazanov 1994). In post 10,000 BC societies, such tools and their early cousins began to be purposefully stored, or rationed in the formation of armies for specific uses in battles, or for pre-defined purposes, such as the ceremonial, widespread slaughter of livestock by a priesthood, or, indeed, in the deliberate organisation and practice of agriculture in early cities (Hillel 1992). The energy distribution and force of the tool therefore sits dormant until called upon, creating a means to control the use of tools, and to link up with other tools, such as orders to distribute the best tools to the best warriors, or commands to make more or adapted tools, or to deploy preferred tools and techniques to produce the best food for societal rulers and others.

It is worthwhile at this point to note that the settlement and territorial designation of a certain place for living and control of nature through agriculture, also has its disadvantages. The push to nomadically follow food sources, to worship movement, and to design and use tools to help with these purposes, such as collapsible and transportable living quarters, for example, yurts; potentially increases the chances of survival, if a particular ecosystem negatively decays, or becomes decimated through drought, flood, or extreme temperature oscillation (cf., Phillips 2001), because the populations can move. In contrast, a settled society, relying on the accumulated knowledge and tools of agriculture and specialists to enact these skills, that have served in the past to survive in that specific place, will become progressively destitute and die out, if this set of knowledges is unable to deal with extreme, unforeseen, environmental variations. A parallel scenario is happening now through global climate change (the Anthropocene), wherein one can surmise that the environmental factors that have led to *Homo sapiens* success in the past have now been altered (the Holocene). Unfortunately, human society today is so widely distributed around the globe, that it is all but impossible to migrate easily to parts of the planet that not have been decimated by climate change (Adamo and Izazola 2010). The prospect is for contemporary human society to become extinct through the very forces that have made it successful, and one of those forces is the establishment of settled agricultural zones and their tool-use (sedentary, agricultural, and defensive, city tool-enhancement). This ironic twist in the fates of humankind, shows how sedentary progress and hierarchical, stabilised civilisations, do not always hold the keys for a continued or better life, and hence we need an escape from this inevitability through education (tN2).

However, at this stage (post 10,000 BC early Neolithic), the tool-enhancement that *Homo sapiens* are principally involved with was still relatively straightforward, shaped and often made of and with stone, and which had become progressively more sophisticated through prehistory, as the hominins learnt to craft new, more specific, and better tools made out of stone (cf., Cochrane 2008). The numerous minor changes and becomings that happened during this extensive prehistoric time (several million years), between the hominin form and the tools that were being deployed to change the environment, therefore mainly revolved around shaping, working with, understanding, imagining and deploying stone for different purposes (Stout and Chaminade 2012). Agricultural tools, as well as the others for changing and adapting the environment, were part of a stone-human unit, that had developed and evolved in stages over several million years. This specific unit involves hand-eye co-ordination, as well as knowledge of the different types of stone that were to be found in the environment, and how to work with them. Large scale middens of stone tools and food remains such as animal bones, have been found around prehistoric sites (e.g., Parkington 2003), that transition after 10,000 BC, into the storage and use of specific tools for agriculture and settlement building. It is interesting to speculate that at some point during the perhaps three million years of hominin evolution of the 'human-stone-tool' form, that harder materials were noticed embedded as ribbons in the stone that the hominins were looking to extract and utilise. At a certain juncture, these harder ribbons were themselves extracted, used, and turned into metal, which was initially in the form of bronze.

4   Metallurgy

The effects of the millions of years of tool-enhancement involving the relations of stone on our bodies, minds, feelings, and in our societies is still keenly felt. However, this transformation and becoming of the 'stone-human-tool' form, made a significant and irreversible leap once *Homo sapiens* learnt how to extract and use bronze. Bronze is created as an alloy of copper and tin or other metals, and is formed due to large amounts of heat being applied to the mixture (firstly to the copper). Bronze can be moulded and polished, it is lighter, more flexible, and potentially enables the creation of more deadly weapons than stone. This next major change in tool-enhancement of the human form emerges after 4,500 BC (tN3), with the incorporation of metal tools in the sedentary tool-arrangements that had been gradually developing since 10,000 BC in the Neolithic cities, and in the new and evolving arrangements of war, agriculture, government, religion and domestic life (cf., Levy et al. 2002). The use of bronze added an extra force and intensity to the tool-enhancement of the hominin form, and augmented the enactment of sedentary power through repetitious acts, domination of the environment and each other, worship-religion, and actions such as cooking, home-building, food storage, and importantly creating the early means for trade and exchange value through the introduction of money.

The movement into the settled agriculture of human society, created a host of different knowledges and skills, that enabled the community to survive in a particular location beyond nomadic or subsistence life. It is straightforward to understand how and why these knowledges might become highly prized, and lead over time to their conservation and protection in hierarchical and defended communities from 10,000 BC onwards (e.g., McIntosh and McIntosh 1981). Furthermore, the introduction of working with and producing bronze intensifies these processes, as the metal objects circulate through society as value-laden, and act as visual, ornamental, and symbolic markers for the technological development from stone. The hominin form henceforth adapts in time to ore mining, working with, understanding, remembering and passing on the knowledge and skills showing how to extract, shape and use metal. In Deleuze/Guattari (1984, 1988) terms, there is a 'becoming with' and through metal of the *Homo sapiens* form, a hardening and focusing from the millions of years of stone-becoming (cf., Hall 2015). Metals are sharper, more noticeable and reflective than most stone, and therefore can take on different imaginative and thought-landscapes in the human mind. Along with the discovery and use of copper, other precious metals and stones were incorporated into the human form after this time, e.g., gold, which increases the potential hierarchy and wonder in terms of adornment and riches associated with these items. In sum, the addition of metals into the human form and their ensuing environment, created a more specific and detailed societal formation (cf., Philip 1988), as metallurgy slowly began to affect and transform thought and human life.

Further, the activities associated with metallurgy accelerated the ways in which *Homo sapiens* transformed their environments, beyond agriculture.

Mining operations had to be expanded and intensified in the search for metals, away from the location of stone in quarries or clay to make pottery. Ribbons of metal ore had to be discovered, followed, and dug out of the ground. Large and intense fires were organised and maintained to smelt the ore. Moulds had to be made from clay, techniques were evolved to shape and finish the metal implements by early blacksmiths (Sherby and Wadsworth 2001). In short, the ways in which the world was changed by sedentary communities, with increasing war capabilities, and better defensive weapons, was accelerated through the incorporation of metallurgic practises into everyday life, and with the organisation of better agriculture, e.g., through the use of metal ploughs (e.g., Aberg 1957). The collective will power of communities was unified and rallied around metallurgy, as it took an unprecedented amount of energy and organisation to function. Admittedly, it was still possible to live outside of these early power and social structures, that were in the process of being transformed by the discovery and usages of metal, but what transpired is that the organisation and coordination of resources around metal production made it increasingly more unlikely that this would take place (cf., McIntosh 2005). Rather, the processes and forces involved with and about bronze were protected and highly prized, and resulted in an intensification of the ways in which settled human society could be conceived and maintained. Nomadic and subsistence societies might learn about the technologies to mine, extract and work with these metals, but without the large scale means to control and defend their cumbersome processes, these societies would inevitably lose out to settlements that could harness everything involved with metal, including fully equipped armies with bronze weapons, and making escape from their remits increasingly more life threatening (e.g., Bergendorff 2020).

Henceforth, highly structured and regulated societies in Egypt, the Indus valley, China, Mesopotamia, and latterly the Minoans on Crete all flourished from 3000 BC, and created many of the codes and foundations for the machinery and inter-relational flows of sedentary society to come through the ages (e.g., Nicholson and Shaw 2000), and specifically in terms of tool-enhancement. Nomadic society was not abolished, and also used bronze in many of its appliances, but these uses and communities, largely existed outside of the controlled hierarchies of sedentary power, often on the fringes, and in-between the society centres that developed over time around pharaohs, kings, aristocrats, priesthoods, bureaucrats and their retinues (cf., Richet 2020). Power was enacted ceremonially during this period in these sedentary societies, and tool-enhancement was mostly deployed at the bequest of the rulers, for example, as a mechanism to build pyramids, to improve agriculture, or to increase the chances of success at war. Populations grew around sedentary power centres and these populations were regulated and controlled by and for the purpose of serving their God-like leaders, that deployed metallurgy combined with agriculture, war, taxes, religion and law, as a means of social and natural control. The next leap forward in the lineage of tool-enhancement came in terms of the development of iron, and its replacement of bronze as the major source of tool-enhancement from 1,200 BC (tN4).

Iron had been previously wrought by the Hittites as early as 2000 BC, yet it was after 1,200 BC, and the collapse of early trading routes that had supplied the connections between copper and tin, that the widespread use of iron began to flourish and metallurgists learnt how to temper iron with carbon to make steel (cf., Maddin 1975), (it is interesting to note that this doesn't happen at this time in China). Further, in the Mesopotamian states of Sumer, Akkad and Assyria, the first use of iron reaches back even farther, to perhaps 3000 BC. There is also some evidence of iron being wrought in Egypt at around this date (Johnson et al. 2013), though Egyptian ancient culture was primarily a bronze civilisation. The use of iron in tool-enhancement required better, more centralised kilns, and larger and well organised labour forces of blacksmiths, to work the iron into tools. One can speculate that the origins of bronze production could have been accidental, when stone laden with the different ores of copper and tin were mixed in a fire. The production of iron requires a more deliberate process, with higher temperatures, and the precise mix of carbon and iron ore to produce a workable metal compound (steel). This correct mix for iron production must have only been achieved through long and hard experimentation with the right elements, and the development of furnace technology to achieve sufficient temperatures (e.g., Amzallag 2009). Larger scale cities in Europe and the Middle East, e.g., Greek, Roman and the Persians began to use iron in everyday tool-enhancement, that improved the production of wheels, barrels, weapons of all descriptions, agricultural tools, shipping, time keeping devices, cutlery and chains for imprisonment, to name but a few. Here we see the development of 'becoming-iron' of the human form, that has been produced through history, and that we still enact today through our everyday lives (cf., Pleiner and Bjorkman 1974), as it relates to and complements every other becoming that we may figure through the ubiquity of iron and steel tools in the Anthropocene. Human population steadily increased during this period, it had been stable at around 4 million for approximately 6 thousand years, but now with better, iron made tools for survival and increasingly sophisticated means to protect and control sedentary societies, and to investigate and probe the forces of nature, human population began to increase to around 190 million by the time of Jesus.

Again, one may state that nomadic societies did not completely die out, but were often put under increasing threat by armies and patrolled trade routes connected to centres of power such as those of the Roman, Persian, Mayan and Kushan Empires, that were engaged in collecting every advantage to maintain and expand their power-bases. It was during this period (approximately 500 BC-100 AD) that the early tool-machinery necessary for our current global society was developed, and many of the elements of the Anthropocene can be traced back to (cf., Humphrey et al. 1998), and even though organised, absolute religion was still an important central plank in these hierarchies and sedentary modes of expansionism, and imperialist control, rational, rules based organisation based on written down laws, and the beginnings of limited democratic debate, started to refashion the ways in which power was distributed and conceived (James 2006). This reorganisation had consequences in terms of how tools were deployed, who used them, why they were put into action, and the ability and reach of tools to refashion the environment, for example, mining activities were expanded, rubbish mounds were organised, wars were fought on grander, imperial, annihilatory scales, trade routes and new connecting towns remade valleys, affected the courses of river beds and transforming vegetation, often without direct replenishment, as the human form connected and reimagined itself in the world through empire and iron (and we can imagine our escape through education (tN4)).

5 Global Trade

History is cyclic and rhythmic. Empires grew and fell, spurred on by the divisions of agriculture, metallurgy and prehistory, and which saw the human form moulded and remoulded through the drive of tool-enhancement. In Europe, the pace of tool-enhancement slowed after the fall of the Roman Empire, yet civilisations elsewhere kept the fundamentals of social organisation and technological development alive, for example, across the Indian sub-continent, Africa, Americas and in China (cf., Hall 2016). Each culture invented and reinvented the technologies and their usages, given different religious and social purposes, thus reinterpreting the tool-enhancement of the human form for their own context. The Neolithic beginnings of agriculture had helped *Homo sapiens* to move from nomadic and subsistence existences, and to stay in one place to build cities, hierarchical societies and eventually to establish empires. Metallurgy had added to this process of urbanisation, and strengthened the city states in terms of projecting and conquering outwards through war, and in some cases into complete empires (e.g., Persian). However, it was not until 1500 AD (tN5) that tool-enhancement took another leap, which could be said to have had a significant effect on the creation of the Anthropocene today. At this time, new empires across the world began to be able to effectively communicate through improvements in long range ships and their concomitant transport technologies (Boot 2006). For example, the invention of printing made written instructions easier to duplicate, and modern empirical scientific methods started to establish themselves in various cultures such as in Europe and China. The result was the possibility for tool-enhancement to create the beginnings of a reproducible culture and products that could be more easily traded and tracked worldwide.

Up until 1500 AD, the expansion of sedentary life by tool-enhancement from its beginnings in prehistory, which was built upon through settled and organised agriculture, and strengthened through the development of metallurgy, reached a culminating point in extensive land empires. After 1500 AD, the technological and social conditions were right for this empire-building to transform through the ways in which tool-enhancement worked and expanded as colonialisation. The problem with land empires was that every point in their extension had to be controlled equally by the central government or ruling royal dynasty (power). This governing was usually performed through might, or by stationing garrisons of soldiers of the central empire organisation at strategic positions throughout the empire (cf., Parker 1997). Clearly, the imposition of such force, the suppression of local identity, and the taking of slaves and taxes, would cause widespread resentment and the likelihood of resistance against the imperial forces. Eventually, every major land empire of the old world disintegrated through internal tension, invasion, climate change, resource depletion and their numerous divisions (cf., Vries 2002). The governance and control of these empires proved to be impossible, but the learnt skills, and technological/social transformations that had been put in place, were carried forward through written records and smaller communities, that could embody this tool-enhancement (tN4), such as specific religious orders in Europe and the Middle East.

After 1500 AD, countries and their states in Europe such as Portugal, Spain, Italy (e.g., Venice) and Holland began to put together the advantages of tool-enhancement that had been learnt from the land empires with long range, seaborne communications and navigational techniques, and looked to secure colonies abroad. There were important land empires at the time, such as in China, that of the Ottomans, in Mali, and as ruled by the Aztecs, some of which had utilised sea routes to extend and expand their trade and power, though they did not militarise and protect these routes in the same manner that the Europeans came to do (cf., Wills 1993). The difference in the tool-enhancement of the Europeans was that they extended their power abroad, not through defended land empires, but through the establishment of global sea routes, that connected colonies to home states. Power shifted over time away from the land empires and began to solidify in and as these global, seafaring colonialists (e.g., McClellan and Regourd 2011). The colonialists combined military with commercial concerns, to rule the colonies in a different mode to the previous and contemporary land empires. The colonialists still used force to dominate and quell resistances to their operations, but looked to encourage semi-autonomous overseas governments that co-operated with the colonialists, whilst maintaining the impression that the newly colonised countries had sovereignty, which is an important point in terms of the quest to escape their influence through education (tN5).

It is at this stage in the journey of tool-enhancement, that a second wave of human knowledges were beginning to be lost. The first loss of knowledges occurred in large scale settlements, when nomadic societies as functioning wholes were absorbed and dominated by the sedentary combinations of agriculture, metallurgy and the remains of stone prehistory. As such, the ways in which human society increased and augmented moved away from the following and tracking of movement, and began to turn towards static, overlaid (repetitive) control, influenced by changes in the seasons (e.g., Preston et al. 2012). Since the time of the first losses of waves of nomadic knowledges, sedentary power had increased and strengthened, and nomadic ways of doing things was progressively forced to the outside of the human mainstream. The second wave of knowledge-losses happened when indigenous knowledges were replaced and subjugated by the colonial powers after 1500 AD, and through the explosion in global trade. One could state that this process has been insidiously going on ever since. The colonial powers used sophisticated, religious, administrative and often racist means (ideology) to account for and transform the local indigenous knowledges (cf., Simpson 2004) that they encountered in their colonies. Of course, indigenous knowledges were not entirely wiped out, and have persisted in a similar form to the nomadic beliefs and practises, at the margins of the settler society and culture, often forgotten, disdained and neglected. Indigenous knowledges were not necessarily nomadic, but concerned the core beliefs and actions of the human societies that had inhabited the land for many thousands of years before the colonial establishment. In contrast, the colonialists were primary concerned with how to live, survive, and profit in their new, displaced lives, often by encouraging trade with their original countries.

The period of colonial tool-enhancement sees the beginnings of many aspects our present day global society of the Anthropocene. For example, the foundations for capitalism can be dated back to this era (e.g., Arrighi 2001). Even though money had been in circulation since the development of metallurgy, it was not until the colonial powers in the world had begun to do global trade, that the system of financial exchanges and protections was evolved. Capitalism is fundamentally about differentials in value and how capital flows between these differentials. In the case of the colonial powers, the value for things was designated by the banks and central powers at the heart of the colonial enterprises. Prior to industrialisation in the colonial powers, the exchange rates were set for commodities and products that came from the colonies, so as to favour the colonial invaders, and they were demarcated as types of bartering systems, or as simply taking the resources from the colonised countries in exchange for very little, some diminished monetary rewards, or supposed benefits bestowed by the colonialists through their organisation skills (cf., Boot 1998). This period also began to see migration and immigration of humans on the back of and in conjunction with the establishment of global trade routes, and the differentiated capital flows by the colonialists. These flows of humans and goods included the commercial set up of slavery during this epoch. The effect of this period of tool-enhancement was that many specific empires, cultures and peoples, were begun to be assimilated into a global culture of enterprise, that established and defended itself through dispersed military power, working through systems of forts, administration and racism (and that we shall attempt to escape from through and as education (tN5)).

This global culture and world interconnectedness that had begun after 1500 AD, took another nonlinear step in 1800 AD (tN6), as the conditions for the creation of factories became possible, through the invention of steam powered engines (cf., Chapter 3), and industrialisation and economics starting to work in unison, creating what we now understand as modern global capitalism. Even though trade at this time was global, it was the colonial countries of Europe that benefitted the most from the differentials in value, labour and commodity that were created after 1800 AD. Vast tracts of the world became utilised to grow crops and provide raw materials for the industrial processes that were being invented in Europe and elsewhere (e.g., Murray 1992). For example, cotton was grown on every increasing scales in the Americas, Africa and Asia, to be transported back to Europe to be made into clothes for sale. The whole colonial and capitalist enterprise depended on the money that was made from the manufacturing of products being enough to pay for every other process, and the cost involved with what was being made. Clearly, this time in history has enormous repercussions for tool-enhancement and its effects on the Anthropocene. Humans and their tools working in colonised countries became subservient to the flows of products and materials back to the colonialists (e.g., Diepart and Schoenberger 2017). Pertinently, in the colonising countries, tool-enhancement meant very different things for the development in hierarchy of human classes. The benefactors of the colonial enterprises could delight at the many ways in which tool-enhancement and their new wealth gave them increasingly pleasurable and sublime experiences. In contrast, workers in the factories became human-factory-wage units, destined to live out their lives in struggle, misery and continuous work for very little reward.

The effects of this period of global trade are still with us in the Anthropocene, even though we have purportedly dealt with some of the more pernicious aspects of colonialisation and capitalism (cf., Popkewitz 1988), e.g., slavery and racism. One of the many problems for changing course in the Anthropocene for a better, more sustainable future, is that the embedded drive of tool-enhancement includes the separation into benefitting from the surpluses of global trade, and being part of the creation of that surplus through labour and resources. This basic distinction, which has been wrought into the human form by tool-enhancement from the time of 1800 AD, has many far reaching consequences, that make the reality of the Anthropocene appear virtually irreversible. It is just a straightforward fact that the benefactors of the colonial and capitalist enterprises starting in and before 1800 AD, will not give up these benefits, and simply become part of the system which creates benefits for them (for example, they would not work in factories). This is why the problematic of the Anthropocene is much more complicated than simply creating 'green solutions' to today's social-economic system – or a Green New Deal (GND) (Barbier 2010). Rather, the embedded drive of tool-enhancement, that saw the colonial and capital separation between workers and owners after 1800 AD, has to be addressed. Otherwise, the global system of exploitation will be left in place that subjugates and controls whole populations and makes them unable to act in different, more sustainable ways. This is why an in depth analysis of the human drives that makes up the Anthropocene and their resolution through education (Nx), is necessary to create the opportunity to change path in this time of environmental crisis (cf., Bauhardt 2014) through pedagogic escape routes. In other words, the industrial, economic and social systems that were set in place after 1800 AD, primarily by colonial countries, but having consequences globally, has to be addressed, if progress is to be made in the complex situation of the Anthropocene.

By 1900 AD, (tN7) coal powered ships, and early land vehicles (not horse drawn) were available to carry an ever increasing number of products for trade worldwide, telephones and electricity (cf., Chapter 5), were beginning to transform business and domestic life, and the pace of social change increased, to accommodate these technological advances. Tools and worker groups were now fully integrated into large machines and factories, cities had begun to dominate the environment and polluted whole ecosystems, warfare was fought on a previously unimaginable, industrial scale. The result of colonialism and capitalism working together for several hundred years was that the West as we now conceive of it, dominated the world scene (cf., Bryant 2006). This nonlinear story of how we have arrived at the Anthropocene is specifically not one of solely British or American emergence, or of any other one nation, but it cannot be underestimated, for example, how powerfully the invention of tools in 19th century Britain has influenced where and how we have arrived at the contemporary situation. A whole plethora of inventiveness complemented advances in science and in the social fields during this period. For example, gun technology was modified and improved, making British armies and other colonial powers amongst the best equipped in the world, and this tool-enhancement, combined with well-designed naval vessels and communication devices, made British invading forces amongst the most formidable offensive force on the planet (cf., Travers 1979). The extension and power of the British Empire at this time has left an indelible mark on tool-enhancement of the Anthropocene through the ways in which its practises have now become so widespread and difficult to escape.

The combined effects of capitalism and colonialism at 1900 AD, was to create a world dominated by trade, and that advantaged those who held the keys to that trade, e.g., the owners of factories, capital, fossil fuels, land, and the controllers of the shipping routes. Along with this system of capitalism and colonialism, there were stock exchanges, the notion of which had begun after 1500 AD, in Europe, and had expanded to many other countries of the world by 1900 AD, (Michie 2011). In effect, flows of investment were controlled via these stock exchanges, and the values of the companies on the stock exchanges and their share prices, became indexes for the wealth of the countries themselves. This system as a tool-enhancement has carried on until and through today, and is one of the oscillatory, stabilising, destabilising and corrective factors that controls the ways in which human society changes and is able to change under global trade. Economic value merges, bleeds and directs every other value, as the domination of one world capitalism begins to assert itself after 1900 AD. There are many nation states at this time, the European states in particular vie for control of world trade through military and diplomatic means, but ultimately this competition is fought out through flows of investment and economic opportunities, often invisible, but relevant to every conflict and play for power around the world (cf., Rosenberg 1985). It is at this time that the U.S.A. begins to assert itself as a world power, and even though the British Empire is still in control of much of the world's vital economic territories, resources and trade, a shift to America starts to happen around this time, as the race to become rich truly begins to accelerate as a personal life goal. Before this time, the notion of being wealthy is mainly connected to inheritance and ownership, rather than recently created fortunes, but just as the aristocrats in Europe start to lose their grip on power, the rise of the commercial classes fills the void, and their values overtake those who had been at the top of society for many hundreds of years previously. Concomitantly, we find ourselves in this same situation today in the 21st century Anthropocene, 120 years later, and this attempt to escape these values through education (tN7)

6   World Machine

Since 1900 AD, tool-enhancement of the human form has intensified to an extraordinary extent. This extension has transformed the flows of world trade into and as part of a machine. The machine is also one of the key concepts from Deleuze/Guattari (1984, 1988), that they introduce in their inter-linked theorisation combining capitalism with schizophrenia. We fit into the world machine as 'desiring-machines', both controlled by and as component parts of the machine and how it functions. Previous distinctions separating humans and their tool-enhancement become redundant, as the multifarious ways in which the machine works merged and diversified. The key to understanding the world machine lies in thinking through how in this period world trade linked to technological development to create mega-cities, and routes between these cities, that sees almost continuous global movement. The world machine is a mega-machine (Mumford 1966), which even though it is inhabited by conscious, reasonable human beings, begins to run itself, which again explains why it is hard to change the course we find ourselves on in the Anthropocene (as education). Enormous, global wars were fought in this period, which saw rapid technological development, sophisticated tool-enhancement designed to defeat the enemy, and human-world machine armies, circling the globe in boats and increasingly in planes, badged under different nations, but with similarly negative ecological and environmental effects. Once we move to 1970 AD (tN8), modern computers were in use, television was commonplace, global industrial powers such as the U.S.A. and U.S.S.R. vied for power on the Cold War world stage, massive cargo ships and large numbers of people on planes travelled around the world. Sedentary domestic life had been completely transformed by consumerism, electricity, world trade markets that never sleep, and modern medicine that had helped to increase the world human population beyond 3.7 billion.

The post-war 1945 AD period has been designated as the time in which the Anthropocene ramps up, as all major indicators of human inhabitation on planet Earth (such as carbon dioxide emissions) begin to move exponentially upwards (Steffen et al. 2015). The post-World War II period sees international agreements between nations not to fight global wars through bodies such as the United Nations, and in this era of relative peace, technological and domestic development accelerates through the world machine of global capitalism. Humans innovate globally to try and make money, create power for themselves and their kin, to improve their status or to stay ahead, and to flourish in an ever changing world. The speed of technological innovation from this period is extraordinary, and far out paces natural processes, as flows of economics, and the ability to copy and reproduce technological designs, which enhances tools with creativity/permutation/adaptation and vice versa; and expands human tool-enhancement reciprocally. The world machine sees humans link up and become parts of other machines, as thinking/feeling/doing/acting components, that interchange and become other, as integrated parts of the ways in which they function and grow. The factories of the 19th century are expunged and/or expanded, locating and relocating globally in the search for cheap labour. At this time, China, Cuba and the U.S.S.R. were communist countries, but in terms of this analysis, these countries only served to temporarily slow down the inevitable one world domination of the capitalist system (cf., Zayani 2000), and all that this entails in terms of the Anthropocene (and for its escape through education). The last of the Marxist revolutionaries are dealt with by the military and police that protect capital interests, the Middle East is militarised to protect the flow of oil. Coal production expands globally, and its extraction is accelerated to power the world's ever increasing thirst for cheap energy.

Today, in 2021 (the contemporary moment) (tN9), we live in an internet and mobile phone connected world: air, car, truck, cargo shipping and train travel are pan-global, there are more than 7.7 billion human beings in the world, most desiring to be sedentary and comfortable on a planet that is thoroughly crisscrossed by 24 hour a day trade routes, roads, planes, electricity supply and generation systems, and ever expanding human cities, all with particular but interconnected, ecological consequences, including irreversible climate change. This one world system that we have produced is thoroughly imbricated through the media, economic speculation on the stock exchanges, and mobile devices that have ever increasing computational powers, as the size and complexity of these devices ceaselessly alters, to make them smarter, more functional, and cheaper to acquire (cf., Zimmerman 1999). The Anthropocene that has been created by us and our tool-enhancement, can be traced back in a nonlinear fashion to its prehistory origins, and the ways that our hominin ancestors began to work with and refigure stone. Now, an unstoppable one world system of capitalist endeavour circles the planet, with machines and humans interlocking and working together to function in a myriad of ways, that are now increasingly mirrored in our digital world. This system only stops for brief moments, ceasing partially, due to global pandemics, as natural catastrophes strike, or as major terrorist attacks temporarily halt the inevitable ticking over of this system, in effect, the world machine is largely beyond our control (the ghosts in the machine sit alongside it, and perhaps only arrest it phantasmagorically) (Cole and Hager 2010). Importantly, this analysis of drives from Deleuze/Guattari (1984, 1988) does not prioritise the tool-enhancement of the contemporary moment over that which has gone before (at any stage), even though we have latterly created an impressive number of machines to interact with and become-other through, we have also produced the precise conditions for our own destruction in the Anthropocene and through climate change (and that is what we are trying to escape (tN9)).

The point here is to realise the very complexity which we are faced with, negates and subsumes techno-solutions to the Anthropocene, such as geoengineering, carbon sequestration, or immediately switching all energy sources to green, renewable, non-carbon emitting technologies (cf., Cole 2020), exactly because of the drive of tool-enhancement. We have built a world machine, and we are essential parts of it. We have to collectively alter the path of this machine, if we are to stand any chance of survival in the Anthropocene. Green capitalism isn't sufficient to divert the machine, as the consumptive, unequal, and non-distributive functioning of the world machine, inherent in world trade (tN5), means that most of the human population will be unable to participate in the new (green) world order, given that tool-enhancement conditioning, inequality, and its consequences, go back millennia (cf., Torrence 1989), and hence, green capitalism fails as a solution to the climate crisis. Similarly, there is no pre-industrial green utopia that we can simply reconstitute, as the structures of the present day tool-enhancement are so prevalent and locked into the very functioning of everyday life (see Chapter 7, for how a Green Utopia as a material future imagining is worked into the multiple educational solutions and social change on offer here). Rather, we require a thoroughgoing, non-linear analysis of the Anthropocene, that shows us how we have got here, what are its drives, and that offers at least some chance of changing things for the better, as an escape route through education. This analysis will be enhanced through the next chapter, that deals with the 'carbon trail', or how hominins developed relationships with energy emitting materials such as wood and coal, that have produced and sustained human society, and under whose sway human life has flourished to bring us into the contemporary world.

TABLE 2.1 Pedagogy of tool-enhancement

Plateaux	Dates	Pedagogy (https://iiraorg.com/tool-enhancement/)
tN1	Prehistory	Examination of how the human form develops in relations to stone
tN2	10000 BC	Inquiry into early tool use in agriculture
tN3	4500 BC	Learning about bronze tools
tN4	1200 BC	Learning about iron tools
tN5	1500 AD	Examination of early world trade tools; e.g., boats, printing press
tN6	1800 AD	Inquiry into the factory as a tool
tN7	1900 AD	Learning about tools such as early cars, coal driven boats and the first electrical tools
tN8	1970 AD	Learning about tools such as television, early computers and trucks
tN9	2021 AD	Inquiry into the contemporary state of tool use

CHAPTER 3

Carbon Trail

1   Introduction

The previous chapter, regarding 'tool-enhancement', could give the false impression that the Anthropocene has been created entirely due to human creativity, tool intent, its functionality, and our combined inventiveness as a species. However, the drive that enhances the human form through tools, which can be traced back to prehistory, and has resulted in the world machine of today (Chapter 2), is only a quarter of the story (and its escape routes, tNx). This chapter concerns another aspect of how humans and tools are creating the Anthropocene; i.e., by interacting with carbon in multiple ways to produce heat (thermodynamics). If human industriousness throughout history had not made heat and released carbon dioxide, we would not be in the situation of global warming and climate change that has been called the Anthropocene. We therefore need to analyse and expand upon the relationships between humans and carbon to the extent that it has become an unconscious drive that underpins climate change in the Anthropocene (and look for escape routes from it). In terms of the Deleuze/Guattari (1984, 1988) historical analysis in this book, the interaction with carbon has been named as the 'carbon trail', because it does not concern a static or scientific extraction of heat from carbon through burning, but follows the ways in which the reactions between carbon and heat have been 'trailed' and explored throughout a nonlinear history (and prehistory). The Deleuze/Guattari (1984, 1988) analysis of the unconscious drive of the carbon trail aligns with tool-enhancement as a figuration of a dynamic history of humans and carbon through time. This chapter reiterates the vitalist aspect of Deleuze's thesis, that aims to rework the ideas of Henri Bergson for a new generation (e.g., Letiche 2000). Vitalism is here not a discredited scientific theory about organic and inorganic life, or suggests that there is anything magical and inexplicable about life (cf., Bennett 2010), but corresponds to how Deleuze picked up and innovated with vitalism as a material concept, and as it had been integrated into French philosophy of science by such advocates as George Canguilhem (Greco 2005). In effect, this vitalism is part of a modified epistemology, that looks to life as holding the key to understanding knowledge of the real. This real as life is many layered, multiple, and does not suggest the propensity to dominate and control other theories or views on or as life. Hence, the Deleuzian vitalism that may be particularly acutely felt in this chapter, is a mode of political and ethical pluralism, that does not impress an authoritarian thesis about carbon upon the reader, but suggests the multiplicity of life itself (Marks 1998) and the escape routes through education from them (as numbered plateaux). Combined with the Spinozian influence, which underpins much of Deleuze's writing with monism and affect (Deleuze 1970/1998), the vitalism of the carbon trail attempts to delve into our instinctual habits that have connected us to fundamentally changing the environment through the control of fire and heat (and to posit escape routes from them, as ctNx).

2 The Discovery of Fire

Modern humans evolved over millions of years from the hominid cradle of Africa. As was argued in the previous chapter, the conditions were right for the evolution of various hominins, who diverged from their hominid ancestors, and began to use tools and spread out in recognisable, human ways from their initial jungle environments (cf., Fox, Pope and Ellis 2017). Fire would not have been ubiquitously present in a wet jungle environment, though the basic photo-sensitivity to the fire of the sun, that would have conditioned primate evolution for many millions of years before the specifics of at hand fire would had gained precedence and become part of the hominin drives, called here, the 'carbon trail'. Sunny clearings in the jungle would have attracted the hominids to gather anything edible that appeared in these bright and warmer spots – further, the direction of the rising and setting sun would have orientated and controlled them. Yet it is not until the hominins moved to the open, drier grass plains that they could encounter substantial at hand fire as part of the environment (cf., Anton, Potts and Aiello 2014). In terms of how, why, and when the hominins went from reacting and avoiding the fire of the plains, to specifically controlling and using it for their own purposes, we can only speculate about this change of behaviour and investigate the archaeological and paleontological records.

There are disputed and variant claims that hominins first deliberately entered the carbon trail, perhaps 1–1.7 (ctN1) million years ago, when *Homo erectus* had recognizably learnt to control fire (James 1989). *Homo erectus* was the first hominin that had extensively spread out over the globe beyond the hominid cradle of Africa, and had settled in colder and harsher climates, so this early evidence of fire use and control coincides with the expansive ability to move, survive, and adapt to the new environments of *Homo erectus*. It is also noteworthy that *Homo erectus* had evolved a substantially larger brain that the earlier hominins such as *Homo habilis*, that has been credited with the first stone tool use, perhaps a million years earlier (Wynn 1993). The point at stake here is that having the cognitive ability to realise how to start and control fire, creates other possibilities for thinking and doing, that *Homo erectus* would have used to their collective advantage/survival. The control of fire (Chazan 2017) is clearly an extraordinarily powerful means to begin to dominate and control the environment, and this increases one's chances for survival, and, further, the understanding and use of the carbon trail of early fire is closely aligned with tool-enhancement and the processes of hominin socialisation; as the warmth, energy, and heating properties of fire encourages tool design, the social use of tools, and a consequently increased tool engineering functionality (cf., Wrangham and Carmody 2010).

Homo erectus learnt how to live and flourish in many different climates around the world. One of the keys to this proliferation was the control of fire. This behaviour opened up new food sources that required heat to eat, and such processes began the deep instinctual relationship between hominins and cooking (cf., Abrams 1982), that is still with us today. Fire contributes to fixed settlements such as caves in terms of constituting a hearth, where food can be cooked, stories told, warmth shared, and tools created. The hominins would have used fire in a variety of manners outside the caves and nomadic settlements, for example, to control animals, as fiery adjuncts to weapons, or for early religious ceremonies that worshipped and shared rituals using the presence of flames. Evidence that our direct ancestors, *Homo sapiens* had begun to use fire as part of a nomadic lifestyle and in cave hearth settlements in dispersed colonies can be dated back at least 125,000 years (cf., Klein 2018). These hunter/gather, nomadic societies (e.g., Matsumura, Hung and Zhen 2017), were not human exceptionalists, but journeyed to search for food in groups that could be cooked on their fires, developed social codes based on shamanism, movement and fire, and worshipped fire as part of their understanding of the seasons and the environments where they journeyed – and in an attempt to survive, flourish, and to deal with consciousness as it developed alongside and through the carbon trails (cf., Hawthorne 1843/2010). The extraordinary speed of the spread of *Homo sapiens* across the world from Africa, helped to wipe out other hominins, and is testament to the complex ways in which tool-enhancement and the use and control of fire in and as part of the carbon trail, were integrated enough to enable quick, effective movement, survival, and societies of robust modern humans, adapted to various environments, and able to compete effectively with other species, and is here taken as our first educational escape route from the Anthropocene in history (ctN1).

3   Fire, Light, and Society

Hominins learned how to control fire in nomadic groups, as a means to cook food, and give light to evening and night activities for more than a million years, according to the scattered charred records of their hearths (e.g., Gowlett and Wrangham 2013). We can speculate that during this extended period, the deliberate use of fire would have probed beyond the human world, to scare prey into traps, to use against enemies in specialised fire weaponry, and to make clearings for basic, subsistence agriculture. The first evidence that we have for more sophisticated use of fire comes from settlements such as those of Jericho and Göbekli Tepe in Anatolia, Turkey, wherein the use and control of fire began to be integrated into an extended, organised settlement, beyond subsistence or nomadic existences (Dietrich et al. 2012). Climatic conditions at this time were still harsh after the last ice age, and it was not until the end of this age, at 12,000 BC (ctN2), and the start of the Holocene, that the carbon trail significantly developed. By that time, in the gap between the Upper Palaeolithic and early Neolithic ages, *Homo sapiens* had colonised every continent except for Antarctica, though were still not present in large numbers (less than 4 million). Noticeably, permanent and designated, integrated settlements beyond cave dwelling for shelter, began to develop after 12,000 BC (ctN2) in places such as Jericho and Göbekli Tepe, and expanded across the fertile Mesopotamian crescent through the beginnings of organised agricultural practices, and the central control of fire to the benefit of a stable society, in contrast to exposed hearths or the camp fires of the nomads; in this nexus, tool-enhancement and the carbon trail functioned in complex unison, to produce the early origins of sedentary culture (cf., Wright and Garrard 2003), that was copied and expanded hereafter.

The most important questions for this Deleuze/Guattari (1984, 1988) analysis of the first two spiralling lines of flight into the contemporary world of the Anthropocene (tool-enhancement/carbon trail), is how and why did *Homo sapiens* transition from nomadic and subsistence existences, who used tools and had become imbricated in the carbon trail through the control of fire, to become settled, larger scale and extended communities, that began to incrementally practice agriculture, breed livestock, build armies, raise taxes, and develop codes and organised religion to regulate and control their societies in a hierarchical manner and from a fixed viewpoint (Marshall 2006). In these early human societies, the worship of a continuous fire deity often remained at the heart of these religions, but altered from being connected to movement, to being concerned with established power. In the nomadic and subsistence societies, or cave dwellers that lived in caves shelter, but not in expanded dwellings, communities expended and received energy in comparable amounts, sometimes many generations of hominins lived in valleys until food ran out, or the climate became unfavourable, which led to their departures, and the consequent replenishment in the specific ecosystems over time. In contrast, the new Neolithic, Holocene sedentary communities (cf., Papadopoulos and Urton 2012), established after 12,000 BC (ctN2), began to remain in the same place for longer, and subsequently developed the means to send out envoys, miners, engineers, farmers, warriors and traders to communicate with other societies, leaving the majority of the population to become static, and integrated into repetitive tasks, therefore creating an oscillatory but stable energy field in and around itself, that constitutes the beginnings of semi-defensive, integrated human structures (cf., Topping 1997). Resources in these stable, sedentary societies had to be replenished within these static, orbital and elliptical fields (in terms of, for example, involving envoys), rather than being envisaged, moved to, or harnessed somewhere else, that was other than the initial stable base, and as a group necessitating moving into the unknown in every sense (physically/emotionally/cognitively/collectively); as had been the case with hunter/gatherer, nomadic societies, or with subsistence cave dwellers, on the occasions that they had to leave their rock shelters.

This monumental change in hominin behaviour, first observed after the recession of the last ice age, is still with us today, in terms of how heat and energy are conserved and channelled in the construction of a society. Previously, fires would have been constructed from at hand materials such as fallen twigs and branches, as the communities moved through the landscape, or settled for a time in caves (sometime lasting for many generations). In the construction of the first cities and urban spaces, the distribution of resources had to be progressively modified, as combustible materials were sourced back to the individual needs of households, and the growing requirements of organised societal practices, such as religious buildings, the initial forms of governance and control, i.e., through the formation of the early rulers of the new societies, their needs, and their military organisation (e.g., Christensen 2004). Thus, the modes in which the flammable resources fed into societal requirements was modified from being in tune with available materials, due to the movement of the human community encouraging a gap in resource harvesting for regrowth over time, to being repeatedly scavenged for, and reused from a single point or nexus. In consequence, the search for fire wood in the early Neolithic communities had to be continually extended outwards from the chosen base, which had the potential to change the local environment away from that base irrevocably. For example, woodland around the first city sites were cut down and grasses grew in their places, meaning that there was a transformation in the ecology from microorganisms to mega fauna (Cox 2004) due to the carbon trails.

The behaviour of sedentary expansion continued for several thousand years, as the earliest cities grew, and sometimes became land empires that dominated whole continents. *Homo sapiens* used the control of fire from these vantage points to reshape nature, and to become increasingly unassailable and potentially lavish in their energy requirements, and specifically because of the manner in which resources were channelled to the ancient rulers (Rich and Wallace-Hadrill 2003). Early civilisations and their extraordinary monuments to the carbon trails, are testament to the paths in which they relentlessly funnelled energy resources back to their hearts, to provide increasingly wealthy and comfortable lives for their kings and bureaucracy/priesthoods. Ancient civilisations in the Levant, Egypt, China and India expanded and retracted with this model in mind, and afterwards locations in Mexico, South America and parts of Africa also used this carbon-heat-model of developing energy resources through land empires and the concentration of fire at a centre (Cline and Graham 2011). In these early sedentary civilisations, rulers were worshipped like Gods, and their control of fire is central to this worship, as it increasingly became involved with everything important that happened to transform the societies. For example, the expansion of agriculture in the Neolithic age coincides with advances in pottery making, houses, ovens and city wide systems (e.g., Mellaart 1965). In short, the securing of enough fire wood to satisfy the energy requirements of these newly developing settlements in different parts of the world, mirrors and reflects the ways in which energy is distributed and used. One may suggest, perhaps whimsically, that there are no clear examples of early, fixed Neolithic communities that respond sensitively to ecological dictates (e.g., Pan, Zheng and Chen 2017). In sum, inequality and different degrees of environmental destruction, seem to be written into the very sedentary architecture and heat/light/energy distribution of these early Neolithic sites. In sum, these first sedentary communities, which broke out from millions of years of nomadic and subsistence life, wrote fixed hierarchical codes into the very origins of human civilisation, which is one of the reasons it is difficult to undo the funnelling of unequal energy distribution today in the Anthropocene (and our reactions to it), yet this action needs to be attended to through education (ctN2), to make a difference to climate change today. It seems that *Homo sapiens* decreed (or it was decreed for us) that there would be protected elites at the hearts of fixed communities from the start, and these elites would most often receive the benefits of fire, light and society, to marshal and respond to the rest of the community's needs (or otherwise).

4   The 'Energy-Life' Threshold

The Carboniferous geological age is a period in Earth's history dated from 359 million years to 299 million years ago. During this time, the climate was relatively warm, the sea levels were lower, and large parts of the Earth's land surface was covered with lush tropical, swampy forests (Scott et al. 1986). These forests were laid down as sediments, and due to specific microbial processes over millions of years, have become the coal and shale beds that we have found across the world, and have exploited ever since we have been able. In the terms of the carbon trail of this chapter (and its escape routes), the discovery of coal is the next major development, and happened at approximately 3,500 BC (ctN3). At this date, there is evidence that coal had begun to be used as a fuel in China to burn in the smelting of bronze (Dodson et al. 2014). The introduction of coal into the carbon trail is a significant step on the path to the global warming of the Anthropocene, because the organised mining and burning of energy resources from the Carboniferous era, constitutes an important step from the hunter and gatherer collection of recently dead wood or detrital carbon to make fire (Anderson 1994). Certainly, coal did not replace wood on any large scale in human communities as an energy source for many thousands of years, but the discovery of the increase in energy yield that coal produces, has major, Anthropogenic consequences, in terms of the drive of the carbon trail, and how *Homo sapiens* have henceforth interacted and transformed the environment.

Nomadic and subsistence humans before the discovery of coal, burnt wood that they sourced from their local environments to cook food, give light, perform shamanic ritual, and to socialise around and perform tasks, such as making useful tools. Early human sedentary society stockpiled and located wood for similar purposes, but from a fixed viewpoint, that encouraged hierarchical society, and environmental destruction around their location, to serve the purposes of the specific, layered, and regulated local society. The use of coal changes this dynamic, because of the increased energy yield that burning coal produces, which could be said to take us through an irreversible threshold between life and energy (cf., Steinberger and Roberts 2010). This threshold may be understood through the release of the trapped energy that had been stored in the seams of coal and shale since the Carboniferous period. Once this threshold had been crossed, it is extremely difficult to go back to the lower energy producing sources of fuel (e.g., wood), as coal burns better, for longer, and at higher temperatures. Coal is more difficult to ignite (Wall, Gupta, Gururajan and Zhang 1991), therefore enhanced technologies and expertise around fire lighting would have been employed to start the fire, which meant that along with the accompanying metallurgy skills (Chapter 2), the control and maintenance of the coal fires was an increasingly dangerous and specialised operation. This specialisation and control of these skills, once again increases the hierarchy around the use and control of fire.

A type of innocence is lost once the energy/life threshold has been crossed. It is important in Deleuze/Guattari (1984, 1988) terms not to romanticise the nomads, as their prehistoric lives in the megafauna would have been extraordinarily dangerous and wholly dependent on a changing environment (e.g., Wandsnider 1999). Rather, what we may understand in terms of their lives, is that movement, displacement, risk, contingency, survival and desire would have been mixed up in the everyday dramas they encountered as they travelled and lived close to nature. Once coal had begun to be burnt in the ancient civilisations that emerge out of the Neolithic agricultural revolution, and the consequent technological developments happened, such as detailed metalworking; the possibility of living apart from every day, potential fear-inducing and life-threatening factors are diminished, as humans are separated from their environment. However, it was not a conscious-choice to give up the nomadic lifestyle, settle down, burn coal, and start to irreversibly change the environment. This is the path that *Homo sapiens* took, it is irreversible, even though we now know that the widespread burning of coal releases carbon dioxide into the atmosphere, and helps to produce global warming (Van Der Ploeg and Withagen 2012). We cannot look back angrily or resentfully at what transpired, at the path that our ancestors took, and wish that we could change the course of history. Rather, what we can do is to take this analysis further, and accept that we have internalised the drive of the carbon trail, which includes the desire to burn coal to harvest its superior energy yield, and look for escape routes as education (ctN3).

The burning of coal by humans sets up a significant energy break, that starts to separate them from nature. The burning of coal and the smelting of metals requires protected areas, and inner sanctums, wherein the energy exchanges of the civilisation can be enacted and celebrated. These spaces are congruent with intensified religious worship, and the strengthening of hierarchies until humanGods were sanctified as pharaohs, kings and emperors (cf., Johnston 2004). As such, an artificial, ceremonial magic and power was enacted by *Homo sapiens* on themselves, as fire, at once distancing them from the brutality and chaos of nature. Again, previous, nomadic and subsistence notions of magic and power are not immediately dispensed with, as the new forms of magic and control take time to be established and accepted. Nomadic power and magic could still be enacted and was meaningful around the margins and in the shadows of regulated and policed society, and by those not subservient to or outside of the power centres that controlled the 'energy-life' threshold of fire. The point here is that there is henceforth a strengthening connection in the human mind, imagination and desire, between the increased energy yield of burning coal, and the ways in which power is mystified and made inaccessible to the majority of the population, for example, in ancient Egypt (Bergendorff 2020).

This inaccessibility and social control of the threshold is in contrast to small scale or mobile communities, where the power systems are predominantly transparent, and the energy-life threshold has not been transgressed, but is followed and worshipped. One can stipulate that the burning of coal and all that this encompassed, gave humans one of their first senses of being above/beyond nature. The tapping into the Carboniferous life-energy threshold by humans, gave them a platform by and through which they saw a gap between themselves and living a natural, entirely environmentally dependent life (cf., Kertzer 1988). This is because coal produces a new type of fire, less natural, and with enhanced smouldering over the burning of wood, which can be associated with the previous Neolithic revolution in agriculture, and what had transpired before in the carbon trails. As such, subsequent human societies were able to produce a new sun, and a new hierarchy, new cultural systems, and new technologies, that helped to set them increasingly apart from nature. This period especially sees advances in money systems and exchange, large scale, organised warfare and taxation (Jördens 2012). As such, the carbon trail deepened as an unconscious drive through the burning of coal, that distanced and changed humans and society ever since, away from a state of nature, and this transformation is to be dealt with today in terms of education (ctN3). However, it was not for several thousand years that this strict hierarchy and social control took another leap along the nonlinear trajectory of the carbon trail, and all that this entails.

5   Furnaces, Mining, and Individual Energy Exchange

Early land empires in the ancient world in places such as the fertile crescent of the Middle East, Asia Minor, China, India, Egypt and the Americas made some use of coal to establish absolute kingdoms that ruled over largely slave-like populations for thousands of years. As such, the benefits of the high energy yield of coal were generally not shared or understood by the populace. Rather, the majority of the population lived in conditions that had no relation to the technological, educational, religious and aesthetic advances that accompanied the higher energy yield of coal burning (e.g., Frye 1984). However, as was seen in the previous chapter, these societies generally did not last, and even though we can still marvel at their monuments, and excavate the archaeological record for the artefacts they produced, the early land empires, and their use of fire, do not in the main serve as models for social, cultural and technological vectors in the Anthropocene. *Homo sapiens* have internalised the drive of the carbon trails that were produced during this ancient period, as we have also assimilated the prehistoric nomadic and subsistence carbon trail drives, yet it was not until approximately 400 BC (ctN4) in parts of Europe (i.e., Rome) and Asia Minor (i.e., the Persian Empire), and North Africa (Carthaginians), that technology, social organisation, and the centralised control of fire developed sufficiently to incorporate the beginnings of the prominence of coal and shale mining and its energy yield into the everyday social fabric of sedentary life and its consequences (cf., Hughes 2014). At this time and afterwards, mining tools were invented to excavate, transport and deliver coal to large scale kilns and furnaces, where coal could be burnt with other flammable objects, and incorporated into useful processes, such as the smelting of iron, pottery making, and the heating of water.

In the ancient world, it is perhaps most pertinently in the Roman Republic and Empire that today's large scale, industrial, worldwide burning of fossil fuel can be traced back to, because the conditions of a stable, expansionist, technologically advanced, pleasure loving society based on rational principles, produced the precise mixture for the widespread use and burning of coal (Cowell 1976). The increased energy yield from the burning of wood to the burning of coal made it more likely that large scale, centrally orchestrated, industrialised processes could be based around this higher energy release, and the expansion and successes of the Roman Empire were built upon on the combinations of wood, coal and iron production, stonework, and the engineering, military, governance, educational and trade structures which this combination enabled (Dunstan 2010). However, there is no compelling evidence that the custodians of the Roman Empire considered the environmental effects from their systematic and industrial scale carbon trail exploits, but they did execute a highly integrated, technologically sophisticated society, that begins the arc and march to the global Anthropocene that we see today.

This Deleuze/Guattari (1984, 1988) analysis does not suggest that the Roman Republic and Empire used coal to the extent that was to follow in the industrial revolution in Europe and beyond. Neither, does it imply that the release of carbon dioxide due to the burning of fossil fuels is solely a product of Western society and technologies, since in the Anthropocene this action is truly a global affair, involving every country on Earth to a certain, but staggered extent. However, in contrast to the models of society, technology and energy distribution that proceeded the Roman civilisation, there was strong, inter-connected knowledge sharing in the ways in which the Roman state spread across Europe, the near East and north Africa, and how its production of energy worked (cf., Joshel et al. 2001). This is because of the governance, religious and educational models at the heart of the Roman state, that were not entirely focused on concentrating all benefits in the hands of a very small elite. Roman society was hierarchical, had slaves, and did produce an elite, though this was not, in the main, the quasi-mystical, absolute leadership of previous societies (with some famous exceptions, e.g., Caligula!). Rather, the education and governance of the Roman lifestyle, though hardly egalitarian, or, in any way completely dealing with the inequalities that were present in Roman society, did make the sharing of the benefits of enhanced energy exchange possible (cf., Runciman 1983). Previous to the model of Roman society, the best one could hope for would be to work for the God-like rulers in some capacity, to envisage the benefits that would come from the carbon trails and tool-enhancement of the time.

The effect of the changes that were apparent after and due to the Roman Republic and Empire, and other places to a certain extent such as in Persia (though power was quite absolute at various times during the different stages of the Persian Empires), was to give the general populace the impression that social advancement was possible (Mathisen 2019). In addition, the reality of this social movement gave birth to a new, educated, middle class, though very different from today, this group actively sought and desired the comforts and pleasures of Roman life, including those provided by the carbon trails. As such, a thirst for enhanced, individualised, energy-exchange was born, and this has locked itself into the human imagination ever since, and is one of the prime movers in the Anthropocene, and the desire for a comfortable global lifestyle that is currently producing global warming through the release of carbon dioxide. The Roman model of society included road works for enhanced transport, new towns, public amenities such as drains, aqueducts, water supplies, new law and tax systems, libraries and schools, and specific heating systems for houses and other buildings such as baths and theatres (cf., Wilson Jones 2000), that were made possible through the design and upkeep of furnaces. Even though such innovations were evident in other parts of the world (e.g., China), it is through the example of the Roman dynasties, that one can see a direct link between an increase in the possible benefits of improved energy exchange and the Anthropocene, because of the inter-relation with the carbon trails, and these linkages have to be dealt with today to escape and/or make a difference through education (ctN4).

The Roman Republic and Empire borders were patrolled and protected by a strong, disciplined, and well-equipped military force (Phang 2008), that fought numerous, continuous wars, in every part of the Roman world. Further, within the confines of that force, trade was made viable and guarded, extensive mining operations for different metals and coal were carried out across the Roman territories, and new innovations led to mechanised modes of mining and transport, plus inventiveness at all levels flourished throughout the Roman world, and was frequently connected to mining and metallurgy. As such, one may stipulate that the prototype for today's global system was born. Even though money was still dependent on the physical separateness and reality of Roman coins, and not the digital fluidity of today's 'capital', the Romans came up with the architecture that links the expansion and defence of a territory, with enjoying and using the benefits of this expansion, in well-serviced urban spaces, and particular, in terms of deploying the material and energy resources that had been successfully harnessed, e.g., building a thriving, educated culture, and relishing its pleasures (Laurence 2009).

Such social linkages created new strings of concepts for groups of *Homo sapiens* in the Roman period, that were henceforth connected to new energy surpluses, such as those relating to pleasure and leisure time, and not having to survive against the odds in a continual state of potentially facing death and ruin (nomadism/subsistence). As such, the Roman energy circuit sits in our instinctual and unconscious responses to the world, as a shared historical memory of how to live well inside and beyond nature. There have even been attempts to track temperature rises across the land mass of Europe through the Roman historic period due to the specific mix of increased industrial activity, agricultural usages (Gilgen et al. 2019), the burning off of foliage, and the use of domestic/civic fuels such as coal and wood. Investigation has found that the Romans did have a real impact on the climate beyond natural variation in temperature, proving the first definite evidence for anthropogenic effects on climate change (Ibid.). These climate effects can be associated with the Roman construction of a new mode of comfort and sedentary living, that deployed intensive energy resources such as mined coal, and made circuits of new energy exchange and distribution. These circuits need to be escaped through education to survive the Anthropocene (ctN4).

6   Steam Engines

The Western Roman Empire fell in 476 AD. Europe descended into what we now refer to as the 'Dark Ages' after this, there followed an age which was characterised by absolute monarchy and feudalism. However, over the next 1000 years, land empires did thrive in other parts of the world, e.g. the Ottoman Turks, the Mali Empire, the Yuan and Ming Dynasties, the Mughal Empire, the

Aztecs and the Inca (e.g., U. Singh 2008). However, one can plausibly argue that the social models of these land empires were based on the earlier, absolute rulership and power systems, that came from the energy/life threshold period in the carbon trails, and in the main did not include the complex, augmented relationships between energy exchange and civil life that we find in the Roman period (Woolf 1992). As such, one can say that in terms of the unconscious drive of the carbon trail, even though civilisations continued to flourish and fail all over the world in the intervening years post the Roman decline, the next important leap on the carbon trail occurs in 1780 AD (ctN5). This is when global trade routes had been well established at sea, colonies were taking over from indigenous powers, steam based machines had been invented, and sedentary societies benefitting from these systems were stable and developed enough to begin to fully exploit coal as a major energy source to power these interconnected systems. Thus, *Homo sapiens* entered into the industrial age, which we are still, arguably in today (for example, most power stations are still types of steam engine, though not always run on coal), through and by which, exponential increases in world human populations are either living out the global steam driven lifestyle, or are exposed to it (hence creating desire), and that has resulted in consistent increases in fossil fuel usage.

The Romans invented systems and devices that allowed for the heating of water to power thermal control over spaces such as homes, baths, and public buildings. The invention of the steam engine expanded this development, in that it provided a means to do work without continuous manpower (such as the turning of spindles with handles). There had been experiments with steam powered devices as early as the late Roman period that had tried to capture the formation of steam to do radial mechanical work, known as the aeolipile (Martin 2016). These early designs were not forgotten, but progressively modified and experimented with, to try and improve the efficiency and effectiveness of the steam engine design. One of the most famous inventors in this lineage of steam engines that began in the late Roman period, and carried through the medieval years was James Watt (1736–1819). Watt patented several innovations that helped to move the design of steam engines onwards, such as the use of a condenser, parallel motion, and the centrifugal governor (Scherer 1965). The result of these inventions over many years, and through his collaboration with Matthew Boulton, were to set up and install Boulton & Watt steam engines to drive the development of the industrial revolution across Britain from the 1780s onwards. The direct effect of these installations was to create a need for large amounts of coal to burn to heat the water in boilers to drive the engines, and this coal needed to be sourced, mined, and shipped to the locations of the steam engines, across Britain.

The majority of Britain was progressively transformed from the late eighteenth century onwards, as the invention of steam engines drove the need for coal. Large scale iron production, factories (especially mills), new towns built to house workers for the factories, and transport networks to feed the industrial landscape such as canals then railways, made enormous inroads into the natural environment (cf., Foster 1994). Again, one should not suggest that Britain in the late eighteenth and nineteenth century, is solely responsible for the Anthropocene, but, parallel and in synchrony with the influence of Rome, it has had a disproportionate influence on the basic ways in which the carbon trails are organised and enacted today (Ruddiman 2013). Initial organisation of the Industrial Revolution in Britain largely followed the feudal systems of the Dark Ages, as the aristocratic hold on Britain was strong, but the desire to emulate and surpass the classical Roman period was profound, and innovations were gradually introduced to create the impression of a prosperous and successful society that would benefit more generally from the carbon trails of the steam engine, e.g., new consumer products and housing (and these incentives enhanced desire for the carbon trails), and these configurations have to be dealt with through education in the contemporary moment (ctN5).

Significantly, this story of the Anthropocene from a Deleuze/Guattari (1984, 1988) analysis, does not assert the superiority of Western, white men from Britain or elsewhere. Rather, this nonlinear narrative incorporates influences in terms of unconscious drives, and the drive of the carbon trail was significantly altered due to the industrial revolution in Britain and in other parts of the world, before and at the start of the nineteenth century (cf., Grassby 1999). The point at stake here, is that the invention of the steam engine, and the uses that it was put to, along with the expansion of the colonial enterprises, and the beginnings of a bureaucratic state in Britain to maintain the linkages between 'coal-resources-work', was now possible. Simply put, the industrial revolution saw a huge increase in the need for coal mining. This coal was transported to the sites of the boilers to heat water to drive the steam engines. These steam engines drove machines in mills that, for example, wove garments from cotton that had been sourced and shipped from one of the colonies (cf., Hills and Pacey 1972). Thus an energy circuit was formed, with *Homo sapiens* fitting into these circuits as component parts. The body and minds of the humans involved with these circuits were progressively transformed from the thousands of years of nomadism and subsistence life, fully connected to the chaos, danger and life of nature, to a component part in an energy system. Even the owners of the mines, mills, commercial shipping lines, and plantations became parts of the system, due to their roles as administrators and overseers.

This reading of the carbon trail and its influence by steam engines and the industrial revolution does not overlook the racism, cruelty, and/or the potentially miserable, confined and exploited lives that factory workers endured at the time (Hopkins 1982). Rather, these conditions are written into the new energy circuits that became increasingly apparent in this period. Numerous military expeditions and protection of these circuits is also written into these circuits for their survival, and it is interesting that Deleuze/Guattari (1988) refer to a 'war machine' in terms of how the military fits in with and works alongside and inside the expansion of the state, as happened in the nineteenth century due to the new energy circuits (cf., MacGregor and Murray 2001). Europe underwent more than a 1000 years of feudal warfare and life after the fall of the Western Roman Empire. This system had to endure attack on its eastern borders from nomadic invaders, including the Mongol hordes, who were a lethal mix of self-sufficient, nomadic warriors, serving an Eastern state, often many thousands of kilometres from where the hordes attacked, and frequently attempting to displace a sedentary (fortified) state. In terms of the carbon trail and its evolution through the invention of steam engines, the implication is that the military, even though responding to and working with the orders of the state, had their own internal logic, predominantly still based on nomadic and naturally grounded principles of war.

Congruent with these developments, and the new energy circuits of the industrial revolution carbon trails, was an advancement in the sciences, called the Enlightenment (Mokyr 2011). Although the Enlightenment was predominantly an activity of rich, white, European men, it had profound consequences in terms of the ways in which the energy circuits functioned alongside and within the industrialisation of the landscape. The scientific knowledge and methods that we have today in areas such as: climate change, environmental studies, ecology, geology and biology, owe much to this period, and whereas these discoveries were not directly or immediately applied to the carbon trails of the time, or the destruction of the natural world that these trails were encouraging, for the situation in the Anthropocene to change, the scientific facts as we know them have to be converted to social action (cf., Cole and Mirzaei Rafe 2017) (and the strategy of this book is to deploy education in this context, Nx). This is one of the basic problems of the Anthropocene, and also one of its paradoxes, in that mechanisms that we have for finding out the truth of the Anthropocene, and the sharing of good evidence about it, coincide with a period of history which pivotally established a course for and as the Anthropocene in the first place. The Enlightenment society, with the steam engine at its heart, working continuously to extend and accelerate the carbon trails, was in the main oblivious to the destruction that it would wreck 200+ years later, due to the release of the invisible gas carbon dioxide. In multiple ways, the now frequently discredited 'romantic science' (e.g., Mitchell 2013), that surfaced after the Enlightenment, with its call to deeply (re)immerse the human and their thinking in nature (on every level, including the unconscious), may be worthwhile to reconsider, as it could meaningfully address negative tendencies that were to follow in the industrialisation of life, and that has resulted in the contemporary Anthropocene. Romantic science is a way to understand the accumulation and deployment of educational forces in this book (Nx), and as responding to the unconscious drives of the Anthropocene.

7   Fossil Fuel Capitalism

We live in an industrial age, and even though the British Empire has fallen away, many of its power structures and mechanisms that control the carbon trails were transplanted and augmented by the rise of America, and what has come in its wake, i.e., one world, global capitalism (cf., Galbraith 1952/1993). After 1850 AD (ctN6), the discovery and use of oil has been added to coal as a high yielding energy source, although oil has many other ubiquitous uses, such as the production of plastics to make a host of products, which has spread the carbon trails even further worldwide. Since the late nineteenth century, human history could be said to be dominated by the use of fossil fuels, which has led to unequal economic development, great wealth being distributed amongst the beneficiaries of the sale and ownership of the fossil fuels supplies, and wars being fought over their exploitation and use (most pointedly in the Middle East). The recent scientific realisation that the widespread burning of fossil fuels harms the environment through global warming and the release of CO_2, has to face the history of the carbon trail, and the drive which that entails, which is inextricably entwined with tool-enhancement as these last two chapters have shown. These drives have been fully enmeshed in the history of modern, global, industrial society since at least the 1850s, and the world view and practice that this history entails, which could be named as fossil fuel capitalism, and this system is the essential challenge to understand, dismantle, and reverse for environmentalism in the Anthropocene (Malm 2016), here understood to stimulate new pedagogy (ctN6).

The carbon trails are deep set and complicated to extricate ourselves from. Enormous tankers full of oil travel the globe on the seas, and are protected by the world's most powerful military forces. Above them, aeroplanes circle the Earth relentlessly, running on jet fuel, releasing carbon dioxide, and carrying hundreds of thousands of travellers every day (even during a pandemic!). On the land, roads criss-cross virtually every section of passable earth, and on them skate cars, trucks, buses and motorbikes, all burning petrol or diesel (there are still only a tiny fraction of electric cars as I write these words in 2020). Enormous cities are predominantly powered by coal, oil and gas burning power stations, and these power sources emit carbon dioxide to generate energy for the ever hungry, consumptive lives of swelling sedentary human populations, and everything that is necessary in these lives (Wagner 2009). Much of this current day, fossil fuel using technology could be imminently replaced by renewable energy sources, but it is clear that this is not a straightforward process, otherwise sensible government policy would have already redirected tax money to achieve this goal, in order to avert catastrophic global warming. However, this is largely not happening (to scale, or not quickly enough), and one of the main reasons for this inaction is that the carbon trails, which this chapter has shown through a Deleuze/Guattari analysis to have an instinctual, unconscious connection to human relationships with fire (ctNx), but are now wholly merged into international financial markets, and how they operate, as well as to the intrinsic high energy yield fascination of fossil fuels, that has broached the 'energy-life' threshold (Smil 2017).

The synchronicity between the vectors and flows of fossil fuels as being intrinsic to global capitalism, is unmistakable and nearly unbreakable, the strategy here to do anything about it is educational (Nx). Capitalism is characterised by booms and busts, as investors stake their earnings on rises in the stock exchanges, and withdraw funds as opportunities fade away. Certainly, the realisation that the burning of fossil fuels causes global warming through the release of carbon dioxide, is a reason for concern for the markets, and has led to some disinvestment in fossil fuel companies (cf., Braungardt, van den Bergh and Dunlop 2019). However, even though there has been a decline in the attractive nature of long term fossil fuel investment, the regular profits that the industry still makes, ensures that the sector is a significant part of the global financial scene, as it proves to be lucrative for investors. Further, there are many countries, and state systems around the world that rely on fossil fuel revenue, such as Saudi Arabia, Russia, Australia, Iran, Venezuela and Kuwait (cf., Morris 2016), plus, there are gigantic fossil fuel corporations and their subsidiaries, that employ hundreds of thousands of workers. In many ways, the carbon trails are too important to economies and individual country prosperity to allow to fail, and are therefore subsidised and supported, even though the potentially catastrophic facts of climate change in the Anthropocene are well known and have been repeated *ad nauseam*.

The carbon trails are essential to the functioning of fossil fuel capitalism, yet these lines are drawn with ever decreasing clarity, like spider's webs in the midday sun. The very ubiquity and indiscernibility of the trails makes them challenging to extinguish (we can try to do something through future-oriented pedagogy, Nx). This point is one of the problems with seeing climate change in the Anthropocene as a quantitative function of reducing carbon emissions by a specific amount in a certain amount of time, to avert dangerous climate change (Steffen et al. 2018). In contrast, the Deleuze/Guattari (1984, 1988) analysis of the carbon trails as instinctual and unconscious aspects of fossil fuel capitalism, admits to the fact that the trails are already immanent to us, they are inside our thoughts and desires, as we need them to do pretty much anything that we want to achieve in the world today. The idea of reducing carbon emissions by a quantifiable amount assumes that these emissions are a static quantity that is simply addressed (as a quantity), or can be balanced by carbon reduction strategies such as planting more trees (Hof, Dymond and Mladenoff 2017). This mathematical approach to climate change in the Anthropocene fails because the very emissions themselves are entirely wrapped up in our lives as carbon trails, that are always in movement, and that take us from A to B (and to dream about it, and to have the energy/imagination to go from A to B in the first place). To reduce carbon emissions, we really need to stop going from A to B, which would most likely see a collapse in the world economy, and would end civilised life as we know it today, thus requiring the expanded now (Nx) as a reimagined education, to avert such a catastrophe.

As an example of this point, we can go back to the 11th of September 2001. I was a teacher in a high school in Buenos Aires, Argentina. On that day, we were alerted to the 9–11 event by one of the students. These were pre-ubiquitous internet access days, so without smart phones or iPads, we gathered around a static computer with internet access, that was showing CNN with live coverage of the attacks. As such, we witnessed the second plane crash into the tower, and the chaos, panic and confusion that ensued in New York. As a result of the attacks, all commercial flights were cancelled in the US and elsewhere for the next 3 days. Analysis of this period has shown that climate temperatures dropped, as the carbon trails above our heads had ceased to be formed, both changing the cloud formations back to a more natural patterns, and reducing the carbon dioxide emissions briefly for those few days (Cain 2016). Thus, we can see what it takes to significantly reduce carbon emissions in the Anthropocene, not as a gradual reduction through calculated, incremental and renewable/transitional means, but as a sudden, dramatic reversal, that would leave millions of people stranded, bewildered and desperate. As a result, no democratic government or authority in the world will actively legislate to enact such measures in their entirety, but they would encourage a new educational means to address these issues as suggested here.

What are the consequences of this Deleuze/Guattari (1984, 1988) analysis of the carbon trails? Fundamentally, to realise any kind of resistance to the way things are, requires a mode of new thinking around the dynamics and force diagrams that have been spelled out in the Anthropocene (cf., Hall 2020), here being drawn out as education. It is not adequate to feel guilty about boarding a plane, or using petrol to drive your car. Real action on climate change requires attending to the carbon trails themselves, and going deeply into the entangled knots that support and enliven them. In effect, a new systems thinking approach that obviates the embedded and multiply efficacious nature of the carbon trails is required, this approach could be linked to Deleuze/Guattari's rhizomatics (1988) and education. Rhizomatics, if implemented, would have the potential to out-manoeuvre the enormous inter-meshed functioning of the fossil fuel capitalist world, because it is a stealth tactic to understanding and doing anything about the problem.[1] Rhizomatics presents a convoluted methodology, that avoids instrumental reason, and acts as a subterranean and/or underground strategy to figuring out, in the case of this book, what has produced the Anthropocene, and how resolution maybe sought through education and social change (Chapters 6 and 7).

Furthermore, in contrast to a rhizomatic approach to climate change action, climate change protesters and protests can become part of the Anthropocene problem, because they attempt to set up a rational dialogue with fossil fuel capitalism, to sensibly lower emissions through renewable and sustainable technologies. However, fossil fuel capitalism does not work that way. The protests and protestors merely become imbricated in its functioning, their agency is (re)deployed by fossil fuel capitalism to help make profits from clean energy products, that don't actually replace or substitute fossil fuels in any way, but simply divert attention from the ever growing carbon trails. A case in point is the funding of the outwardly radical anti-fossil fuel group, 350.org by the Rockefeller Brother Fund (2020). Why would a foundation that is attached to one of the largest fossil fuel companies in history (Standard Oil) fund an anti-fossil fuel movement? The reason is that in this way they can control and limit the group to acceptable activities, such as peaceful protests and rallies, whilst carbon emissions continue to escalate. In effect, the Rockefeller Fund use, what is for them, a very small amount of money, to make the public believe that something is at last being done about climate change, whilst the extraordinary revenue from oil is protected, hidden, augmented and channelled. The carbon trails act as capital, which Deleuze/Guattari deal with through their conceptual analysis as linked to schizophrenia (1984, 1988), as the actions of capital flows can literally drive you mad. Capital flows do not care about human agency, subjectivity, identity, culture, the truth or values, but are only set to work in the world to make profit, which is the primary ideology to be overturned through enhanced pedagogic action in this book (ctN6). As such, capital has created an unreal world, called in the next chapter along with other influences as: 'the phallocene'.

TABLE 3.1   The pedagogy of the carbon trail

Plateaux	Dates	Pedagogy (https://iiraorg.com/carbon-trail/)
ctN1	1.7 million yrs	Inquiry into the prehistory control and use of fire
ctN2	12000 BC	Examination of fire as the hearth and religious focus of early cities
ctN3	3500 BC	Learning about the earliest uses of coal in society
ctN4	400 BC	Learning about ancient city thermodynamic processes (e.g., Rome)
ctN5	1780 AD	Inquiry into the nature of the steam engine
ctN6	1850 AD	Examination of the uses and deployment of oil

Note

1   Here translated to new pedagogy, hosted at https://iiraorg.com/education-the-anthropocene-and-deleuze-guattari/

CHAPTER 4

The Phallocene

1   Introduction

The previous chapters on tool-enhancement and the carbon trail have drawn out two inter-related and enmeshed lines, that merge in the Anthropocene. These two themes, though incredibly important, and fundamental to the ways in which humans are currently transforming and warming the planet, do not go far enough to explain how the Anthropocene has been created. Humans are tool creators and have become instinctually attuned to fire and carbon for millions of years, yet they are also biological animals, programmed to reproduce through mammalian sexual intercourse. This aspect of the Anthropocene cannot be overlooked, and Deleuze/Guattari attend to it by positing desire at the very heart of their philosophy (1984, 1988). However, their theory of desire, and the consequent theory of the drives (and its escape routes through education) that is being presented here in terms of a non-linear history of the Anthropocene, is not a psychoanalytic, Freudian rendering of the unconscious as operant through symbolic or metaphoric means, or understood as the expressions of repression and catharsis (Freud 1905). Rather, Deleuze/Guattari (1984, 1988) reject personalised and sexually familiarised (human) Freudian concepts, such as the Oedipal subject and the 'Id', and instead render desire to be operant in the collective, social field. This intellectual move has vast consequences for their philosophy, and how humans function in the world, as sexuality and its effects are removed from private secrets that are repressed, and that one may be embarrassed about, and that should be kept from prying eyes in a subconscious. Rather, the whole social world and everything that we do in it contains and relates to sexuality (including, in the context of this book, constructing the Anthropocene and education). As has been previously suggested, humans are hyper social animals (cf., Fox, Pope and Ellis 2017), therefore, the approach to the Anthropocene of this book is that the social world that we have created for ourselves in the Anthropocene is also a hyper sexualised one. Hence, the Deleuze/Guattari (1984, 1988) analysis of this chapter is in line with their theory of sexuality as a socially circulating mechanism, augmented by global capitalism and its spectacular media machine. The title of this chapter, 'the phallocene' reflects this hyper sexuality, but also works on the level of a double entendre, in that the phallus, as represented, is also 'fallacious'. This chapter will henceforth help to explain how we have got to the state of ubiquitous, mediated 'fake news', and the ways in which the hyper sexuality of the human species has undergone transformations through an account of its non-linear history. Let it be noted that in no way does the naming of the Anthropocene as the phallocene attribute male sexuality above or as better than female sexuality. Instead, the sexuality of the Anthropocene as the phallocene, is an outwards, circulating, material field of sexual interaction and becoming, that gives us an indication as to the current state of humanity, and its effects on the planet Earth, in these times of environmental and climate crises.

2   The Phallic God-Heads

The extensive prehistoric conditioning, instinctual and unconscious forces that constitute tool-enhancement and the carbon trail do not figure in/as part of the phallocene (these drives in Chapters 2 and 3, explore human life dating back several million years). This characteristic of the phallocene comes about because these extensive periods (pre-Holocene) were not subject to dominating sedentary powers that had attempted to augment, curb and control sexuality for their own purposes, and to the benefit of a state system (cf., Bullough 1976). Again, it is important that we do not idealise or romanticise the hunter/gatherer, prehistoric, nomadic and subsistence period of human history, as simply being better or 'more natural' that contemporary life, although one may stipulate that in this period, humans were more closely connected to nature. The contrast between pre and post Holocene life is important, not because *Homo sapiens* lived in an innocent, 'state of nature', or before their sexualities have been euthanised by civilisation, but due to the translation of the Anthropocene into a workable concept according to the Deleuze/Guattari (1984, 1988) analysis of this book, and its treatment through pedagogy.

The concept of the Anthropocene in this book starts to work as the phallocene when tool-enhancement and the carbon trails are sufficiently enmeshed to require a third term for their evolution. In this context, the fundamental problem for the Anthropocene is not its scientific definition, or when it officially started, but how to translate the reality of the enmeshment of tool-enhancement with the carbon trail into controlled (human) actions. This problem of human enactment through the drives and the consequent control of human life, touches upon and includes the sexual and imaginary, desirous aspects of the Anthropocene, which I call, after Liz Kinnamon, Jess Mach, and the SCUM manifesto by Valerie Solanas (1968), as 'the phallocene' (cf., Cole 2017a). The phallocene is a reworking of human instinctual history using Deleuze/Guattari (1984, 1988) philosophy. Feminist arguments and how they have come to permeate educational practice (cf., Hennessy 2012), run through much of this chapter and book in terms of its focus on materiality, and the questioning of a unified subjectivity through the four drives of the Anthropocene. The specific argument in this chapter concerns the mode that the lineages of tool-enhancement and carbon trail has been coming together and augmented through and by the phallic imaginary as a drive, which this writing will demonstrate through a non-linear history of the phallocene, and as an aspect of the force/energy/lines that have created the contemporary Anthropocene (and its subsequent educational escape routes).

The integrating processes of tool-enhancement and the carbon trails through the phallocene began approximately 4000–3200 BC (pN1) in Egypt and Sumer, through the gradual centralisation of nomadic, shamanic religions into one faith, controlled by a hierarchical priesthood, and directed to the worship of a pharaoh or king-God (cf., Assmann 2003). This relocation and transformation of religion was an incredibly arduous process, as the hunters and gatherers/nomads had been practicing their particular religions based on separate ecosystems, movement, having visions, prophecy, and survival for hundreds of thousands of years. The prehistoric animisms had been locally directed, worshipped a range of Gods from the variant environments where the hunter/gatherers lived, deployed shamans as a means to predict the future, and to aid with important functions in the tribes, such as healing and understanding nature. Early centralised religions managed by theological bureaucracies, firstly had to convince the populations of their relevance, and latterly had to replace over time the deep-seated animist beliefs in the populations with the ceremonies of pharaoh or king directed, multi-pantheon, phallic God-head worship (cf., Kunin 2003).

Civilisations in the fertile crescent of the Middle East (the Uruk period) and Egypt had begun to establish themselves after 4000–3200 BC. The practise of agriculture, the emergence of urban life, pottery, armies, bronze smelting and absolute monarchs supported by religious and administrative retinues, demonstrate how tool-enhancement, the carbon trails, and the phallocene had begun to work together to order and reorder human life as drives, that set them apart from their 'closer-to-nature' predecessors. The early civilisations took the shamanic and animist notions of a multiplicity of Gods that interacted with them, but transformed them into hierarchical and representable forms in terms of paintings, writings, and enormous monuments such as temples and statues (e.g., Trigger 1993). The sheer scale of the religious monuments that have survived since this period, show how intensely the rulers had to work to convince populations of the veracity of the new religions. In many ways, the new religious orders had to convince the populations that they had the power of life over death, and that the new hierarchies of Gods were better than the old shamanic orders. Admittedly, this process doesn't happen everywhere at this time, and, for example, we do see west Asian civilisations still adhering to nomadic modes of existences, later collectively titled under the rubric of 'the Scythians' (Rolle 1989) by the Greeks.

It is through the ancient Greeks and their extensive mythology, that we have the most detailed account of how the phallic God-heads worked. Again, and as has been argued in the previous chapters, this book is not a solely western account of the evolution of the Anthropocene through a Deleuze/Guattari (1984, 1988) analysis. Rather, the Greek Pantheon is one of the most intense, familiar (for many readers of this book), and as such, extremely well developed example of a multiplicity of Gods interacting with the everyday lives of humans (Sissa and Detienne 2000). The fabulous stories that we have from ancient Greek mythology are filled with Gods interacting with humans, sexuality, intrigue and extraordinary drama. The Greek mythological universe is a 'more-than-human' world, which isn't only intended to emphasise the ignored aspects of the universe that are non-human (and our relations with them), but augments the powers that flow through humans that are greater than us, and can lead to the consideration of bigger issues. The Greek ancient society was a mix of nomadic warriors with a sedentary layered base, and became an expansionary empire under Alexander, and after the defeat of the Persians, but it is through the mythology that we have direct access to the vitality of this society.

The phallic God-heads of the ancient Greek religion did not repress sexuality, but in many ways made it stronger, by creating imaginative and incredible scenarios whereby human and God-like sexualities could interact. Thus, citizens were not controlled and repressed by this institutionalised religion, but were augmented by it to greater action. In a very explicit way, the Greek mythological effect on the psyche is to expand and exult sexuality and its intrigues, and not to diminish their impacts on thought. Pleasure is a central aspect of this religion (Foucault 1983/1990), and even though one could state that the ancient Greek Pantheon does count as a stepping stone on the road to climate change in the Anthropocene through the phallic God-heads (which are not animist), and how they have helped to constitute the phallocene, the attractiveness and power of the ancient Greek Gods is undeniable. After reading the Greek myths, one must concur with Nietzsche (1887/1989) in his assessment of the ancient Greek life as being full, exciting, and as casting a long shadow over the dull lives that we frequently lead today, and that could be enhanced through new educational practice (pN1).

3   One Phallus-God

During the rule of the ancient Egyptian pharaoh, Akhenaten (1353-1336 BC) approx., there is evidence to suggest that the Egyptian Pantheon of Gods were dismantled, and he replaced it with the worship of one God. This God was called Aten, and was the God of the Sun (Goldwasser 2010). One can state that this move by Akhenaten was risky, as it had the potential to alienate Egyptian society, and especially the specific priests and their retinues who served the worship of particular Gods. The consequence of Akhenaten's change in worship and ritual, was to concentrate the supernatural world, and hence people's imaginations and thoughts on one almighty God, rather than a host of different Gods. This change in direction is therefore more likely to make the worship of one God part of an other-worldly practice, disconnected from the everyday fears and thoughts of the Egyptians (Allen 1989). Further, the abstract nature of the one-God worship, relieves God of the sexuality and possibly physicality of, for example, the Greek Gods, and their often lusty and violent ways. However, Akhenaten's revolution in monotheism did not last, and when he died, the Egyptian Pantheon of worship was restored. It is not until the surfacing of the Jewish faith, about 800 years later, that the one phallus-God started to operate in earnest, beyond the confines of one pharaoh's rule.

At approximately 500 BC (pN2), the multi-God religions started to break down into monotheistic religions in Israel and elsewhere, as a result of phallic directness over time, and worship towards a God-like king (Becking 2001). Even though multiple gods in religions remained in place, and to this day, animism and polytheistic religions such as Hinduism still importantly exist, and are practiced around the world, the tendency towards one God worship, phallic monotheism, and how that relates to tool-enhancement and the carbon trail in terms of social and cultural codes and scales, are a guide to understanding how and why we have reached the predicament of the Anthropocene as we perceive and imagine it (Conty 2019), and how it may be escaped through education (pN2). One could argue that all polytheistic and animist religions had elements of monotheism in them, but they were not formalised into the worship of one God, and the retinues of multiple gods had not been eradicated. However, the point for the phallocene is that once the polytheistic order starts to break down, ancient religions such as Judaism begin to take its place, and the scene is set for global regimes of conditioning. This statement is important, because the transcendence into one ineffable God takes away locally directed modes of worship, and, for example, the adoration of particular natures in these localities, as connected to notions of natural gods, and such means to worship could help in terms of local eco-regeneration in the Anthropocene.

It is vital to understand that this process of monotheistic transcendence, that has seen whole sectors of the human population become detached from and live apart from nature in the phallocene, has happened over the span of several thousand years (cf., Grimes 2014). The establishment of monotheism amongst the polytheistic religions, caused a rupture in the thoughts and dreams of humans, that over time has disconnected them from a multiplicity of gods, and has attempted to reconnect them to one, transcendent, almighty, and all powerful God. This reconnection is phallic, because it necessarily works on the unconscious and imaginative levels, where sexual desire operates to create yearning and love for an almighty being. One may surmise that such desire was transposed to an almighty leader such as king or pharaoh, in the case of the Jewish tribe, to strong leaders such as David or Solomon and their images (Knoppers 1995). Further, the introduction of monotheism encourages bureaucratic and administrative structures to gather around worship, invited by the transportation to nothingness, and the void that is created by an empty pantheon of gods. The multiple god, polytheistic religions were already bureaucratic, and did have a clerical class of priests administering the rights of the particular gods, but this tendency was solidified and centralised under the turn to one God.

Alongside the increase in bureaucracy and administration of monotheism is an increase in law. The Jewish Torah are a set of instructions on how to live that have supposedly come from God through the revelations of Moses. The Jewish religion relies heavily on the written word of the Old Testament, a sacred text that needs to be studied and learnt amongst the believers (Batnitzky 2013). Thus, language was introduced and formalised as worship, and even though there are parts of the Old Testament in which sexuality is glorified, such as the Songs of Solomon, in the main, the introduction of one phallus-God through the written word is to make literacy compulsory and physicality secondary. As such, another step away from the animist and shamanic religions is formalised. Knowledge of the holy traditions through text is passed on from generation to generation via literacy and the written word, and even though oral traditions are still extremely important in the Jewish faith, reading and writing become increasingly utilised and dominate sacred communications (Shahak 1994). As such, worship, faith, and prayer are transposed from taking place outside and in specific natural locations, and happen in relation to holy books that have to be protected at all costs.

Accordingly, humans learn to read the word of God from the holy texts rather than reading nature for signs of life, as they would have done for thousands of years before. The nature of what is holy and sacred therefore changes, as do the skills and requirements for understanding the nature of the divine. In effect, a specialised class of administrators (we now call Rabbis) was born, that read and analysed the holy books, and spread their teachings amongst the people (Kanarfogel 2011). The Rabbi were part of a strict religious hierarchy, that served the ancient rulers of Israel, and included sages and prophets, and many different categories and types of priest. In effect, the one phallus-God, in all (his) majesty and mystery, encouraged a large clerical class, that were the accepted experts in the laws of God. This class shielded the rulers from the populace, due to the ritual and faith they administered, but they could also become a threat, as power could be concentrated amongst their ranks (cf., Neusner 1969). The clerics of one phallus-God could call on the holy power that had been divested in them, to act in unison against the royalty if necessary. This is one reason (amongst others) why the line of Jewish Kings did not survive, and their power became transmuted to the heads of their community, and as they spread around the world. In terms of the pedagogy that we may glean from the one phallus-God (pN2), one may question how the cleric class gains and distributes power on the basis of a transcendental God through textual practice.

4   Establishment of Phallus-Worship

The switch from a pantheon of multiple gods to one God is one of the most momentous changes in human history. Multiple god worship more closely mimics and echoes animist nature worship and shamanism, that were attempts by early humans to understand the forces in the natural world, and to be united with them through religion (cf., Harvey 2005). Multiple god worship became institutionalised through the early civilisations over thousands of years, but the ways in which absolute, God-like rulers subjugated their populations started to break down along with the formal structures of polytheism in society, when they were combined with the move to one 'true' (unknowable) God. However, the movement to one God remained relatively discrete, until the most important date in this material Deleuze/Guattari (1984, 1988) analysis of the phallocene, 600 AD (pN3). Even though Christianity began before this date (Teeple 1992), it was with the start of Islam, in combination with Christianity, that the phallic imaginary of One God begins to change global human behaviours, highlighted by mantras such as: 'the father, the son, and the holy ghost', and that gives us a vital pivot to work through as education in the Anthropocene.

The Deleuze/Guattari (1984, 1988) analysis of this book is not anti-Christianity or anti-Islam, but seeks to understand how self-same repetitions, set up and augmented by phallic logic, and seen, for example, in the inability to steer a course away from the reality of the Anthropocene, or to do anything about it, and that are notably present in the notion of human exceptionalism (Haraway 2015), have come to pass (and how to resist them through education). We cannot go back in time and 'unstart' Christianity or Islam, but we can question the domination and centralisation of human concerns over anything 'un' or non-human, and how these deep-seated prejudices have helped to create a form of blindness to environmental matters contained in, for example, capitalism, colonialism and neoliberalism (cf., Comaroff and Comaroff 2008). The phallic logics of insertion into and exploitation of nature as an infinite resource, and not working with or reciprocally as part of nature, defines a common and widespread belief system and set of drives, that has pushed humans forward into the black hole and event horizon of the Anthropocene extinction, and that are attempted to be realigned here through education (pN3).

The reason that 600 AD is an important date in terms of the phallocene, is because it demarcates a time since when two major world religions, and others that have followed, e.g., Sikhism, have set out sets of rituals and beliefs in a one phallus-God (G. S. Singh 2008). This one phallus-God worship represents a tremendous movement and synchronisation of human bodies and minds, as and when they attend Christian mass, or listen to the imam in the mosque (cf., Goddard 2003) and pray. It goes without saying that Christian and Muslim worshippers are not literally worshipping phalluses. Rather, investment in the rituals and rites of the Christian and Muslim faiths, represents a diversion, and channelling of sexual energy towards one ineffable, transcendental God. The object that the worshippers desire becomes an unknown, but, at the same time, an incredibly powerful force in the universe (human and latterly environmental). God is everywhere but nowhere, and worship of whom shows us how to live the good, moral life (and enter heaven). Thus, Christianity and Islam provide blueprints for (human) living, they write codes in the worship of one God for the masses, and the control of human life through phallic-directedness. In contrast, pre-phallic religions, such as animist and shamanistic worship, establish rituals and rites through direct relationships and insights into specific and local ways in which humans and nature interact and function together.

Thus, after 600 AD, the possibility of connecting one's religious and spiritual imaginations with many local gods and nature was incrementally diminished through the establishment of the regimes of one-God phallus worship (cf., Van der Toorn 1996). At the same time, multiple God religions such as Hinduism, Shinto, Buddhism and animist traditions and practises still existed, and are extremely widespread to this day, but this story of how we have arrived at the mind and behavioural state of the phallocene in the Anthropocene, was initiated and begun to spread as major world religions after 600 AD. The thinking connection for this chapter to make is between the unified movement to one-God worship, and the breakdown in environmental understanding, sensitivity, and ultimately action, that one-God worship encapsulates, and how to treat these actions through education (pN3). This breakdown does not mean that Christians and Muslims cannot be environmental activists, be aware of, or help with environmental matters (e.g., Boyd 1999). Rather, the point and problematic for this chapter, is to describe how the widespread one-God phallus directed worship, has related to the environmental problems and the consequences that we see today, and how it may be attended to through education (pN3).

Firstly, we have experienced an alteration over time from understanding and reading nature, to cognitively putting emphasis into the reading of books (becoming literate). Both Christianity and Islam placed literacy centrally in terms of reading their holy books, and as a pillar of their religions. This combined religious action meant that literate codes and their consequences in terms of how people acted, became sacrosanct and central to social life, replacing the codes and manners that people had lived in and as part of nature for millennia (Peoples, Duda and Marlowe 2016). Further, privileged readers of the holy books were placed as gate keepers and experts in the reading, explanation, and interpretation of the holy books. In effect, a specialist class of literate cleric was initiated in Christianity and Islam, that held power through their textual learnedness at the centre of the religions, and worked in unison with others in non-religious hierarchies, such as aristocrats, military and civic rulers, to maintain and extend that specific power. The holy books contained the words of God, and as such, they were to be revered and exalted by the populace, beyond the everydayness of living in nature, or understanding how to best respond to nature's forces (cf., Tremlin 2006). Consequently, the phallocene emerges as a practice and system of thought over time, in which the variations in human nature are understood as a result of the ritualised writing down of what is holy, here to be attended to through pedagogy (pN3).

For example, theologies around interpretation of the holy texts grew up in Christianity and Islam, that have influenced the humanities, philosophy, education and science through the ages. The essential contention of these theologies concerns how to uphold the existence of an abstract, non-verifiable God, and how to connect this existence to the everyday moral behaviour of humans (e.g., Punt 2005). Such a thinking project can extend and make inroads into the nature of the universe in terms of, for example, understanding the notions of zero and nothingness (e.g., Lanzetta 2001). However, the problem of the phallic directedness towards one-God over time, is that the real and concrete nature of everything not connected to zero and nothingness, becomes more obscure and difficult to understand. Established, well-argued, and extremely articulate theological positions have evolved over time since 600 AD, to justify and back up Christian and Muslim worship, these positions have moved whole communities, and continue to be extremely important and widespread nexuses of thought in the world (e.g., Jeffries and Tygart 1974). The wide ranging and extensive reiterations of these positions, can be one of the reasons why it can be so contradictory to act on climate change, despite the direct evidence from science, and why these systems need to be questioned through an expanded education practice (pN3).

Science has objectively proven the reality of anthropocentric climate change, but it remains difficult to act upon. One of the major reasons for this problem is the self-reciprocating vision of humans as being connected to one-God (Waldon 2010), and the consequent divine nature of humans. The phallus directed worship of one unknowable, but almighty God, puts humans potentially in touch with something outside and beyond nature, and thus elevates the position of humans as being special in the universe, and, for example, as possessing a non-transitory soul, that might exist beyond the direct, experienced, sensory, natural human life. One might say that this specific problem of and for the phallocene, is beyond questions about duality and/or the truth of the mind/body division. Rather, and following this Deleuze/Guattari (1984, 1988) philosophical analysis of the Anthropocene, the question of how human exceptionalism works in the case of joining the soul to God and back to morality and action, is one of circuits, vectors, and energy flows (e.g., Barker 1995). Here, these factors are understood as components of the phallocene, which as a machine, has redirected human energy and life towards the worship of one-God, and all the mysteries that this encourages and incorporates into the passing of everyday life (and those which it dismisses). Hence, the task at hand it to reconnect consciousness to everyday life through education (pN3).

Furthermore, the phallocene works in unison with tool-enhancement and the carbon trails to make in roads, lines, and to hence situate the human drives as relating to and as being about the Anthropocene. In terms of phallus-worship, churches and mosques have been built, empires and societies have been run under, through and because of the names of these religions, and all that they constitute and believe. It is interesting that even though peace and love are central axioms of both Christianity and Islam, their spread and take up has frequently been accompanied by war (cf., Jenkins 2007). This connection has come about because the phallic directedness into and as being about an ineffable, unknowable God, and as postulating life after death in heaven as being the main goal of life, makes self-sacrifice, and a fanaticism according to these postulates written into the codes of these one-God religions from their initiation (Toscano 2017), as well as the need to proselytise. Questions about and suggestions regarding life after death are written into all religions, but it is in Christianity and Islam that these directions and postulates are particularly marked. In both religions, there exists the fundamental paradox that human life is valued above everything else (because it is connected to God), yet personal sacrifice for the religion is simultaneously highly valued and esteemed (but not suicide). Along with the relationships with death that these religions establish, comes the requirement to proselytise, or to actively seek converts.

The tendency to actively seek converts makes Christianity and Islam progressive and predatory religions, looking to spread knowledge about their beliefs and practices, and to gain believers from non-believers. In the beginning of the religions, communication was restricted to those who had access to sermons and first-hand knowledge from largely hand written Bibles and Qur'ans (cf., Badry et al. 2018). As technology advanced, from printing presses, and now to global, electronic texts, understanding and discussion about Christian and Muslim beliefs and practises has become commonplace. In effect, there is now a widely held notion and link between being religious or spiritual at all, and having a set of beliefs that relate to Christianity and/or Islam in some way. This linkage further obscures and blurs any other sets of beliefs that might handle religion differently, or aid with the human-nature relationship, by resetting human sexuality away from overwhelming phallic directedness, which we seek here through education (pN3). In addition, the phallic directedness of one-God worship has linked to capitalism, and made the return to a pre one-God space for belief even harder, as the conditioning of one-God has become absorbed in and by money.

5 The Working Phallic-Week

After the establishment of the great monotheistic religions of Christianity and Islam, that have been transposed to most corners of the world over the span of the following thousand years (post 600 AD) through conquest and trade, the next deepening of the phallocene comes about after 1820 AD (pN4), and the phallic same, repetitive, industrial notion of work, tied to economics. By this time, tool-enhancement and the carbon trail had been linked to such an extent, that it was possible to lock in a notion of monetary work as being entirely compatible and transposed with 'life', and, as a basic energy inter-relationship and exchange. The phallic logic of the self-same is henceforth played out for the majority of the population by work in terms of wages and payment, the working week, and the consequent organisations of the family, government and companies, plus any other social organisation around and due to these structures, including leisure-time, travel, and in the ways in which groups interact, people learn, and identity develops and is inhibited, all of which can be attended to through education (pN4).

There has been much speculation about the nexus between capitalism, Christianity and Islam (e.g., Weber 1904–5/1992). For the purposes of this study, the particular naming of branches of Christianity, such as Protestantism or Calvinism, or the different Islamic sects such as the Shia and the Sunni, and their connections to the intensification of capitalism or otherwise, are of less importance than the ways in which the establishment of phallic worship through the one-God religions, has transmuted into the repetitions of the working phallic-week. Primarily, one-God phallic worship connects to the working phallic-week by clearing out over time the other nuanced and subtle ways in which human action may relate to the environment (Tawney 1926/1998). The worship of one entirely mystical, unknowable God, has erased the subject of specific and knowable connections to the divine, (i.e., a multitude of gods in specific/ variant, natural places), and in its place, the worship and abeyance of commercial and monetary concerns, has been encouraged to take hold through history. The Deleuze/Guattari (1984, 1988) analysis of this book is not linear or causal, but figures these relations through a material analysis of the energy flows, and their subsequent modes of control and action, that the schemas for transference that have been allowed and encouraged (abstract machines). At the heart of these interactions is the ways in which one-God, phallus worship, has proven to function effectively and efficiently at the centre of capitalist and colonialist empire building (pN4).

Christianity and Islam, with their voracious need for converts, has been successfully transplanted into different parts of the world, and made subject numerous ethnic populations, from every social class (cf., Bikhazi and Gervers 1990). Alongside this shift to global one-God worship, has come military conquest and trade, and the setting up of the world economic system, as has been explored in the previous chapters on tool-enhancement and the carbon trails. However, the benefactors of this global system are in the main a tiny minority of the population, who by birth, or (quite rarely) industry, own the means to production, and are able to reap the profits from any surplus value that is established in the system (cf., Kordela 1999). For the global economic system to work in this intrinsically differential manner, the majority of the population have to work productively for little monetary reward, in effect, becoming enslaved by the unequal economics at play. The hub of this trick, is to make the majority of the population worship at the altar of possible economic success, whilst, at the same time, actively serving the needs of others. It is at the pivotal date for the phallocene of 1820 AD, that we see this 'Möbius strip' of energy interaction and exchange functioning as a model for the destruction of the environment, and what is to come in terms of the Anthropocene, and what needs to be reversed through education (pN4).

The working phallic-week is monotonous, repetitive, devoid of outside/exterior interest or distraction, yet underpinned by flows of money, the imaginary (e.g., masturbation), property, family, and bodies doing work together (cf., Raknes 2004). The tying of the working week to human sexuality after the industrial revolution in Europe and elsewhere, is one of the most important conditioning programmes that has ever been invented. Such a movement is a vital staging and distancing action from nature, from curiosity in and knowledge of nature, and moves us towards the creation of a whole regime of human interiority connected to work, financial survival, and money-labour (Read 2009). This point of dislocation is focused through and by the contrast, for example, between working in a factory, and being part of a hunter/gatherer community, going about their everyday lives. The working week for the factory worker has a repeated start time and end time, every day is the same, with a task or set of tasks as part of a production line, set out in advance and from above by the owners, managers and designers of the factory machine. The factory worker has to become integrated into the machines in the factory setting, their minds and desires are free to wander to an extent, yet their bodies and movements must stay focused on the tasks at hand. In effect, the duality of one-God phallic worship fits seamlessly into the duality of the factory worker, with their bodies integrated into and by machine tasks, whilst their minds can desire to be one with a mystical God, or anything else, to fill the boredom and emptiness of their repetitive, mindless jobs (pN4).

Contrariwise, the hunter/gatherer community has no organised, working phallic-week. Rather, community members continuously look for food, bring the food back for preparation, and take part in entirely local, social, sexual and religious activities (cf., Peoples, Duda and Marlowe 2016). There is no stark duality in these communities and their lives, as the other (spiritual) world is accessible through ritual and ceremony connected to local shamanism, and that everyone has a full stake in. The hunter/gatherers demonstrate immanent lives, as the whole human-natural world for them is inter-connected, and comprehensible from particular, local perspectives (Harvey 2005). The introduced, artificial dislocation of the factory worker's existence, who lives in an abstracted industrial landscape fed by capital, is incomprehensible from a hunter/gatherer perspective. The creation of meaning becomes a central question for the factory worker, as the monotony and subservience of their existence to capital demands some kind of answer. The hunter/gatherer has no such propulsion to question the meaning of life, as their actions and thoughts are entirely combined in local tasks and desires, with no active concern to be other than they actually are in every moment that they live, and this is what we want to return to through education (pN4).

The danger at this point is similar to many others in this Deleuze/Guattari (1984, 1988) analysis of the drives, in that we may romanticise the ways in which prehistoric communities lived. The contrast between prehistoric living and that of a factory worker is illuminating, and demonstrates a point about the phallocene, in that our connections to nature have been diminished and mutilated over time (e.g., by factories), and that a dislocation has been introduced between humans and nature (Grimes 2014). This dislocation has helped to produce scepticism, denial, and disbelief in the ability of humans to create (and fix) the Anthropocene, due to the ways in which the phallocene operates as the working phallic-week, and in conjunction with tool-enhancement and the carbon trails. The creation of an interiority tied to capital and work makes the conditions possible whereby the thought of a natural life is unimaginable. Extending from this notion that the natural life is unthinkable, how could a thinking subject conceive of climate change, when their outward perception of natural change has been disavowed by the artificial determinations of the working week, and as the phallic self-same repetitions of factory life (cf., Engels 1845/1987)? Thus, such 'nature thinking' needs to be reintroduced through and as education (pN4).

Admittedly, the domination of the phallic-week in terms of perception, understanding and living in nature is not absolute. There will be moments when the factory worker will experience nature, they may be able to live outside of the rigour and routine of the factory, and they should be able to still dream of the freedom to explore nature unexpectedly and chaotically (Portelli 1988). However, the rhythms of the factory are brutal, inevitable, self-determining and real. Nature becomes the unreal world for the factory worker, not as a concrete dualism of nature/culture, but as the indeterminable, inexplicable, fear-inducing outside. The Deleuze/Guattari (1984, 1988) analysis of this book does not emphasise the phenomenology of the experience of being a factory worker, but looks to induce a thoroughgoing material analysis of the field, which is historic, as it has non-linear roots in 1820 AD (pN4), and the industrial revolution, but carries on to this day (Hopkins 1982). Further, as there have been different varieties of factory throughout history, and around the world, many have introduced innovations and new means and benefits for labour, some of which attend to the negative impacts of the working phallic-week and its dislocations from nature (e.g., by introducing plants onto the shop floor). Yet we can say with confidence that the overall rhythmic conformism of the working phallic-week remains in place, and its force in the drive of and to the phallocene is unassailable, yet contestable through education (pN4).

Alongside the move to interiority of the working phallic-week, came other subsidiary effects of industrialisation, that go largely unnoticed by the increasingly robotic lives of the factory workers. Foremost amongst these effects is pollution, the desolation of the natural environment, and the destruction of ecology around factory sites (Mokyr 2011). One may state that in the main, factories act as black boxes. They are machines to primarily transform inputs into outputs, to make profits for the owners and managers of the factories. However, these machines are leaky and are not perfect, along with the outputs that the factory produces, are waste products and ubiquitous other toxic excretions (e.g., Sousa et al. 2009), including carbon dioxide from the burning of coal, when used to create energy and power the factory. Over the next two hundred years, most urban spaces in the world developed industrial zones, where the working phallic-week and concomitant effects, such as pollution have been played out on a continuous basis, adding significantly to climate change. Waterways and wetlands have been decimated. Trees and grasslands have been bulldozed and built over. Urban planners have redesignated the areas in terms of how many factories can be slotted into these city spaces, they have made provision for power and transport services, and the availability of a qualified workforce. Whole economies have come to rely and relate to these industrial zones in very specific ways, as they have frequently been nominated as engines of growth in the local and global economy (cf., Chapter 6, and the global thinking matrix), (pN4), at least until the digital revolution, and the transference of many of these self-same phallic energies into the infosphere.

6   Digital Phallic-Endeavour

The working phallic-week is still with us, and it functions to alter time, habits and beliefs for the majority of the population under capitalism (and that shall be attended to through education in Chapter 6, and as the plateau, pN4). The working phallic-week has been strengthened and prolonged, as capitalism has become a one world, non-culturally-specific, ubiquitous system (cf., Bradley and Cole 2018). However, congruent with the working phallic-week, the development of inter-connected digital tools and their concomitant technologies, such as personal computers in combination with the world wide web, and the rise of global, highly structured, and capitalised corporations, and computerised manufacturing techniques, has seen the intensification of the phallocene after 1996 AD (pN5), and a new 'post-work', digitally mediated definition of human life has begun to emerge (e.g., Rifkin 1995). Whilst this post-work environment challenges the hegemony and coherence of the working phallic-week, that has digressed from typical factory assemblages, the new post-work scenario simultaneously extends the penetration of the working phallic-week, by making work accessible and actionable 24/7 (cf., Crary 2013), and not dependent on the physical space of the factory. The definition of post-work, whether it concerns raising one's profile via social media, or taking part in digital, social, cultural and political mechanisms that aim to gain attention in the infosphere, function as embedded offshoots connected to the phallocene, and dominate contemporary globally mediated life, to be addressed through education by this book (pN5).

Hence, the argument of this chapter is that one might draw a line between the phallic God-heads that corralled human sexuality away from the immanence of nature post-Holocene, and digital phallic-endeavour, that sucks the life out of existence, and dumps it on the internet (e.g., Pettman 2016, 2020). This line of argument is called 'the phallocene', which contributes to the Deleuze/Guattari (1984, 1988) analysis of the Anthropocene in conjunction with tool-enhancement, the carbon trail and atomic-time (Chapter 5), to move us towards our own extinction (as a combinatory death drive), and performs a sense of nihilistic climate change, never before realised or realisable in history. This epoch is an age of fake news, fake information, fake facts, and potentially fake climate change, and markedly fake climate change solutions (cf., Vargo, Guo and Amazeen 2018). Any fact or position is potentially 'up for grabs' in the digital infosphere, hence, every statement should be rigorously checked and double checked for authenticity. Yet how is this possible, given the ubiquity and density of the information on the internet, how can one navigate such a terrain? This chapter suggests that the key to this mapping and emergence is understanding the dynamics and the drives associated with and constituted by the phallocene as education (pNx).

Such a comprehensive action as the determination of the phallocene on the internet, carries on from earlier work into libidinal economies, and how the linkages between sexuality and money carry with them weight and propulsion, and that drives many of the exchange mechanisms through and by which capitalism functions (Cameron, Nesvetailova and Palan 2011). As Jean-Francois Lyotard (1974/1993) has stated:

> Are we, intellectual sirs, not actively or passively 'producing' more and more words, more books, more articles, ceaselessly refilling the pot-boiler of speech, gorging ourselves on it rather, seizing books and 'experiences', to metamorphose them as quickly as possible into other words, plugging us in here, being plugged in there, just like Mina on her blue squared oilcloth, extending the market and the trade in words of course, but also

multiplying the chances of *jouissance*, scraping up intensities wherever possible, and never being sufficiently dead, for we too are required to go from forty to the hundred a day, and we will never play the whore enough, we will never be dead enough. (133)

Lyotard, writing in the 1970s, could never have imagined how much these words would be magnified and extended in the contemporary situation of digital publication and exchange. Now, the impetus to produce has reproduced infinitely, everyone is a publisher, or at least a blog writer, or commentator through social media on this, that, and the other. The point here is that the libidinal economy exaggerates a messy connection between things, that at the same time, coincides with the notion that mediated critiques of how things work usually miss the point, and have no firm grasp of the real complexity involved (Grodin and Lindlof 1996). This libidinal action is happening in the contemporary situation of the Anthropocene, for example, with respect to where and how to apportion blame for its evolution (and hence its solutions). Many look to capitalism, others to colonialism, others still to western civilisation, to men, and to the over-consumption of the rich (e.g., Lent 2018). However, the truth is that we all live and partake in and of the contemporary situation, we are all connected to the libidinal economy and the phallocene, whether or not we are communist, feminist, anti-Western, or anti-colonial (pro-Indigenous). Therefore, the understanding, learning and mapping of the processes involved with the libidinal economy and the phallocene has to start with ourselves as digital users (pN5).

This statement about self-cartography has never been more true than today in the Anthropocene (Rousell 2021). This proposition means more than working out one's carbon footprint, though this should be an important and central, formative educational activity of the Anthropocene (Mirzaei Rafe el al. 2019). Rather, the mapping and educational resolution of the phallocene has to start with an understanding of our daily lives, and how they relate to climate change. No-one can play the 'religious or romantic' other in this game, even those espousing deep ecology and/or total withdrawal from everyday life (Cole 2013). To change the system through and by which we currently live, we need to recognise our part in it, and attend to these parts as functioning components of the whole. We cannot relay responsibility for change to others in the Anthropocene, it is too important, critical, and late in the day for this to be effective. We must admit that we are phallically invested in the Anthropocene in some way, and that we have a part to play in changing things. This leads us to the central problem of the Anthropocene, here figured as the phallocene (pNx) and as education backed up by social change.

As has been argued so far in this book, we are enmeshed in the Anthropocene in complex and frequently unanticipated ways (cf., Cole 2019b). This point comes to the fore when we have to take action, as is necessary to avoid future climate collapse, and the acceleration of the sixth great extinction event. The conundrum exists that we should actively encourage transformations in our lives that could make our economies weaker, our job security more vulnerable, and in sum, our lives more diffuse in terms of money and economics. Such action goes directly against the phallic self-same conditioning that has steered us to desire more economically, and to preserve at all costs the advantages and forces that make us prosperous (cf., Whitehead 2014). Furthermore, this self-same phallic conditioning is intensified and exaggerated by digital phallic-endeavour (pN5), as any message can be relayed, copied and transmitted through the digital medium, for example, false, misleading and doctored images of wealth and prosperity, that circulate with regularity, and with little critical attention (here to be processed through education).

Hence, in a situation where we are dreaming about being rich and powerful through the digital celebrity gloss of the internet, that is upheld by pornography, capital, energy flows, and lies (the phallocene), doing anything meaningful about climate change becomes an anathema (cf., Sprenger et al. 2019). The environmental challenges that are at hand are so grave, so in depth, and so fundamental, that we might think it better to coast along and avoid the issue. Better still, leave the problem to the experts, who will surely come up with a fix that will magically solve the problem. But the problem at hand is precisely how to figure out a new education leading to social change, that has to be enacted by the majority of the population to avoid catastrophic climate change (Dryzek 1997). Such a change agenda is stymied and halted by the phallocene, as the rational, ethical, and sensible changes that should take place to avoid climate disaster are sieved through the unconscious repetitions of the self-same, now present as and in digital phallic-endeavour (pN5). As a result, we must work to break the linkages between sexuality and economy through (re)education to move action on the climate, now routed through mediation in the digital infosphere (Hroch and Stoddart 2015), otherwise, we will be caught in the impotency, narcissism and disaster of the self-same repetitions of the phallocene.

So, what is to be done, how can we combat the phallocene? Does any of this make a difference in terms of climate change and its ensuing politics? The debate here has to move the argument on from simple, discursive 'left-right' politics, that either look to carry on as normal, and lie about carbon production outcomes and emissions, or suggest magic solutions, that might immediately produce radical social and political change (e.g., Barbier 2010). I would like to suggest a middle path, that is at once political and philosophical, and attends to the ways in which this chapter is framed from a Deleuze/Guattari (1984, 1988) analysis. The story starts with their first combined text, *Anti-Oedipus*, which was written in the shadows of the May 1968 student uprising in Paris, an event that proved that social change through education is possible, even though it did not result in the major overhaul that is required to address climate change. In *Anti-Oedipus*, the take on capitalism echoes that of Marx, but not necessarily of Marxists. There is a respect for the power and efficacy of capitalism in the book, that does not directly mean that you become a capitalist or a straightforward left wing reactionary, but that you take into account the forces that capitalism has unleashed. Such a 'taking into account' includes understanding how capitalism wrecks the environment through 'deterritorialisation', and in its endless search for exploitable resources to make profit and use (Malm 2016), and how the capitalist system lies about these inbuilt manoeuvres and consequences (because corporations are engaged with softening their environmental images to remain relevant in the Anthropocene), and these insights are major components of the (re)education being suggested here (pN5).

The point is that the deterritorialisation of capitalism cannot be straightforwardly arrested through discussion, rational argument, opposition, or, indeed, dialectics alone (Deleuze 1994). Rather, the dynamics of deterritorialisation play out through complex, fluid processes, that have progressively come to resemble natural phenomena. To understand how this works, and that advances the argument of education in the phallocene (pNx), one might think how deterritorialisation may be recast in the Anthropocene (Figure 4.1).

Figure 4.1 shows how Deleuze/Guattari concepts may be updated for the Anthropocene. This updating is a fluid and thoughtful updating, that avoids concepts becoming concrete as molar ideas, that indelibly mark out research and thought on and in the Anthropocene (as phallic-directed and hence in a self-repetitive manner). Rather, this updating, which is one of the purposes of this book as a whole on Education, the Anthropocene, and Deleuze/Guattari, is part of the nomadic science and politics that the deployment of a Deleuze/Guattari analysis necessitates (1984, 1988). As has been argued, tool-enhancement, the carbon trail, the phallocene (and atomic-time in the next chapter) have worked together through time to produce the situation in which we find ourselves (the Anthropocene). We cannot artificially dissect and separate these entwined processes, or simply try to oppose them. Rather, the ways in which advanced capitalism works, in the current age through digital phallic endeavour (pN5), challenges us to become as fluid and entwined as the processes that we are trying to unravel through education. Furthermore, we cannot state that

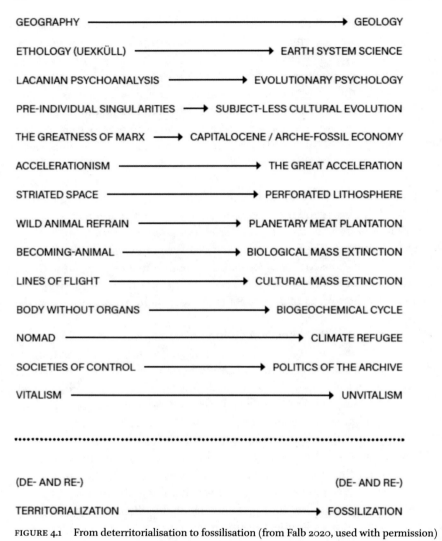

FIGURE 4.1   From deterritorialisation to fossilisation (from Falb 2020, used with permission)

the future will proceed in a predictable and orderly manner through a set of principles that we can determine as heading towards a better, more environmentally friendly world and life (cf., Chapter 1). In the context of this chapter and the phallocene, this consideration of the future means working with and through the forces of deterritorialisation of capitalism, not as simple voices and bodies of complaint, but as forces in and of life itself as education (pNx). As Tim Ingold (2011) has stated:

It is of the essence of life that it does not begin here or end there, or connect a point of origin with a final destination, but rather that it keeps on going, finding a way through the myriad of things that form, persist and break up in its currents. Life, in short, is a movement of opening, not of closure. (4)

In sum, working with the phallocene, requires a great openness to the forces and manners in which sexuality and economics have transpired through human activity in time to destroy the environment (pNx). Only such openness will lead to environmental action and social change through education, to make a difference in the Anthropocene, and challenge the paradoxes of time in which we are enmeshed (Atomic-time).

TABLE 4.1   The pedagogy of the phallocene

Plateaux	Dates	Pedagogy (https://iiraorg.com/the-phallocene/)
pN1	4000–3200 BC	Examination of earliest establishment of state religions outside of shamanism
pN2	500 BC	Inquiry into earliest monotheistic belief, e.g., Judaism
pN3	600 AD	Learning about the establishment of Christianity and Islam
pN4	1820 AD	Examination into the working week
pN5	1996 AD	Inquiry into the development of the internet

CHAPTER 5

Atomic-Time

1 Introduction

The previous three chapters on tool-enhancement, the carbon trail, and the phallocene, all occur in time, and have dates attached to important events in their trajectories, that act as educational escape routes from the inevitability of the Anthropocene as plateaux (Nx). However, these trajectories with dates do not constitute a traditional, linear, historical or modernist account of events, which have simply accumulated into the situation that we find ourselves in today, called the Anthropocene. The nonlinear imposition of dates, sequences, and escape routes from the events depicted in these chapters, attempts to read time as emerging separately at every juncture as 'planes of immanence' (Nx). Consequently, adjacent to this reading, the time dimension has its own properties and effects, that can be read beyond the imposition of recorded, accumulated, or sequential time, and this nonlinear theory of time was one of Deleuze's prime concerns throughout his career (e.g., 1994), and why a separate time chapter is necessary to add to the 'problem of the future' (Chapter 1), and the three other timelines and Deleuze/Guattari (1984, 1988) analyses of the Anthropocene drives (Chapters 2–4).

This chapter is called 'atomic-time' because this time juncture is where we have arrived, post 1945, and the dropping of the nuclear bombs on Japan at the end of the Second World War. This piece of writing is specifically a nonlinear story of how we have arrived at a sense of atomised and 'apart' time. The Deleuze/Guattari (1984, 1988) analysis of time, history and events, does not suggest that this sense of time was unavailable pre-1945, nor that it is attached to every event post-1945 in a uniform or universal (top down) fashion. Rather, the designation of atomic-time runs through this chapter as a stream that was possible to be thought and approached previous to 1945, but that could not have been fully appreciated before the nuclear bombs were dropped. Pertinently, the dropping of the nuclear bombs has proved that humans can destroy the world of their own volition, and hence the relationship between humans and the world/nature has been hereafter over-turned and re-arranged, a process that continues to this day in subsequent events (cf., Cole, Dolphijn and Bradley 2016). The Deleuze/Guattari (1984, 1988) analysis of the unconscious drive of atomic-time complements Deleuze's solo work on time, and suggests how the drives have evolved in time through human society. This chapter presents a narrative about how we have got to the stage of being aware that we are able to destroy the world, and it fills in important time-induced gaps, that underpin the complex relationships between tool-enhancement, carbon time and the phallocene overall (as unconscious drives). The further, adjacent excavation of the time dimension, acting throughout the ways in which tools, carbon, the phallocene and human inter-relationships presently function (in time), can be understood as an important aspect of the thinking practise that this book on the Anthropocene is enabling, and the educational escape routes that it offers (aNx).

2   A Universe of Atoms

With respect to the last three chapters of this book, this chapter is the least situated in prehistory. Similar to the phallocene, the concept of 'atomic-time', wherein and whereby we are atomised, only becomes pertinent once humans begin to look out at the world and speculate as to its atomised nature. We have records that this speculation begins at approximately 500 BC (aN1) in India with the Indian philosopher, Kanada, and latterly in Greece with Democritus (McDonnell 1991, Nene 2005). Pertinently, this speculation about atoms does not mean that *Homo sapiens* did not have the thought that the universe may be made of atoms prior to this date, or that all human thought after this date contains the apartness that a universe of atoms suggests. This Deleuze/Guattari (1984, 1988) analysis of the unconscious drives of the Anthropocene does not cognitively define humans, and speculate as to the origins and reasons behind the development of consciousness, and in the context of this chapter, a consciousness of the atomised time dimension, and its implications for our lives, however interesting this speculation might be (e.g., Glynn 1990). Rather, it looks to explicate and understand the inter-related forces and drives that have propelled us to the era that we now find ourselves in, the Anthropocene, as a platform, and in the continuous search for escape routes in education (Nx).

The contrast and phase change that happens when *Homo sapiens* start to think of 'a universe of atoms', is that it is the beginning of thinking that the world around us is not constituted by an ever changing, full, and inter-connected whole. One can speculate that the tendency of atomisation in thought and human life begins with this date, and has carried on ever since. *Homo sapiens* before 500 BC already had the abstract thought of time, and had begun to measure and incorporate it into their everyday lives and religious codes in several ways. For example, the practises of agriculture and hunting both require the thought and use of time, though it is not of an atomised nature (cf., Rowley-Conwy 2001).

Agriculture necessitates understanding when to sow and harvest crops, which links calendar time with these actions. Hunting animals for food involves linking the movement of animals with the times (and places) where and when they have appeared. The difference that post 500 BC human society produces, is that atomic-time henceforth begins to be incorporated into the functioning of sedentary society, and the hierarchies and orders that these societies extol and practice (aN1), and that are to be attended to here through education.

Pre- 500 BC society still had many of the codes and functions of nomadic society, that had been developed and had evolved since *Homo sapiens* started to permanently move away from the hominin well spring of Africa. Once the early hominins left the environmental conditions that had sustained and nourished them for millennia, a sense of time would have been essential to guide them in their ongoing quest to survive (cf., Steinert and Leifer 2012). More specifically, a speculative sense of time is written into shamanism in term of prophecy, and trying to foresee and understand what will happen in the future. Shaman worship and its belief systems are connected to revelation, movement, change and the environment, and not the repetitive spiritual re-iterations that the majority of religions practice today, and as was explored in the last chapter on the phallocene (e.g., inducing mass at the same time each week). Thus, the non-sedentary thought of time of nomadic societies is one that is more wholly entwined with and in nature, and consequently includes all the contingencies, accidents, horrors, vagueness, and open-ended pauses to thought that this movement-connection necessitates (cf., Winterhalder 2001). In many ways, the nomadic thought of and in time, is the very opposite of thinking about the universe as a collection of atoms, and the ordering logic contained by atomic thought (aN1).

At 500 BC, we have the first records of thinking of a universe of atoms from India and Greece. However, this was also the age of the greatest extent of the Achaemenid Empire, and thus the influence and power of the ancient Persian Empire is simultaneously written into the timeline of the first atomised perceptions of the universe (cf., Kuhrt 2013). That is not to say that the perception of an atomised universe has cultural or social markers. Rather, it is at this stage of history (500 BC) that human society conceived of and recorded the atomised notion of the universe for the first time (as far as we know), and this is an ordered, sequential, and sedentary thought, as it attempts to capture the nature of the universe (as speculative, logical thought). Science as we know and practice it today, primarily takes place in and originates from sedentary culture, that harnesses resources to further what is known, and then tests this knowledge to verify its truth (cf., Deming 2014). Similarly, written into the atomic perception of the universe, is a sedentary view of the universe, that attempts to freeze time, and to apply an ordering logic to the universe, to explain how each atom in the universe inter-relates and acts. Such sedentary thought patterning could only have emerged from a society that was sufficiently distanced and stable enough to pinpoint atoms and their potential relationality (Ibid.), and that is being treated here as pedagogy (aN1).

By 500 BC, human society was sufficiently 'stable' (though I use this term advisedly), to project and record a map of the universe as atoms. Time stands still in this map, or it is at least subjected to the constraint of atomisation, that means it is taken apart and reassembled as individual pieces. It could be argued that the projection of a universe of atoms is one of the bases for the modern scientific description of the universe (e.g., astronomy), and all the knowledge that this project has entailed since 500 BC (cf., Chadwick 1984). However, understanding a universe of atoms conjointly includes humans being powerful enough, and, some might say, beyond nature, in that they can imagine time stopping, and contemplating the universe as specific atoms. In a nomadic society, this would not be possible, as every moment is spent fully enveloped in, and as part of, the natural processes that constitute and move life. From a nomadic perspective, the ability and power to stop time, and break up the universe into component atomic parts is inconceivable. That's not to say that the nomadic imagination is not potent and creative, it's just that it is not possible for it to conceive of a universe of atoms, due to the stasis, equilibrium, and time paralysis that this conception consists of, and that we are here questioning in terms of education (aN1).

Democritus (Berryman 2016) was a re-Socratic philosopher, and a member of the blossoming of early Greek philosophers, who have helped to found western thought, including atomic theory, and suggested that everything works according to natural laws, thus eliminating God as an 'unmoved mover' in the universe, and diminishing man's elevated place in the universe (ego). Therefore, there is double bind (cf., Chapter 8) contained in the conception of the universe of atoms from Democritus, in that at the same time, it shows that humans have consciously moved away from their nomadic ancestors, and were able to functionally project their thoughts and imaginations, beyond the processes that rip through them at every moment, in a type of sedentary immobilisation of the universe, and that this extraordinary thought mechanism reveals through reciprocation that we are but tiny dots, indeed, atoms, in a vast, bleak, and terrifying universe; we are, in fact, merely so many irrelevant microbes, living by and large trivial lives (cf., Cole 2017a), a double bind we are attempting to get to grips with here in teaching and learning (aN1).

In effect, one might say that the universe of atoms post Democritus, could be conceived of as a mode of Lovecraftian horror (1921/1973), in that as a progressive realist perception, it denotes the extreme, repetitive, and unfaltering meaninglessness of everything (nihilism). Again, such thought pivots in on a motive tension and aporia at the heart of this chapter (and book), in that the unfolding scientific description of the universe, which will become more accurate, as this story and chapter of atomic-time continues, is also an unequivocal invitation to hopelessness, or the 'black hole' of the Anthropocene. In effect, the increasingly clarity of atomic thought accompanies a descent into the void, perhaps between the very atoms about which Democritus wrote (cf., Berryman 2016). Atomic-time, whilst separating and individualising us as atoms, and as components in an atomic whole, concurrently makes any claims that we might have as to power, essence, meaning and dominion questionable, given the atomic logic by and through which we knowingly, abide and live (aN_1). Atomic-time therefore cuts away at the thought that we could be Gods, or be in any way connected to Gods, and in the case of this book, that we can act in a manner that will change the course of the Anthropocene in a magical/supernatural way, and that is why the chosen mechanism of this book is a material theory of education (Nx) and its consequent social change. The thought of the universe of atoms, and our small part in it, is a motive pressure to be realistic, whilst retaining the energy and drive to carry on: i.e., by simultaneously realising and defying atomic-time as learning (aNx).

Further, the contemporary time of the Anthropocene could be characterised as a 'dark time', this is time as a 'Black Sun' (Cole 2017a), because of the extinction singularity (Moynihan 2020), which we are being dragged towards, that is at the centre of a black hole created by the repetitions of the human drives (in and of ourselves, and our actions), and as a combination of tool-enhancement, carbon trails, the phallocene and atomic-time. The 'dark time' of the Anthropocene is parallel but entwined with atomic-time, because of the many ways in which society has become progressively individualised and separated, and how it is especially difficult to act collectively, or, indeed, to act at all, in the face of overwhelming climate change, that is largely beyond our direct control. Additionally, atomic-time exists at the same time, and coheres with the phallocene (Chapter 4), that has augmented the homogenisation of society away from living in and as part of the multiplicities of hunter and gatherer collectives, and their requisite transversal nomadic behaviours (in a complex nature). As a result, the phallocene has moved collective human society towards the worship of one abstract male (human) God, in a herd-like, unquestioning manner (cf., Nietzsche 1887/1989). Many of us therefore find ourselves in the contradictory position of being trapped in One-God belief by the domination of the phallocene (total projected idealism), whilst at the same time, being separated, and subjectivised, by the forces of atomic-time (complete subjugation to micro forces). To understand this state-of-affairs further, it is worth examining the remaining material cloud, and line of flight of atomic-time, with its origins at 500 BC in Greece and India (and influenced on a parallel axis through history by Persia). At this time, speculative philosophers such as Democritus (Berryman 2016), imagined the universe was made up of atoms, and this thought was to remain largely unchallenged, but buried by the belief in one-God, until specific developments in science in the nineteenth century in England and elsewhere, here to be worked though as education (aN2).

3 Atomic Theory

We know about the early atomic theory of Democritus due to the Roman writings of Lucretius (Huby 1978). Time passes between Democritus, the Indian scholar, Kanada, and the next plane of intensity wherein atomic theory was accelerated, and was significantly added to in 1803 AD (aN2), through the atomic theory of John Dalton (cf., McDonnell 1991). One can speculate why the development of atomic theory happened at this time, and in this place (the north of England), in terms of the accompanying industrial revolution, and the re-examination of the thoughts of the ancient Greeks and Romans in the Enlightenment. Again, this Deleuze/Guattari (1984, 1988) analysis does not look to re-centre the Anthropocene in terms of a western, male, privileged and/or human emergence in thought and life, but attempts to make the connections (and escape routes) that have produced the atomic-time of the Anthropocene, in which we find ourselves embroiled today. The imaginative visualisation of atomic structure by Dalton, is seen by many as the foundation for modern chemistry and physics, in that he laid the groundwork for the scientific and atomic discoveries that constitute the model of our explained science world today (Rocke 2005). Dalton was not from an especially privileged position in society, but has managed to leave an important mark on the history of science and thought, through his precise observations and creative application to the problems that he saw around him. Energy and heat exchange theories had been well-established, and steam power was already driving industry in Dalton's locality and throughout many parts of Britain at the time. However, what was not properly understood was functioning at the atomic level in basic exchange processes, which had been largely unconsidered since Democritus, and its Lucretian retelling. Dalton's designation of atomic theory (aN2), helped to overturn the now obsolete scientific theory of caloric exchange, that stipulated that a separate fluid called 'caloric' flowed between substances at different temperatures (cf., Erlichson 1999).

One might say that it is important not to misunderstand the multitudinous effects that Dalton's visualisation of atomic structure, and the consequent atomic theory has had on our lives, and its place in the Anthropocene. Previous to Dalton, other than the speculative arrangements of Democritus, Kanada, and the retelling by Lucretius, the notion of an atomic level of interaction was virtually inaccessible. Thus, it was very difficult to correctly understand material processes, that involved, for example, changes in nature, weight, temperature and form (cf., Bader and Nguyen-Dang 1981). For example, abundantly observable changes in the nature of water from liquid to solid and gas in the world, could not have been explained in terms of the changes in energy distribution and molecules of the same atomic structure, i.e., H_2O, but would have been thought in any number of sometimes magical ways, as the workings of mystical powers. Admittedly, scientific knowledge of the structure of atoms and its consequences for many of the basic natural processes that constitute the universe and how it changes, was not divulged or distributed amongst the majority of the population for many years to come (cf., Furley 1987). What is significant here, is how the atomic theory of Dalton, and the consequent filling out of the atomic level of interaction and life, has gone into our unconscious functioning as the drive of atomic-time, and how this has joined up with tool-enhancement, the carbon trail, and the phallocene to create the Anthropocene, and how to escape these conjunctions through education (aN2).

After Dalton, the tendency for scientific, explanatory thought of the material universe and its processes, has been to delve into increasingly minute and microscopic detail, to observe atomic structure at work (cf., Lappert and Murrell 2003). Thus, a need for accuracy and precision has been produced alongside this sense that we must look into ever smaller parcels of the universe to understand how it works. Clearly, such a tendency requires specific, advanced, atomic investigation apparatuses (e.g., ever better microscopes), technical skills to operate and read these apparatuses, and the conditions and funding to sustain such an apparatus. As such, a cleavage in thought has been produced post Dalton, with increasingly more expensive and resource hungry investigations, yielding important new knowledge with respect to atomic structure and the material processes of the universe, and a simultaneous, reciprocating blindness to think coherently about 'the big picture', which is, for example, vital in the current state of the Anthropocene, and that will not be executed by examining the atomic nature of the universe (cf., Lewis and Maslin 2015), and doing anything about it, here as stipulated through education. As an example of this cleavage and significant influence in the production of atomic-time in the Anthropocene (aN2), wherein time is divided between investigations of the micro world and explanation of the macro world, I will take the current

COVID-19 pandemic, which I am living through as I write these words (in 2020/21).

Microbiologists have a crucial role to play in investigating the atomic structure of the novel coronavirus. National governments and private companies worldwide are funding these investigations in the race to map, understand, and find solutions, such as vaccines to stop the spread of the pandemic. There is a specific time associated with this micro analysis and often competitive race to observe the atomic details of the coronavirus. However, simultaneous to this time of micro analysis of atomic structures to understand the nature of the coronavirus, is a macro necessity to comprehend the world economic, political, ecological and social effects of the pandemic, and the congruous effects of a global shut down of business involving human face-to-face socialisation (e.g., Abel and McQueen 2020). This entirely divergent path for investigation, explanation and complex relationality, opens up a significantly different vista on time from micro investigation, it is a global, inter-connected, overview of and on time, a time of the world pandemic, a time of social isolation, a time of unemployment/underemployment, and a time of working from home (if you still have a job). National governments, and international agencies such as the WHO and United Nations are working on the global dynamics of the pandemic, yet are faced by the separation and problematic opened up by the simultaneous investigation into the atomic structure of COVID-19, and comprehending the social and world consequences of the pandemic.

Post Dalton scientific investigation (aN2) incrementally became an occupation of highly specialised academics, requiring purposeful training, laboratories, and substantial funding to investigate the atomic world and beyond (e.g., Risler et al. 1974). Yet the problem remains to think the whole, to extrapolate from the micro world, and to understand how these atomic discoveries function at different, more expansive levels. There is a parallel dynamic at work in the Anthropocene and this book, including the move to simultaneously produce new educational action (Nx). At the micro levels of atomic theory, the chemistry and physics is straightforward, we have to limit as far as possible the emission of carbon dioxide to decrease global warming, and its inter-connected effects. However, the emission of carbon dioxide is involved in nearly any activity currently undertaken by humans at the global level, as, for example, an invisible bi-product of trade, commerce, and basically any substantial human movement and socialisation as such (cf., Hall 2020). Thus, global warming requires that we fundamentally change our behaviours in order to cut emissions. But what is the consequence of this? Should we never go out, do no trade or socialise at all, and not use electricity if it is still being created through the burning of fossil fuels? As a result, we would be effectively cutting ourselves off from mainstream human activity, and condemning ourselves to the life of a hermit. Yet at the time of the coronavirus, this is exactly what we are being told to do (social isolation to limit the spread of infection), and in terms of education, this move is embodied by remote learning and its consequences (Engzell, Frey and Verhagen 2021).

Hence, a congruity is reached through the pandemic and the Anthropocene that is accessed via atomic theory, post Dalton (aN2). Both the pandemic and the Anthropocene require enormous behavioural changes, and that are, as such, modes of behaviourism (cf., Crawshaw 2013), both about us and 'as' us. Governments and international agencies such as the WHO and United Nations are reverting to behaviourism to get their messages across, and we have suddenly become children in classrooms again, subject to behavioural constraints, this time not emanating from the teacher, and the teacher-power bestowed by the school (and the state), but through our television and screen devices, telling us to stay home, wash our hands, and to obey social distancing rules. Governments around the world have been mobilised to rely on operant conditioning (Ibid.) due to the public health danger, and they are repeating these messages daily, obsessively, until they have become the global norm. In contrast, no such effort has been concertedly carried out and/or achieved with respect to climate change, that perversely holds a greater existential threat to humanity (i.e., as widespread extinction) in the long run than the pandemic. Thus, in the congruity between the pandemic and the Anthropocene with respect to atomic theory and time, is a simultaneous incongruity with respect to how it is being handled by contemporary governments and agencies. After Dalton heralded the beginning of modern atomic theory through his sketches of atoms, important advancements were made in the field, such as the development of the laws of thermodynamics (Erlichson 1999), the expansion of the periodic table, and a century of discovery and investigation with respect to the atom (the 19th century), that ultimately culminated in one of the most important modern discoveries that has been pivotal in terms of understanding how we have got to 'atomic-time' in the Anthropocene (and how to escape it): electricity, which was increasingly and ubiquitously harnessed and put to use in growing, global, industrialised societies (aN3).

4   Electricity

Trying to envisage a time before electricity is almost inconceivable. Thus, we can see that electricity is intimately connected to and with atomic-time, because it has become so enveloped in and as part of our imaginations and lives. If we are to imagine a new life and consequent system for the Anthropocene (aN3) through education and social change, the problem of electricity, and how we relate to it, is crucial to the realignments necessary in the Anthropocene and future beyond. Admittedly, observation and experimentation with electricity had gone on for many thousands of years throughout history, with one of the first recorded experiments that we have being Thales rubbing amber with cat's fur to produce static electricity (Williams 2012). Latterly, Benjamin Franklin is credited with proving the existence of electricity via flying a kite with a key attached to a dampened string in a storm, and observing sparks and a flow of electricity in 1752. During the 19th century, investors and scientists such as Michael Faraday and Thomas Edison pushed the understanding, control, and use of electricity forward, until in 1904 AD (aN3), the existence of electron was theorised by J.J. Thomson (cf., Achinstein 2001) and others, and the large scale use of electricity to power cities and towns had begun to be well-established in many parts of the world, and this date acts as the plane of immanence for electricity-pedagogy.

Atomic-time is concurrently electrical time. The discovery of electrons and how to control and harness their movements in electrical currents, is one of the fundamental shifts in human history, that has helped to define what is happening in the contemporary era called the Anthropocene as a drive (aN3). Even though early attempts to wire homes and other appliances using electricity, were often shoddy and dangerous, the shift from heating homes with coal and wood, and lighting homes with candles, to using electricity for these tasks, and, furthermore, the immense and manifold changes in the running of industry by deploying mechanical power (e.g., from steam engines) to using electrical power, once achieved, was irreversible (cf., Panofsky and Phillips 2005). One of the most startling and important images to think about with respect to understanding the Anthropocene (aN3), is how planet Earth is now lit up by electricity at night, and, therefore, how humans have effectively changed the visage of the planet through their activities (Figure 5.1).

In effect, humans have changed the way the Earth looks from space through electric lights (Figure 5.1). Further, electricity has become integral to our lives at every level, and is connected to most activities that we do in some way. In the terms of this book, and the Deleuze/Guattari (1984, 1988) analysis, we have 'become-electric', in that we have formed a system and a whole with and through electricity (aN3), that powers much of the world in which we live and our participation in that world (Panofsky and Phillips 2005). Undoubtedly, there are hierarchies, slippages, and holes in the 'electric-human-world' system, in that the supply, efficiency, cost, and

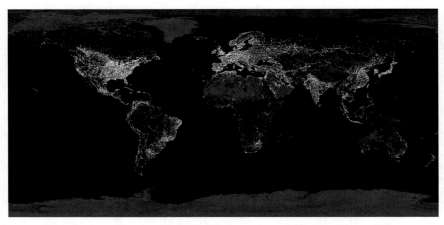

FIGURE 5.1　The view of Earth with electrical lights. Source: Wikimedia Commons licence: https://commons.wikimedia.org/wiki/File:Earth%27s_City_Lights_by_DMSP,_1994-1995_(large).jpg

distribution of electricity is not uniform around the globe, yet even in the most remote and economically deprived regions of the planet, the production and use of electricity has penetrated the environment to some extent. Hence, humans have turned the world electric, and the new Earth that has been created is a mixture of electric-human-natural structures that bleed and feed into one another, with hazy fluxes in-between. Further, in 2017, it has been calculated that fossil fuels generated 64.5% of electricity worldwide (WNA 2020), and hence the production of electricity is a continuing major source of global carbon dioxide emissions, that should be dealt with here through (re) education.

The transition from the fossil fuel production of electricity to renewable sources that do not emit carbon dioxide is one of the greatest and central challenges that we face today, as well as eliminating other sources of carbon dioxide emissions, such as transport and machinery using petrol and oil. Similar to many aspects of atomic-time, the path to renewable energy for electricity creates and inserts a cleavage in thought, that is at once global and local (Şener, Sharp and Anctil 2018). At the local level, every effort could be made to convert from fossil fuels to renewables, such as installing solar panels and predominantly using electric cars. However, these switches in lifestyle and the production of energy at a local level to renewable and non-carbon dioxide emitting sources, can be expensive, and out of reach for the majority of the population. Hence, it is vital that the switch to renewable sources of energy is taken up and implemented at the global level in terms of the production of electricity (aN3). Yet many governments are still using coal, gas and oil power stations to power their countries, and major international fossil fuel companies and countries such as Saudi Arabia, Iran, Canada and Australia still make tremendous amounts of money from extracting and selling fossil fuels (Dayanandan and Donker 2011). Therefore, one may conclude that the global capital flows that include investment in fossil fuel companies on stock exchanges, back up and support the continued global use of fossil fuels in energy production, and this will only be diverted to renewables when capital ceases to flow in and out (and because) of these (re)sources (see Chapters 6 and 7).

The twentieth century was the century of 'fossil fuel-capital-electricity'. Wars have been fought, huge amounts of electricity have been produced, inventions were made to harness the increasing control and global availability of electricity. All of these waves of combined and inter-linked activities has produced desire and longing in the human species and society, as knowledge of electricity and what we can do with it has extended and penetrated around the globe (Winther 2008). As such, the 'human-electric-psyche' has been born, and is irreversible, notwithstanding a wholesale breakdown event in the organisation of the human species, a generalised crumbling in societal structures, and a consequent inability to generate enough electricity to support the 'electric-dreams' of the human animal (aN3). The nature of electricity and what it can do, flows through and produces atomic-time, as a separating and continuous force against realigning and reaffirming strong ecological ties to and with nature. One might state that abstracting oneself from the power, force and allure of electricity, is vital to coming closer to what is necessary for the ecological revolution to come in the Anthropocene, and when diverting from the sixth great extinction event, here being asserted through education and subsequent social change (Chapters 6 and 7). However, there are two more stages of atomic-time, before we may conceive to the fullest extent what is necessary to avert the 'Black Sun' of extinction, in terms of time, pedagogy and multiple agency.

5 Quantum Mechanics

The first stage of atomic-time post-electricity-nexus is wrapped up in quantum mechanics, and the fact that previous models of atomic structure had been too static and uniform. By 1926 AD (aN4), the theory of quantum mechanics had helped to delve into and calculate the wave patterns and energy forms that move atoms, and Niels Bohr, Erwin Schrödinger, Albert Einstein, James Chadwick and others had progressively come up with more sophisticated models of atomic structure, that were consistent with empirical observations, and that have lasted until today (cf., Motz and Weaver 1989). Work into quantum mechanics in the first half of the twentieth century saw the disciplines of physics, mathematics and chemistry combined in an exceptional way, to push forward atomic investigation, and that has helped to dispel the perception that atomic structure is fixed and continuous. Rather, quantum mechanics and its related empirical experimentation at the atomic level, has demonstrated the chaotic, unpredictable, and complicated nature of atoms, their energy and wave exchanges/formations, and the relativity of time (aN4), which are crucial for the educational practice being imagined here.

At this point in this chapter about 'atomic-time', we fold back in Deleuze's quest for a philosophical reading of time, that includes every level of interaction from the natural to the cosmic and sits parallel to the Deleuze/Guattari (1984, 1988) analysis of atomic-time in this chapter. Deleuze's reading of 'pure time' comes largely from philosophical sources, such as Kant's syntheses (Deleuze 1994), Spinoza's monism, and Bergson's vitalism (durée) (Deleuze 1966/1991), yet at every point, Deleuze looks to sidestep the notion that a conscious thinking philosopher is simply projecting a rational theory of the universe onto the world, and coming up with a thought conception of the world, of which the time dimension is an important part (aN4). As such, Deleuze is at odds to resist and critique an idealist notion of time, as coming from a philosopher's mind, and thus being a 'human-constructed' framing of time in the world. At the quantum level, in the first half of the twentieth century, a similar process transpired, as theorists' notions and models of time were modified and extended, as comprehension of atomic behaviour was adapted given new empirical observations and experiments at the atomic level. Deleuze's philosophical thought experiments (e.g., 1994) are similarly designed to reach a natural conception of time (or threshold in/as time), beyond human measurement, linearity, and imposition on the complex unfoldings in and of time (as a thing apart), here carried forward for teaching and learning (aN4).

Deleuze was not a scientist. Rather, he mobilised scientific concepts and notions to challenge a fixed, human-centred, and brittle conception of time, one that would fall apart given new conditions and evidence that proves time acts contrary to previous conceptions. Thus, Deleuze mobilised literary conceptions of time from Proust and Kafka, alongside philosophical and mathematical conceptions of time from Simondon and Riemann (Smith 2003). Deleuze extended and played with time to approach 'natural or pure time', that is not an assumption, that can be ignored, and hence not accounted for in one's approach to things (ontology), yet simultaneously not an over-theorised or over-coded axiom, that defies variability (epistemology). The developments in quantum mechanics in the early twentieth century helped to dispel notions of the fixed (T) in mathematical renditions of the atom, as the universe of atoms was increasingly realigned and remapped as wave and energy patterns, with time being part of this entanglement, and not a fixed axiom along which atoms pass in one direction (e.g., Feynman 1942/2005). One can experience time in variable manners as a function of subjectivity in, for example, dreaming, memory, focusing exclusively for a long time on a difficult task, or just longing for something. What Deleuze's time conception does is to make an important connection between changes in the conception of time due to quantum mechanics of the early twentieth century (aN4), and the variable nature of time, that can be experienced in the real, but can be easily quashed by linear, repetitive, intrusive notions of time, for example, as embedded in conjunctions between 'labour-money-time-profit' (cf., Chapter 4), or as presented by fixed and time-tabled educational practice, that we are resisting here through an expanded time dimension (N).

The first half of the twentieth century was a tumultuous time, with two world wars, the financial crash in 1929, and a consequent global economic depression. It is almost as if the discoveries at the atomic level were translated into world events, as world history became wave and flux like (Roberts and Case 1999). The time period between the two world wars, with the famous Wall street financial crash and depression, especially seems to correspond to a pre-defined wave function, with the First World War (and subsequent pandemic) setting off a wave pattern that ended in 1945, and leading to the next phase change in atomic-time (aN5). Furthermore, the first half of the twentieth century, defines many of the parameters of the contemporary Anthropocene, in the very wave and flux patterns of human society and economic activity that dipped, rose and fell, as different approaches to manage the expansion of the modern, fossil fuel, electrified mass society were tried, such as communism, fascism, and liberal democracy, that sits alongside unbridled and expansive capitalism (cf., Cole 2014). On the scientific level, thought and experimentation with respect to the atom was set free in this period (aN4), and on the human scale, many societies saw a global period of growth and diminution never before experienced on the planet Earth, and that can be explored through education.

Human population increased significantly during this period, but this was only a precursor and foundation for significant increases in population to come (post 1945). Likewise, economic growth in many parts of the world saw an unprecedented upsurge during the first half of the twentieth century, especially for those who were already capitalised, and able to take advantage of the upswing, however, both human population and economic growth were still subject to 'natural' downsides. The two world wars, though terrible, destructive and responsible for enormous death and destruction, briefly slowed growth in the economy and world human population (McNeill 2001). Thus, the wave and flux cycles of material expansion in human activity, though accelerated by the global use of fossil fuels and electricity to drive industry and life, do not match the exponential growth figures and that were to follow post WWII (aN5). As such, the first half of the twentieth century acts as a case study of inter-laced, industrial-commercial, scientific, artistic and political/social experimentation (aN4), but without the runaway human surge that has created the Anthropocene in terms of climate change since 1945 (aN5). It is not until after the Second World War in 1945, and the dropping of the first atomic bomb, that the last phase change in atomic-time was reached, and that we are still living through today as a continuous learning experience (aN5).

6   The Atomic Bomb

On August the 6th, 1945 AD (aN5), a uranium-based bomb, that was called 'Little Boy', was exploded above Hiroshima, and 72 hours later, a plutonium-based bomb, named 'Fat Man', was detonated above the population centre of Nagasaki. These events are extraordinarily important in terms of the Anthropocene (e.g., Bonneuil and Fressoz 2016), this Deleuze/Guattari (1984, 1988) analysis of the unconscious drives and, pointedly, in terms of the specific human ability to destroy the world through harnessing the energy of/in atoms, to be addressed here as education.

The consequence of the first atomic detonations was to create an uneasy standoff between the major world industrial powers, that now possessed the ability to destroy the world many times over. In this muted and mutational atmosphere, consumerism, subjectivity, learning and change have all become compromised, as the false equilibrium of nuclear détente has pushed along the deadening effects of one world capitalism into and as a negative and false 'space-time', wherein any enduring reason to live otherwise has become harder to imagine, as the American novelist Kurt Vonnegut (1969/2000) has said, as an example of how atomic-time and the other elements of this analysis of the Anthropocene work together: "Like so many Americans, she was trying to construct a life that made sense from things she found in gift shops" (39). Atomic-time is a repetitious, dead-time, built upon sedentary behaviours, division and stasis, wherein capital flows are capable of (and likely to) take over subjectivity and thought, as there is nothing left to do other than watch TV, or try and enjoy the spectacle of the universal, global standoff, and as we fall, at the same time, relentlessly, effortlessly, into the Anthropocene. Nuclear accidents such as Chernobyl, Long Island and Fukushima may puncture the boredom and numbness of nuclear capitalism, yet the invisible nature of nuclear radiation (aN5), combined with the release of CO_2 can make us shrug our shoulders, again, which is characteristic of the atomic-time of the phallocene/tool-enhancement and carbon trails; as Vonnegut (2000) has said: "How nice – to feel nothing, and to still get full credit for being alive" (105).

As such, we reach the apex of 'atomic-time' and its effects on/in the Anthropocene. This time is opened up by the Deleuze/Guattari (1984, 1988) analysis of the unconscious drive of atomic-time, Deleuze's philosophical approach to time, and as demonstrated by Vonnegut (2000), wherein a complex, interrelated, entwined, multi-level post-war time is depicted, for example, in his novel *Slaughterhouse 5*, in which the main character, Billy Pilgrim has become 'unstuck in time'. This means that Pilgrim can move about in time between his birth and his death, and experience moments of his life as disjointed and 'out-of-place', but always referring back to the bombing of Dresden during the Second World War (aN5). Pilgrim has gained the power to move about in time due to being kidnapped by aliens, the Tralfamadorians, who are able to perceive of time as one entity, and thus can experience the universe through four dimensions, i.e., with a separate time dimension as Deleuze (1994) has theorised as 'pure time'. Pilgrim's experiences life with the aliens as a continuous utopic and erotic dream, with the enhanced ability to jump in and out of time episodes, and the rest of his life on Earth as a disjointed, fateful, non-linear nightmare, that has no discernible meaning, sequence or truth, but is only rendered comprehensible by the slaughter that he experienced during the air raid in Dresden (in this book reality is rendered sensible as N/education).

Similarly, atomic-time is possible to understand through the augmentations involved with the dropping of the two atomic bombs in 1945, and the post-war acceleration in human activity since that date (aN5). These augmentations include the neglect, denial, obfuscation and reality of living through a time of known planetary environmental degradation, which has brought on a simultaneous, unprecedented expansion in the human domain and power (McLeod 2018), that is parallel to Vonnegut's portrait of Pilgrim's post-war fortunes. Pilgrim becomes an optometrist, and settles into a comfortable, suburban lifestyle, somewhere in America, and simultaneously carries with him the horror and destruction that he experienced during the Second World War. One might state that one is numbed into conformity through a slice of material wealth, by capital accumulation, and the luxuries that it brings, and we are henceforth trapped in the pursuits of pleasure, comfort and capital, and at the same time, the environmental effects of our lifestyle is overlooked and forgotten. Further, every imagistic technology that has been taken up on mass since the end of the

Second World War, such as cinema, television, the internet, and more recently social media, have added to the power of the image of the human and the maze of mirrors that we are led into from birth (Deleuze 1985/1989). It's as if capital and technology have colluded to augment the ways in which human dominion can be expanded and connected in a protective shell against the chaos and uncertainty of nature since 1945 (aN5). Further, this shell is ribbed and lined with the radioactive micro particles of the atomic bombs that were dropped, and the nuclear arsenals that have signalled from their bunkers to stop all out global war since the horrors of Hiroshima and Nagasaki.

Moreover, there have been a significant number of other writers, philosophers, cultural theorists, film makers and sociologists, who have tried to come to terms with the reality of 'atomic-time' post-1945 (aN5), in addition to Vonnegut, such as: J.G. Ballard, Michel Houellebecq, William Burroughs, Philip K. Dick, Ursula K. Le Guin, Jean Baudrillard, Frederic Jameson, Andrei Tarkovsky, Lars von Trier and Haruki Murakami. These creative thinkers (and many others) have tried to make sense of the post-war period in terms of the expansion of a particular milieu in capitalist lifestyle and thought largely emanating from the U.S.A. (or countries/economies that predominantly refer to the U.S.A.), and the global responses/changes/understandings and complications that are associated with these knots in thinking, values and life. In a straightforward sense, the expansion in and of human activity around the world in the uneasy global peace that has been produced since the atomic bombs were dropped (aN5), has led to opportunities and improvements in life, and millions have been lifted out of poverty through increases in the numbers of jobs, employment, capital and human movement. However, this expansion, sometimes termed as 'globalisation' (cf., Cole and Woodrow 2016), has come at the cost of local cultures, environmental safeguards, and the continuity of strong communities. Thus, the thinking required in the Anthropocene and atomic-time, involves this double-edged and complex knot in/of simultaneous expansion and excavation, here being treated through teaching and learning (aN5).

Parallel to the action of an atomic bomb and the waves of radioactivity and destruction that it unleashes, the thinking that this chapter is proposing conforms to wave patterns and fluxes in/as the complexities of time. Absolute, 360°, or turnaround change is hence less of an issue than understanding the ways in which time wraps around and through itself to produce change (Deleuze 1989). Further, of vital importance to comprehending the Deleuze/ Guattari (1984, 1988) analysis of the Anthropocene (and its escape routes) presented here, is the way in which tool-enhancement, the carbon trails, the phallocene and atomic-time have combined and become embedded in our drives as parts of the automatic and unconscious ways in which we act. The dropping of the atomic bombs (aN5) has been absorbed into our thinking and imaginations, as the ultimate threat and power to destroy the planet of biodiversity and life, at least on the human, mammalian level or greater (some microbial and insect life could survive a nuclear holocaust, e.g., cockroaches). In the shadow of this threat, the Anthropocene is being produced as a 'one world capitalist system', with economic activity ramping up around the globe post-1945, and encouraging what has commonly been described as 'economic development' (cf., Wallerstein 1979). The fall of alternative systems, such as communism and fascism to run major economies and nations, and the consequent spread of liberal democracy, as the foundational political mechanism to uphold a universal market based on capital exchange across the world, and everything that has evolved due to these systems since 1945, has been obliquely set as the (only viable) path for humanity to follow. This is at least in part due to the image of thought produced by the dropping of the atom bomb, which is to create the possibility of global death accompanied by a reciprocating image of the new being bound up in the dropping of the bomb (aN5), as constant artificial renewal under conditions of nuclear détente. The image in Figure 5.2 from the Japanese manga comic, Akira, depicts this image of thought, as the explosion of the bomb carries universal fear (death) alongside a clearing away of the old, and a promise of the new, rising from the ashes of the nuclear explosion.

This image (Figure 5.2) of a nuclear explosion exemplifies the juxtaposition in thought that atomic-time encourages (aN5). In the path of the explosion is the complexity of human civilisation, which is entangled in and with nature and history in a non-uniform way. Yet the explosion is drawn as smooth, enveloping, radiant and constant, analogous with a perfect sphere advancing from a hidden point in the centre of the city (an egg). This is, in many ways, an image of the atom itself, now drawn as enormous, menacing and potent, and as an absolute reversal from the reality of tiny particles, that are hardly noticeable (Figure 5.2). The ensuing atomic-time (aN5) combines the ways in which the overpowering, massive atom links with the complexities of human life to complete transformations at every level, and which can be seen, for example, in post-war Japan, and as a test case for learning in this thesis (aN5).

Japan since 1945 has been exemplary in terms of the proposed concept of atomic-time in this chapter. After the Second World War, and the devastation of defeat, Japan went about rebuilding as a liberal, democratic country, that practised capitalism as the *modus operandi* for economic development (cf., Rosenbaum and Iwata-Weickgenannt 2014). Until the Fukushima disaster of 2011, Japan used nearly equal combinations of natural gas, coal and nuclear power, after the disaster, the percentage of nuclear power included in the mixture of Japan's power sources has reduced dramatically, and now barely

FIGURE 5.2 Illustration of the atomic bomb taken from manga comic Akira (1993).
Source: AKIRA / アキラ by Katsuhiro Otomo

figures in the energy sources of Japan (Zhu et al. 2020). Japan's economy is yet to substantially embrace renewable sources of energy, despite the science of climate change, and the abundance of, for example, hydroelectric power sources. Japan's economy, which was for many years the envy of the rest of the world, and a veritable post-war miracle, is high in energy needs, and hence adds significantly to carbon dioxide emissions. Japan still has a large manufacturing base, and makes a range of important goods and products for the global market, such as: cars, air conditioners, other consumer electronics, computers, pharmaceutical products, agriculture and bio-industrial products, ships, aerospace, textiles, and processed foods. However, this path to high productivity, capital and success, has come at a cost to the environment and local culture (aN5).

On a recent, pre-pandemic trip to Tokyo (2019), I was amazed and delighted by the sights, sounds and smells of this cosmopolitan, impressive city. I tried the local food, enjoyed the nightlife, and was intrigued by a performance of the Noh theatre, that I was given a glimpse of along with other delegates in the conference that I was attending. However, about half way through my week long stay in the heart of Tokyo, in the Shinjuku district, I was suddenly struck by the lack of local wildlife and the consequent ecology of the situation. It was summer, late June, and the weather was hot. There was a 3-day camp before the main conference, and it was being held in a room adjacent to an art gallery, with long, sliding glass doors. As it was very hot, the organisers opened the doors to their fullest extent, I was shocked and surprised by this action, for where I live, in the Blue Mountains close to Sydney, Australia, opening doors in this way would be an invitation to be inundated by insects. However, it was not a problem here. Next, I went to several parks close to my hotel, that had once been royal playgrounds in the heart of old Tokyo. I expected to see birds, insects, perhaps a few squirrels. But I was disappointed, the parks were only full of people and plants. One day, I noticed a squashed cockroach on the Tokyo metro, and stopped to gaze at it approvingly, before I was engulfed by a wave of commuters, and forced to move on from my low level wildlife observation.

In short, even though Tokyo is a buzzing and exciting metropolis, there is something missing, that I missed, and that is now out of reach, and this is direct contact with nature (of a non-human, but living form). I can appreciate how people might want to kill bugs, as they can be annoying, but when I could find none, I missed them. In sum, Japanese society at its zenith and most dense, such as in the middle of Tokyo, is a machine, and this machine processes everything in its domain. Nature has been processed and forced to the outside of this machine, perhaps due to the possibility of interrupting the clean and linear functioning of the machine. Bugs can act as distractions to the working day, animals need food sources, water, and their own specific paths to roam on, that do not correspond to the constraints of a neoliberal democracy, with its capitalist exchange values, which primarily has to make a profit. Hence, Japan is a case study in and of atomic-time (aN_5), wherein time has been synthesised according to human constraints, and has been made to bend to the forces of production. In Japan, atomic-time can literally be applied to the everyday working week and its consequences in the high tech cities with their unenviable complexity, and lack of nature. That is, until events such as natural disasters, the Fukushima nuclear accident (Cole, Dolphijn and Bradley 2016), or the global pandemic of 2020/21, shake the Japanese out of their somnambulistic work and life rituals, and the continued gleaming success post-1945 (aN_5). In the next chapters (Chapters 6 and 7), the synthesises of tool-enhancement, carbon trail, the phallocene, and atomic-time will be drawn out through education and social change to augment the substantial pedagogic opportunities provide by the last four chapters as plateaux (Nx).

TABLE 5.1   The pedagogy of atomic-time

Plateaux	Dates	Pedagogy (https://iiraorg.com/atomic-time/)
aN1	500 BC	Inquiry into the early description of a universe of atoms
aN2	1803 AD	Examination of Dalton's model of atoms
aN3	1904 AD	Learning about the early development and uses of electricity
aN4	1926 AD	Examination of the quantum theory of the atom
aN5	1945 AD	Inquiry into the details of the first atom bombs and their consequences

CHAPTER 6

Teaching and Learning Differently in the Anthropocene

> **Special Note**
>
> This chapter, in conjunction with Chapters 2–5, is designed to evolve new resources, pedagogic action, and lesson/unit ideas for educators at each point Nx.[1]

1   Introduction

This chapter asks the fundamental question: *How can we teach differently in the Anthropocene*? The previous four chapters have attended to the forces and processes that have flowed through us in time to produce the Anthropocene (cf., Wallin 2017). At every point and date, figured as expanded planes of interaction and thought presented by these chapters, new pedagogic opportunities have arisen as escape routes from the reality of the Anthropocene, as plateaux (Nx). Clearly, as these chapters have shown, these forces and processes are deep set, have become instinctual, and have produced a type of conditioning, that complicates resistance, – in fact, this conditioning is commensurate with our drives, and works through unconscious functioning (Figure 6.2). The question that arises is therefore, what can we do about the Anthropocene? The thesis of this book, following a Deleuze/Guattari (1984, 1988) philosophical analysis, is to turn to education, and the ways in which the forces and processes of the Anthropocene as now (N) can be manipulated, played with, and reimagined through pedagogy as escape routes in the continuous but changing dimension (Nx). Of course, we almost immediately hit a barrier of sensation, in that education is not a homogenous system, and is practised in a multitude of modes, and in different places and stages, from the kindergarten to university, and it is increasingly mediated online, and in 'lifelong learning'. Further, education has become embroiled within global systems of capitalism and the unceasing exploitation of the natural world, and that is largely productive of many of the negative effects of the Anthropocene (cf., Steffen et al. 2018). The most basic task for education is henceforth to extract us from the constraints and systems that have controlled and dominated teaching and learning, and have aided in the production of the Anthropocene, so that the new pedagogy of this book may be realised, as divergences from the unconscious drives (Figure 6.2) that have created the contemporary world (and from the plane of globalisation below).

At its most basic level, education is an encounter, a nexus between teaching and learning, wherein something happens, which we might call an event (cf., Deleuze 1994). To do this differently is the point of this book and chapter, with the aim of changing what happens in the Anthropocene (and not merely as a political cliché or as a short-term fix). Teaching and learning differently in the Anthropocene is therefore about recognising and acting upon the impulses and organisational constraints that work through every level of our communal lives, from the microscopic to the cosmic, to enforce and augment the momentum that has resulted in the Anthropocene in time. As such, this book is primarily about translating the findings from the previous four chapters (Nx) into teaching and learning differently, not as static, top-down, enforced and artificial structures of coercion and prescription, that sit on top of complex and fluid situational contexts, but as fully entwined with and in the flows of the educational world as they currently exist (Cole 2019a). Teaching and learning differently in the Anthropocene is not an ideal or 'best practice' set of teaching and learning instructions, (even though the imaginary is a substantial part of this schema for change in terms of the forces that it is calling upon), but it is co-existent with the material flows that pass through us every day, and that we experience as life. The following analysis about teaching and learning differently in the Anthropocene is designed to be realistic yet integral, practical, non-moralistic, non-prescriptive, and able to attend to the drives that have formed the Anthropocene as the non-linear cloud analysis (Figure 1.2), to 'make a difference' as a new timeline of 'now' (Nx). The following conceptual analysis adds a holistic, in depth, non-capitalist, original approach to existing research and practices, and contributes a new ontological and epistemological analysis to climate change education as it currently exists, in the forms of environmental education (e.g., Payne 2019), Education for Sustainable Development (ESD), and/or education that follows the Sustainable Development Goals (cf., Anderson 2012, Kopnina 2020).

2 Attending to the 'Forces of Control' at the Local Level

Every act of and in education, however small, comes from a context. Hence, the first job of this conjunction between education and the Anthropocene, is to initiate an ongoing, situational analysis of the particular effects of the Anthropocene on and in a locality (Mannion, Fenwick and Lynch 2013). This job is historical, geographical, scientific, philosophical and political; i.e., it is entirely interdisciplinary (also understood through and as 'assemblage' (Deleuze and Guattari 1988)).[2] Teachers and lecturers may proffer the notion that they are not trained in the specifics of the Anthropocene, and do not have the expertise, knowledge and skills to bring the interdisciplinary aspects of the Anthropocene sufficiently together to deliver a satisfying and rigorous curriculum (cf., Metzger, Blockstein and Callahan 2017). Certainly, in tandem, the position of this book is to question any narrow specialism, as this propensity for knowledge formation does not unlock the forces that are at work in the Anthropocene, nor explain the conjunction of and in forces through the inter-connections that they are making in time, and therefore does not begin to resist the unconscious drives of the Anthropocene (Figure 6.2), to the benefit of future generations and the planet Earth, as is the intent of Chapters 2–5 (Nx).

The first consideration in terms of local and specifically educative matters, is the drive of 'tool-enhancement', as it has been explained in Chapter 2 with dates for its evolution tNx: (two and a half million years to the contemporary situation). As was shown with the non-linear, historical drive analysis, tool-enhancement is a well-spring of human creativity and imagination, and as such, it is one of the keys to a purposeful transition in the Anthropocene to arrest climate change, and to move towards a better future (cf., Mithen 2007). As a result, lecturers, teachers, students and the communities in which they live, will shift the tool-enhancement that results from their teaching and learning modules, to enhance the possibility of surviving the sixth great extinction event. In sum, one might surmise that most of what is presently taught in the contemporary curriculum, relates in some way to tool-enhancement as its core function, and hence, the point here is to question the direction of said tool-enhancement, with respect to the knowledge and skills that the curriculum imparts (cf., Reyes-García et al. 2010). At the moment, skills are frequently taught and learnt with no understanding as to why or how they might be used, thus disabling the point of education at its base. Thus, many talented students emerge due to the processes of education, having learnt great skills and knowledge, and being able to function brilliantly in terms of 'tool-enhancement', yet they end up working for businesses that are precisely damaging the planet with respect to climate change and ecology. The major problem that we face is that money, desire and power displace populations away from putting tool-enhancement at the service of environmental causes, because the desire for environmental solutions has been co-opted by capitalism (Collins and Barkdull 1995).

Hence, teaching and learning differently about tool-enhancement, is a multi-levelled and inter-connected process, of thinking through the different aspects of making and using tools. For example, what materials are used in the prospective tool making, where do these materials come from, and how well integrated into natural cycles of use and decay are these tools? (e.g., Jarzabkowski and Kaplan 2015) Clearly, the over-use of plastics, rare earth metals, and any materials that are toxic or harmful to the natural environment, can be limited in the processes of tool-enhancement, as well as the connection to fossil fuels, in terms of the production of the materials. In short, it is for educators, administrators and researchers to think clearly and purposefully about the ways in which the tool-enhancement of the activities they organise adversely adds to environmental damage, and, for example, exacerbates the negative effects of climate change through pedagogy and skill transference (Læssøe et al. 2009). This pedagogic action requires research and understanding about what constitutes specific instances of tool-enhancement in education, as well as fully thinking through the consequences of tool-enhancement, so that education has a better chance of serving pro-environmental purposes, rather than being merely exploited by capitalist power. This schema for change is enhanced by attending to the specific dates and impetus for innovation in tool-enhancement in Chapter 2 (tNx), that includes opportunities for new, relational, pedagogic action (cf., West et al. 2020).

Secondly, teaching and learning differently relates to the carbon trail ctNx: (1.7 million years ago to 1850 AD). Again, educators might wonder about this aspect of teaching and learning differently in the Anthropocene, as they may not consider themselves to be sufficiently knowledgeable to understand the carbonisation of everyday life, and not powerful enough to do anything about it. These are real issues for educators looking to make a difference in the Anthropocene, because fossil fuels and the capital that accompanies the circulation of fossil fuels in everyday lives, have become so integrated, that separating them out, and doing anything about them, can be an insidious process (e.g., Cole 2013). This is one of the reasons why the Deleuze/Guattari (1984, 1988) philosophical analysis of this book has been chosen, as it gives the educator the freedom and licence to experiment with their curriculum and pedagogy, so that the particular level of understanding of the cohort may be understood (with respect to in this instance the carbon trail), and hence, the realisation as to what they can do about it in terms of reducing particular carbon footprints is possible (ctNx). For example, going entirely off grid, and using solar and wind to replace fossil fuel generated electricity, would most likely not be realistic for many communities due to cost, and the ability to source and install such devices. Likewise, buying electric cars could be prohibitive for the majority of the population, due to the price and availability of such vehicles. In sum, going entirely green in terms of the emission of carbon dioxide due to the burning of fossil fuels might not be possible for many communities for practical reasons.

As such, educators can research and make a plan with their cohorts in terms of understanding how best they would be able to work with the carbon trails as they exist in their specific locality (cf., Mirzaei Rafe et al. 2019). Every context is different, with variant mixes of energy supply, car usage, industry and other transport options that in combination burn fossil fuels, such as jet planes and trains. Subsequently, the plans for working with and through the carbon trails will vary for every context, with educators and cohorts making connections and through-lines between the current state of the carbon trails in their locality, and a possible future to effectively deal with them, and using Chapter 3 as a blueprint to experiment with how the carbon trail has eventuated in now (and can be escaped, ctNx). Working with the imagination and coming up with creative, ideal plans, that may not always be realizable, are not excluded from this teaching and learning experience, as they will extend and challenge the thinking that takes place as a result of and in conjunction with the carbon trail, and its dates as planes of immanence, as depicted in Chapter 3 (ctNx). The local nexus with respect to thinking through the carbon trial sits alongside and integrates with tool-enhancement, as both inter-link and entwine in terms of teaching and learning differently in the Anthropocene. In a sense, this suggestion of inter-linkage comprises of an 'inside-out', constructivist environmental education, combined with an awareness of human carbon usage, and as a purposeful educational experiment for the contemporary moment (cf., Maggs and Robinson 2016). The pedagogic result oscillates between realism (what can be done locally in terms of climate change in the moment), and ideal, imaginary utopic construction or fabulation (as a projection to a post-carbon society, cf., Chapter 8). Teaching and learning differently at this point is an educational plan that relates to social ecology (Guattari 1996b), combining thinking through the consequences of the Anthropocene socially and ecologically, with doing something purposeful about climate change. The pedagogy of the carbon trail involves diving in-between the dates and marks of the formation of this drive (Chapter 3, ctNx), and in finding its escape routes as education (N).

The phallocene is part of this educative scheme for teaching and learning differently in the Anthropocene in terms of avoiding the self-same repetitions that are characteristic of phallic logic pNx: (4000 BC to 1996 AD). As was shown in Chapter 4, phallic logic sets up repetitive tasks and orders that have become unconscious behaviours, and that can dominate our thinking and lives (Deleuze 1994). If we wish to move beyond the forces that have set up and dominate the Anthropocene, we require new through-lines and thinking strategies that take away the impetus and directedness of the phallocene as a whole. In a straightforward manner, teachers can apply feminist educational strategies (e.g., Hawkesworth 2006) to the practice of knowledge inquiry in the Anthropocene, that significantly takes account of the bodily, subjective, and positional stances that exist in and as a result of teaching and learning (affect). Thus, this aspect of teaching and learning differently in the Anthropocene involves investigating the body, subjectivity, and positionality in the contemporary situation, as a result of the dates and plateaux as depicted in Chapter 4 (pNx). In simple terms, teachers and students can organise against the negative aspects of climate change, environmental degradation, and the ways in which industrial processes, backed by big business and capital, has caused environmental damage and will continue to destroy nature (cf., Wakefield 2020). As a more complex education event caused by the phallocene, teachers and students can sketch social-cultural through-lines that extend and enhance the analysis of Chapter 4, and create transformed ways to see the future as new (or as a continuously changing now (N), and that removes phallic influence (-p)).

Furthermore, challenging the phallocene is a process of teaching and learning how to explore and purposefully work through affective feelings connected to the destruction of the natural world. The teachers and students do not have to become committed environmental activists as a result of their feminist inquiry into the present situation, though it is not excluded from this non-prescriptive schema for change. Feminism at its most purposeful and directed, can help teachers and students focus their climate critique on the phallic means to reproduce the self-same in their local domain (cf., Konior and Granata 2018). In terms of climate change, phallic logic will attempt to perpetuate what has gone before, for example, the wholesale use of fossil fuels as energy supply, and as an integral part of global capitalism, but this logic will cover up the usage, and divert arguments and inquiry away from understanding how fossil fuels remain in the mix, despite the science of climate change, and what can be done about it (cf., Malm and Hornborg 2015).

Lastly, in terms of teaching and learning differently in the Anthropocene at the local level, teachers can think about time, named as 'atomic-time' in Chapter 5, aNx (500 BC to 1945 AD). Schools and universities are often organised in time as mechanical and repetitive, with timetables that cut up and separate knowledge-areas and their requisite thinking skills, hence making any mode of interdisciplinary inquiry and its emergence as new life-forms that this book requires, challenging, if not impossible to implement (Cole 2011). Hence, teachers and lecturers can redirect the time separating processes of the normal top-down and divisive curriculum into time-producing processes, that which Bergson called *durée* (Deleuze 1991), in and through which cohorts work together on plans to do something purposeful and integrated with respect to the Anthropocene. Altering the direction of humanity in the Anthropocene is not straightforward, as it involves not only augmenting the collective intelligence to understand what is wrong with respect to humanity's path, but engendering the will and making the effort to change it. Reading the separate dates of Chapter 5 (aNx) as plateaux, to enable thinking out of atomic-time, and its translation to a purposeful pedagogy, is one way to achieve this 'will to change' (e.g., Neyrat 2019). Such modification will not be initiated from one source, and fan out to the rest of the world, and hence, local attention to the forces of control are connected to what is taking place globally to have impact, beyond specific, local climate, and/or ecological problems. Further, time is not limited to one locality, but extends across the universe, and, as such, the impetus to teach and learn differently in 'atomic-time', involves encountering interconnected, cosmic time, in, through and as education (cf., Naughton, Biesta and Cole 2018). Cosmic time extends time beyond the remit of being atomised and separated in time and hence fixed to one order of and in time, to positively using and working with time in a complex and variant manner as teaching and learning, and as it flows through the universe (Nx). One way to do this is to reformulate education in terms of the global and to critique contemporary processes of globalisation as timeless.

3 A Global Thinking Matrix

Climate change is a global concern that complements its local effects as the Anthropocene. Most pedagogic practice in environmental education and Education for Sustainable Development (ESD) stops at the remit of local effects (cf., Jickling 1992). This chapter insists that the global thinking matrix that follows (Figure 6.1) purposefully adds to environmental education and Education for Sustainable Development (ESD), because it augments how these practises inter-relate to other critical human activities such as the economy (cf., Kopnina 2014). The effects of carbon dioxide emissions and the consequent global warming are being felt across the world, and this will continue for the foreseeable future (Steffen et al. 2018). Hence, teaching differently in the Anthropocene has to encourage students to think globally, and to address the current state of globalisation, and how we have got here as an inter-connected 'eternal-now'. In this section, I interpret the philosophy of Deleuze/Guattari (1984, 1988), and the four-line approach to the Anthropocene (Chapters 2–5)

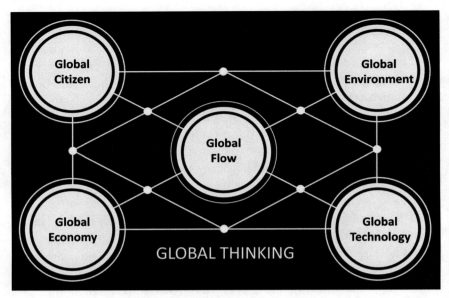

FIGURE 6.1 Global thinking in the Anthropocene: 'Citizen, economy, technology, environment and flow' (© Cole 2020)

and its pedagogic escape routes (Nx), as being inter-related to critically exploring contemporary globalisation (see Figure 6.2), not in order to endorse or augment it, but to open up thought (and escape) about globalisation in the Anthropocene, to create something new in education, and in particular, to understand how its component parts come together and function to preserve the status quo (international one-world capitalism). Globalisation is an area that has been much discussed, studied, and applied to educational thought and practice (e.g., Cole and Woodrow 2016, Cole and Bradley 2018). For the purposes of this chapter and book, and to understand how to relate the topic of globalisation to the Anthropocene, the educational parameters of globalisation have been divided into five overlapping/connected areas:

1. *Global citizen*: thinking through the components of changing identity and personal becoming in a global context.
2. *Global economy*: realising that all economic activity is connected, e.g., through international electronic networks.
3. *Global flow*: examining the differentials and push factors between countries and regions, which make the global economy work.
4. *Global technology*: understanding that much of the impetus of contemporary globalisation comes from technological development.
5. *Global environment*: including the impacts on the environment of accelerated and expanded human development due to globalisation.

Whilst all five elements above (Figure 6.1) are in themselves extremely important in terms of comprehending how to teach and learn differently in the Anthropocene, and potentially suggesting vast topics for study and discussion, it is vital to simultaneously work on their inter-connectedness, and to try to understand how and why they function together. For example, it is clear from study of the global economy, global technology and global environment, that they change together in complicated and inter-related ways, yet it is imperative to understand how exactly this inter-connection works for education in the Anthropocene, as vectors Deleuze/Guattari (1984). A case in point is the formula for increased activity in the global economy (growth), via the extensive use of global technologies, necessarily having a detrimental effect on the global environment, and this action being mitigated incrementally through the use of new, environmentally less damaging and sustainable processes (e.g., Şener, Sharp and Anctil 2018). However, the absolute ubiquity, of, for example, plastics and other materials in and as part of industrial processes, makes the separation and judgement regarding better or worse increases in global economic activity, the spread of global technologies and their environmental effects, part of an inter-laced, global mapping process. Further, the interconnections between the five global elements above exemplify a thinking matrix (Figure 6.1), to understand how the complex changing aspects of globalisation relate to, for example, education in the Anthropocene (e.g., Cole and Woodrow 2016, Cole and Bradley 2018), and this matrix can be superimposed as a plane on the four unconscious drives of the Anthropocene as conical spirals (Figure 6.2).

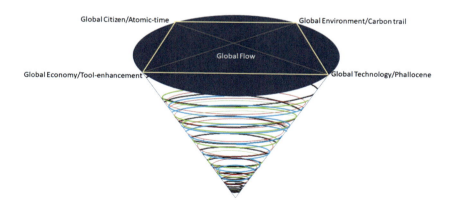

FIGURE 6.2   Global thinking in the Anthropocene: 'Citizen', 'economy', 'technology', 'environment' and 'flow', as a plane superimposed on: 'Tool-enhancement', 'Carbon trail', 'the phallocene' and 'Atomic-time' as four conical spirals (© Cole and Baghi 2021)

The superimposition of the matrix on the inward conical spirals of the Anthropocene shows how globalisation may be seen to be an important figure in terms of doing something about the Anthropocene through education (Nx), but that it is a one dimensional analysis of the drives.

The analysis of globalisation sits upon the four unconscious drives of the Anthropocene as a plane (Figure 6.2). This is because globalisation spreads out synchronously. Globalisation is the contemporary latest extent of the global capitalist situation, and, as such, does not penetrate into the depths of time, as does the analysis of the drives (cf., Wakefield 2020). In terms of education, the four drives of the unconscious diagram provide opportunities of teaching and learning at every date in their emergence (Chapters 2–5, Nx), whilst globalisation provides a planar matrix for analysis, global thinking, and subsequent pedagogy.[3]

3.1 Pedagogy of the Global Matrix

The first global citizen element of the matrix (Figures 6.1 & 6.2) involves questions about who the students and teachers are, and who they will become. In an increasingly connected, global world, nobody can think of themselves as truly isolated, or separate from the global community. This connection happens because we are continually related to world events as soon as we engage with the media, further, we form complicated relations with global identities when we travel, work and think about where we sit in the world, and how we act (cf., Rigby 2009). There has been movement to halt the effects of globalisation on identity, for example, as espoused by political nationalisms, yet these movements are primarily reactionary, and often rile against an element of globalisation that they don't agree with (e.g., immigration or import tariffs); however, it could be argued that no-one can hide from the effects of globalisation on the collective formation of individuals in the long run (cf., Bradley and Cole 2018). The global citizen segment of this analysis of teaching and learning differently in the Anthropocene, asks teachers to think about the identity resources they bring to education, and how their knowledge-work relates to global citizenship. Elements of the flux-like identity and knowledge-work that teachers can perform with reference to this element in the Anthropocene include:
– Citizenship: What does citizenship mean for the students, teachers, parents and the community of your school/college? Governmental and official documents related to citizenship will give a certain perspective on what it means and how one should perform it (cf., Stromquist and Monkman 2014). However: Do governmental resources on citizenship resonate with community expectations? How well can students articulate the concept of citizenship, and does it provide a platform for their codes of ethics? What specifically is (your national) citizenship, in addition to global citizenship, and are they compatible? These questions can be explored through the examination of

documents, literature, and critical discussion about what citizenship means in the Anthropocene.
- Multiculturalism: One of the consequences of globalisation is the formation over time of multicultural communities. One can ask: What does multiculturalism mean for students, teachers and community? How do students engage with the reality of multiculturalism in their context? Questions about multiculturalism and diversity can be deeply personal, especially if any of the community has experienced racism (cf., Au 2009). These elements of the formation of global citizens need to be dealt with sensitively, and teachers can explore the best ways to treat the subject in their context of the specific effects of global warming.
- Values: Values are passed down from generations and between members of society, sometimes in complicated ways (Cole and Mirzaei Rafe 2018). However, one could ask, does the current reality of globalisation in the Anthropocene, demand a new set of global values, and new modes of transmission of these values? Teachers can engage with the values in their communities, how they relate to global values, and which take into account global interpersonal relationships.
- Jobs and careers: The global movement of people and access to global information has opened up the international jobs market (pre-pandemic). Students can begin to think about how they fit into the global job market, and the sorts of skills that global workers require (e.g., Malone 2004). This element of a global, Anthropocenic thinking module needs to be handled with their contexts in mind, especially if there have been local environmental problems due to global business decisions (e.g., mining), yet as part of this important pedagogic conversation, students may have valuable experience and knowledge in this area from their parents or other contacts.

The reality of contemporary globalisation and the Anthropocene, is that we live in a fluctuating global economic situation. Whilst historical information about why and how this has happened is significant, and can be dealt with through specialist studies in economics and history, the present day dynamics of the global economy is of interest to this critical study of education in the Anthropocene, and how they inter-relate (Figures 6.1 & 6.2). These contemporary dynamics of economics for the Anthropocene can be understood through the following elements:
- Products: the contemporary global economy means that students interact with products from all over the world on a daily basis, as well as being part of communities that manufacture and distribute international products. This element of divergent education in the Anthropocene asks teachers and their students to become aware of and understand the global nature of the products which they interact with every day. Where do the products come

from? Why do they use global products and not local ones? Which products are produced in their locality, and where do they go? Teachers need to enable their students to become literate in terms of reading the labelling of products and understanding what they mean (cf., Masny and Cole 2012). This element of teaching and learning differently in the Anthropocene is not about teachers and students being experts in product design, but equips them with the skills to understand the global movement of products in the Anthropocene and their consequences.

– Skills: Just as the products which we use can come from anywhere in the world, depending on various factors, such as the costs of manufacture and labour, ease of distribution, and product marketing and sales, the skills for the global economy are subject to inverted and flux-like forces (Malone 2004). This element of new education in the Anthropocene relates to global citizens, and suggests that learners can think of themselves in relation to the global economy and the skills that they are learning. Speculative, imaginative and joined-up thinking is required, to enable students to engage in the types of skill development required for the future in the Anthropocene, e.g., rethinking food production, carbon emissions evaluation, local energy use, climate change prevention and eco-lifestyles.

– Exchange: the global economy is a vast exchange market. Products and skills are 'for sale', and this exchange has been augmented through technological developments, such as cargo shipping, planes and the internet. This element of a different education in the Anthropocene initiates teaching and learning scenarios that come to grips with exchange-values and how to transform them given today's environmental situation, and that human beings have been preoccupied with for many years (Stromquist and Monkman 2014). Investigation into the ways in which commercial exchange happens, will benefit learners as a critical Anthropocene thinking skill.

– Sales: Once markets with prices have been organised and set for products and skills, these items have to be sold. Standing out in a crowded marketplace, is an important part of the dynamics of the global economy (Malone 2004). This element of a different education in the Anthropocene does not have to be additive, as teachers do not have to become expert sales people. However, critically understanding the sales and marketing environment of the global economy as a thinking exercise, aids knowledge of the forces of the Anthropocene, and how they control us.

The global economy works due to 'push' factors. For example, products are made in countries where labour and the costs of production are lower than the countries where the products are sold (Scott 1996). The products therefore 'flow' from countries of production, to countries of sales/distribution,

where they are bought. These 'flows' that are happening due to the global economy (Figures 6.1 & 6.2) have consequences for communities, work and the life choices of individuals in every part of the world. These consequences can be figured through elements that define teaching and learning differently in the Anthropocene with respect to global flows:
- Migration: One of the most contentious issues connected to global flows and ecological and economic collapse in the Anthropocene is related to the international migration of people. This element has to be handled delicately by educators, so not to provoke the politics of anti-immigration (Au 2009). Hence, this aspect of differentiated education in the Anthropocene cannot augment negative, racist or xenophobic reactions, but allow students to positively investigate the facts and projections of global migration (that will increase as climate change effects worsens) in a safe environment.
- Developing world: One consequence of the global flows of people, products and capital in the Anthropocene, is that the world has been classified in term of its developmental status. The 'first world' relates to highly industrialised countries, which have over time, become the gross recipients of the benefits of globalisation, including the massive burning of fossil fuels (Scott 1996), and 'third' or even 'fourth world' countries, which have been largely bypassed in the 'progress' of globalisation, and have experienced negative consequences of these changes, such as poverty, wars, and the decimation of human rights.
- Money: Behind the global flows that we are experiencing in this phase of contemporary globalisation in the Anthropocene, is the unprecedented flow of capital/money through inter-connected electronic markets and their algorithms. Students and teachers can discuss how price setting in global markets has consequences for local communities (Ibid.); e.g., agricultural communities will have specific knowledge about issues connected to the financing of their enterprise through the pricing of their products, whereas urban communities, whose primary connection to global finance might be through investment projects, and, for example, the pricing of service industries.

In terms of element four (Figures 6.1 & 6.2), globalisation in the Anthropocene is enacted, maintained and enhanced through the development of global technologies. Teachers and students will be able to think through the technologies with which they are familiar, and explore how they are interacting with and changing their lives. Amongst the global technologies which could be explored through teaching and learning differently in the Anthropocene are:
- The Internet: perhaps the most obvious and abundant global technology that students and teachers know is the internet. This recent technological development was one of the drivers for the acceleration in globalisation

that was experienced throughout the 1990s. Enhanced digital interconnections between peoples and places have seen the abilities of individuals and groups to communicate in ways which were previously unimaginable (Pettman 2016). Perhaps one could argue that the educational promise of the internet has not been fully realised, in term of achieving internationally cooperative learning communities, yet the manner in which social media and the increased access to open source scientific materials, does signal huge inversions in knowledge and informational environments (e.g., Crary 2013). Teachers and students can inquire into their internet usage, for what purposes they use the internet (e.g., environmental activism), and the messages and skills necessary for knowledge creation, comprehension and interaction on the internet given the facts of climate change.

– Television, screen devices and cinema: the global spread of the ability to record and broadcast events has risen exponentially since mobile devices have had digital video recording facilities incorporated into them (cf., Cole and Pullen 2010, Cole and Bradley 2016). Today, a mixture of traditional and online broadcasting companies around the world deliver an overwhelming plethora of content to worldwide audiences. Teachers and students can explore their television/screen watching habits in this element, as well as discussing where the programmes that they watch come from (e.g., the U.S.A.), what the values and messages are in the programmes, and what the programmes mean for them with respect to the Anthropocene.

– Transport technologies such as planes, cars, trains and ships: masses of the human population are able to move around the planet with a freedom and ease as never before (ignoring restrictions due to, for example, the COVID-19 pandemic). Technologies to aid the interconnection of economic activity and people in recreation, has grown to such an extent, that we can take it for granted to travel anywhere in the world, and that we are able to exchange goods and services globally (Malone 2004). This element of global thinking in the Anthropocene (Figure 6.1) asks teachers and students to inquire into global transport networks, and to critically analyse its consequences, for example, in terms of carbon emissions.

Perhaps one of the most unambiguous, yet frequently overlooked elements of globalisation, is the effect that it is having on the environment, which is a priority in terms of the Anthropocene. The two sides of the fifth element (Figures 6.1 & 6.2) about the effects of globalisation on the environment come down to:

– Globalisation is having an enormous impact on the environment, and this impact is largely negative. One could name: global warming, industrial pollution and other processes such as agriculture, models of human development based on greed, exponential human population growth, and unsustainable resources usage (e.g., Hall 2020); which are amongst many factors that are contributing to the notion that the environmental effects of globalisation are overwhelmingly negative. Of course, exploration of this element in teaching and learning differently in the Anthropocene, could lead to despair, especially because many political leaders do not seem to be across the facts with respect to how severely globalisation can impact on the environment (cf., Dryzek 1997). Teachers and educators might explore this element of the Anthropocene differently, so not as to create fear amongst students, but to purposefully realise how the effects of globalisation on the environment can be shared. What we can do, and how to deal with the impacts on the environment that are being caused by globalisation, are questions to be engaged with at the local level, whilst requiring binding and extensive international agreements on climate change action of an unprecedented nature, for example, to combat the effects of global warming (Hall 2020).

- The solution to the negative impacts on the environment lies within the dynamics of globalisation. Many may wonder how, or if they can make any difference to the ways in which globalisation is having an impact on the environment. However, one can state that the most readily available educational solution to this problem is critical and militant consciousness raising, with respect to the very processes of globalisation (cf., Cole and Bradley 2018; Chapter 7 (this book)). Global thinking in the Anthropocene is required in this context that links local actions with global processes. Education is key to this thinking effort, and how we deal with globalisation going forward, as the creation of positive learning communities are vital. However, there is a political reaction against the effects of globalisation worldwide, and this includes taking seriously the impacts of globalisation on the environment (Cole 2020). Climate sceptics and climate change deniers can be challenged, and the often confusing and contradictory information that students may encounter about global warming has to be corrected, so there is at least the possibility of concerted, effective action in the Anthropocene.

The fifth element in teaching and learning globally in the Anthropocene needs to be handled precisely. It is straightforward for teachers and communities to work in their local context, and to directly address environmental issues with their cohorts, e.g., by clearing up rubbish, or examining the pollution in their waterways. The more complicated, thinking, and action challenge, comes when students and teachers expand outside their locality, to address global environmental matters, and how they can change them (i.e., as the Anthropocene, and as depicted in Figures 6.1 & 6.2).

4   What Is Pedagogy of/in the Anthropocene?

Education at its best is involved with making a difference, and the most differential aspects of pedagogy need to be carried forward to make an attempt to change things in the Anthropocene according to the precepts of this book, i.e., the Deleuze/Guattari (1984, 1988) analysis of the unconscious drives. This prospect of a change agenda foregrounds a complex and elongated task, because systems of fossil fuel consumption and capitalism through history have previously controlled and limited our actions and thoughts at every step (cf., Malm 2016). Clearly, teachers and educators need to be aware of the gravity of the situation, and integrate such awareness into inventing new pedagogies that shape and mould the next generation into positive action, that will make a real difference in the Anthropocene (Nx).[4] This book suggests that pedagogy in the Anthropocene is more than an addition to environmental education and Education for Sustainable Development, or a discrete subject, placed in the curriculum to aid comprehension of climate change and what can be done about it. Rather, following the Deleuze/Guattari (1984, 1988) philosophical analysis of this book, and the specific Guattarian influence, that manifests in this chapter, as the three ecologies (1996b), and as a mode of 'climate change techno-shamanism' (cf., Cole 2007), one might divide pedagogy of/in the Anthropocene (Nx) into three inter-linked, but separate areas:

1. Differentiating the self: As teachers, we are shaping the characters and personalities of the next generation. Given the philosophical analysis of this book, one might legitimately ask whether or not a stable human self can be salvaged, given the inter-connected Anthropocenic drives that have been described to flow through us in Chapters 2–5, and that can be escaped through education as (N). However, in a very pertinent sense, teachers and lecturers are frequently concerned with the individuals that they are influencing. These individuals have dreams and desires for the future, as was explored in Chapter 1. The reality of climate change and what is happening as a result, is that we need to prepare for a different future, other than the present and past, one with zero consumption of fossil fuels, lifestyles that work to enhance the ecology of the planet, rather than continuously using up resources until they have been exhausted, and with little or no regard for the consequences outside of our pleasures and benefits (Lent 2018). One could argue that human nature is fundamentally greedy and selfish, and involves establishing an enhanced position for one's self, and with little true thought for others and nature. Hence, the differentiations of the self that are part of the transition to a future for humanity wherein we survive and avoid our own annihilation in the sixth great extinction event, is connected to successful pedagogy

that encourages individuals to turn away from planet and life destroying choices, such as leading careless, consumerist, self-absorbed lives (cf., Chapter 7 + Nx). Educators can demonstrate the options open to students to not become trapped in and part of the ever expanding, capitalist, annihilation and extinction machine (Cole 2019b).

2. Differentiation of society: Along with demonstrating the differentiation of the self through pedagogy, educators can model how society may change to have a chance to survive into the future (cf., Chapter 7). Enhanced collaboration and agreement on issues to protect Earth resources, and the move to a model wherein they are not exploited and used for profit is important (e.g., Valentine 2012). Further, the obscene inequities in societies around the world can be mentioned and addressed through pedagogy (Nx). Different models for society and the social changes to get there can also be debated. History is replete with good examples of societies that have lived collectively and collaborated with respect to resource sharing, so that the society will not become extinct in the environment on which is depends. For example, the nomads of the Mongolian plain developed a complex social structure and codes that have avoided the sedentary exploitation and domination of nature without replenishment through millennia (cf., Deleuze and Guattari 1988: 351–424). Admittedly, it is impossible to wholly reproduce nomadic society in the contemporary situation, but we can move towards the resource and social integration of the nomads, that inter-locks society with ecology more thoroughly. At the moment, children are progressively schooled away from nature, as the lessons they learn and the skills they acquire are geared towards the current, global, industrial-capitalist model of society, with its value system embedded in profit-making, and the perspective on nature as resources to be harvested and sold (Moore 2016). Making a meaningful reconnection with nature through nomadism could subtract from the propensity to exploit and use nature in a sedentary fashion, in short, these societal differentials taught through pedagogy could be an important contribution to the Anthropocene in terms of future differentiation as now (Nx).

3. Differentials in the environment: Lastly, pedagogy in the Anthropocene has to be realigned to address the environmental damage and harm that we have caused. As has been mentioned, the environment is most often currently addressed through environmental education, or as a discrete knowledge area for study in science. Environmental education frequently receives little or no attention in the curriculum. It is the hypothesis of this book that the engagement, attuning with, and immersion in nature, tend towards positive changes that are necessary in the Anthropocene (Cole 2019b). Hence, environmental education will be elevated and moved from

the periphery to the centre of education, so that all children and communities experience a worthwhile and strong connection with nature, something that they may carry with them for the rest of their lives, and that will help them deal with the changes that will come due to climate change. Enhanced sensitivity and understanding of nature will emerge from being closer to nature from an early age, and not being artificially isolated from the environment in a classroom, or only seeing it as an abstract diagram of scientific principles on a whiteboard. Pedagogy in this context is akin to the Aboriginal Australian 'walkabout', which is a ritual designed for members of the community to experience 'Country', and which is a deep, ancestral connection with the land (Cole and Somerville 2018). At the moment, children learn through a standardised and universal knowledge-based curriculum, that abstracts them from the very environments on which they depend (Cole 2019c). This perception is repetitively enhanced through the majority of the modern aspects of our lives, such as supermarkets with food wrapped in cellophane, as this food is unrecognisable as coming from the Earth. A differential in the environment through pedagogy in the Anthropocene involves students, teachers and groups of learners realigning themselves closer to nature, understanding the ways in which it is changing, and realising the impacts that human inhabitation is having on the Earth. Only after these teaching and learning experiences have been achieved, can we begin to plot a way forward as a collective society, and live in the world in a different manner (Nx). To enable this movement, changes in society need to be addressed that directly relate to teaching and learning differently in the Anthropocene (Chapters 6 and 7).

Notes

1 These strategies can be viewed and shared on https://iiraorg.com/education-the-anthropocene-and-deleuze-guattari/
2 The specific results of this experiment in pedagogic evolution may be seen at https://iiraorg.com/education-the-anthropocene-and-deleuze-guattari/
3 Examples are collated here: https://iiraorg.com/global-thinking-matrix/
4 See https://iiraorg.com/education-the-anthropocene-and-deleuze-guattari/

CHAPTER 7

Incremental Movements towards a New Society

> **Special Note**
>
> This chapter acts as a purposeful underpinning to the creation of new educational materials and episodes with reference to the previous chapters (Chapters 2–6): Nx + global thinking matrix.[1]

1 Introduction

This chapter asks the question: *What mode of social change complements teaching and learning differently in the Anthropocene?* The overall problem for this book is that the chosen motor for transition in the Anthropocene is education, and this is a major component in the apparatus that maintains the status quo; i.e., capitalism (e.g., Cole 2019c). Marxist theorists have attempted to co-opt education, and have evolve a praxis of 'critical pedagogy' to move society towards a socialist revolution through education (e.g., McLaren et al. 2004). However, the flaw in this schema for change is that teachers and educators have to be in ideological agreement with this alteration in society, that could deliver positive ecological and environmental outcomes through collective governance if implemented (this is not the proposed, divergent change processes of this book). Furthermore, educational philosophers such as John Dewey, Paulo Freire (1996), bell hooks and Ivan Illich have theorised education with respect to different aspects of social change. In contrast, this book has chosen a new (multiple) path to previous philosophers of education in terms of differentiating pedagogy from the maintenance system for one world capitalism, to being an engine for social change. The process of this book is: (1) Posit the future as the Anthropocene to create an expanded conception of 'now' (N), into which new educational practice may be fitted (Chapter 1); (2) Analyse the four drives of the Anthropocene through history to create opportunities for pedagogy that subverts these drives, Nx (Chapters 2–5); (3) Augment these opportunities (Nx) at the local level, and expand to connect them globally through a thinking matrix (Figure 6.2) (Chapter 6); (4) Apply the resulting educational practice to social change (Chapter 7). Hence, this chapter follows on with the intent of opening up education in order to *act in the Anthropocene*, and adds the layer of social change, as decisive strategic thought (tactic) (cf., Cole 2019a).

Human society changes for many reasons, as the analysis in Chapters 2–5 has showed (Nx), by drawing out the unconscious drives, and due to composite factors such as power, money, population, culture, food, starvation, technology, war and, pertinently for this book on the Anthropocene, climate change (e.g., Clarke 2014). Theories for social change include: Evolutionary Theory; Cyclical Theory; Economic (Mandan) Theory of Social Change; Conflict Theory, and; Technological Theory (e.g., Corning 1987). The approach of this book, based on the philosophy of Deleuze/Guattari (1984, 1988), is to suggest that none of these theories wholly describes social change as society alters due to complex, inter-woven material factors, and often in a non-linear fashion. This book presents a theory of mutual and inter-related change, that expands materiality from human power, struggle and hierarchy (e.g., as capital), to include natural aspects of modification proved by science and other sources such as indigenous knowledges; and does not suggest that human society is being perfected, or that there is a pre-defined path to salvation (e.g., through technology). Rather, the theory of social change on offer through this book is one that is routed through the unconscious and education, and does not avoid the distortions that dreaming about social change can bring, but, indeed, looks to augment them. Education as a practice is crucial to the social change that is suggested here, but it is education as coming from a bottom-up, chaotic, and multiply divergent perspective; as a situational response to the analysis of the unconscious drives (Nx) of Chapters 2–5, and not one mired in already established power-formations and structures, that frequently represent hindrances to differentiation (cf., Cole 2011). Hence, everything presented in this chapter (as elsewhere) is meant to stimulate difference, as well as being an analysis of the routes to social reformation in the Anthropocene, and that adds to the directions of social morphology as suggested by the previous chapters as education and pedagogy (Nx + global thinking matrix).

If we take the model of social change from Deleuze/Guattari (1984, 1988) in the Anthropocene as being encapsulated by social ecology, (i.e. as differentiating the psyche, society + ecology), derived from Guattari (1996b), such a heterodox praxis enables three inter-related, radical, pathways/nexuses, that will be presented and analysed below in terms of their dynamics and educative potential: (1) *A 'degrowth' path*, wherein micro societies actively work towards a sustainable future, in which what we know about living a life in harmony with nature (and not exploiting it through capitalist growth/surplus value) is acted upon, and with these actions, climate change is stabilised, and ecology is enhanced (cf., Brossmann and Islar 2020). "Degrowth is a planned reduction of energy and resource throughput designed to bring the economy back into balance with the living world in a way that reduces inequality and improves human well-being" (Hickel 2020: 2, Kallis 2018, Latouche 2009).; (2) *A change of consciousness model,* wherein the thinking and imagining processes of living a better life, in tune with the vicissitudes of nature, and as more responsive to the tenets of climate change, are fully considered, and as a result, are more likely to be acted upon (Hamilton 2010); (3) *A critical, political, and planetary model of immanent change,* wherein the dominant and guiding capitalist forces of our time are challenged and critiqued: i.e., this model of social change leads to a holistic eco-revolution. It is only when large scale systems and institutions of our time are challenged (i.e., capitalism/government/corporations/universities), that there will be a noticeable effect on global warming in the Anthropocene, a reduction of carbon emissions and an enhanced ecology. However, as was noted in the previous chapter, with respect to globalisation (Figures 6.1 & 6.2), the pervasive mechanisms of global capitalism that currently make enormous profits, and that are entirely inter-laced with the use of fossil fuels, will be the most resilient and stubborn forces in the world to change.

2 The Great Leap Forward – A Green Utopia?

Utopias have been sketched out to describe better, indeed, perfect societies since Plato imagined a Republic, ruled by philosopher-kings (Plato 360 BC). Famously, Thomas More described a utopic island state in 1516, with no money exchanges and strict rules about how to live to enforce his imagined and designed Utopia (More 1516). Hence, it is straightforward to see how the notion of Utopia, which is deeply embedded in the western social imagination, might intensify, in terms of thinking about the required shift to a green, renewable, sustainable, and more egalitarian and ecological society, especially in the present day, critical state of climate change in the Anthropocene. One could argue that to improve society at all requires a utopic imagination, yet in the light of the enormous disparities in wealth that have been created by global capitalism in recent years, and the fact that this (continuing) world system is largely run around fossil fuel infrastructure and profits, one might ask the question: *What is utopic thinking in the Anthropocene?*

Firstly, this chapter posits the notion of Green Utopia as a wholly material consideration and not idealism, and that it is central to small scale, degrowth models of society, and how they perceive and intend human communities to be modified in the Anthropocene (Brossmann and Islar 2020, Muraca 2012).

The problem with contemporary human society in these terms, is that it is wasteful, massive, and has had inequity and pollution programmed into it, due to how capitalism produces surplus value. Proponents of degrowth models of human society point to advancements in regenerative farming, renewable energy sources, the ability of telecommunications, and using the internet to make distant learning and work possible, and other technologies and modes of small scale social organisation that induce sustainability, ecology, and decarbonisation more than unrealizable, utopic dreams (e.g., Kerschner et al. 2018). However, it strikes me that the fulfilment of such programs hits a barrier when the actual living conditions under which we are currently exist are taken into account. I am fortunate, in that I live close to nature, in the Blue Mountains of New South Wales, Australia, an environmentally protected, World-Heritage listed area, I already have solar panels, and could install a solar battery and water collection unit for rainwater, and turn my small patch of land into a relatively fertile growing area. Moreover, it would be easy to approach my neighbours to change our lifestyles, as we live in a cul-de-sac, and we would be able to pool resources, to fabricate a small scale, degrowth type community, through which we could share resources such as power production (e.g., from solar panels, small wind turbines, and electrical battery storage), grow our own food, and communicate about other shared needs, such as helping out with house, garden, and perhaps car and other mechanical repairs (cf., Alexander and Gleeson 2019), However, I can say without fear of contradiction, that we cannot unhook ourselves from the current financial/social system, due to mortgages and the high cost of living in Australia, and, in addition, frankly, I don't know if my neighbours would be interested in establishing such a degrowth community at the present time, due to the practical implications of having to commit themselves to such a project. Hence, even though degrowth models of human society are possible, actual implementation remains unlikely, at best patchy, and it is certainly unpredictable.

Hence, in affluent societies, practical obstacles to establishing degrowth communities remain inhibitive to implementation, and, as such, those from rich societies continue to live under the premises of large scale capitalist societies, dependent on economics, flows of capital, debt, supposed monetary growth models to encourage investment, and international lines of commerce and trade. In contrast, for those living in less wealthy countries, the notion of living in a degrowth community might already be a daily fact of life, as they don't know of any other reality (cf., Müller et al. 2013), yet this fact will not stop them from wanting to emulate countries where wastefulness, consumption, surplus value, and the pursuit of luxury items are the accepted norm. This is one of the fundamental problems with climate change and differentiating society in terms of imagining a Green Utopia, in that even though the degrowth model for human socialisation and flourishing is possible, its opposite, i.e., continually looking to enhance economic growth by living through capitalism and consumerist (i.e., as monetary opportunities), and the concomitant wasteful lifestyles, and their sets of values, are a wholly attractive, yet contrasting set of options to degrowth, and that pro-capitalism is plugged into and pursued by human desire, and perpetually augmented through mediated images of high growth, wastage, and anti-environmental lifestyles through the media (cf., Cole and Bradley 2016). Hence, even though the notion of a Green Utopia is an important schema for the imaginary of the degrowth path of social change, and the degrowth Green Utopia sits beneath the remit of small scale environmental sustainability and renewability, it is surrounded by the realities and stories of present day economic human growth (cf., James 2014), that are underpinned by fossil fuel consumption, and all the images through time that this pro-growth, high carbon emission, consumerist behaviour has produced and relies upon. However, the reality of what we face in the Anthropocene necessitates degrowth as a differentiating program, to stave off societal collapse (cf., McLeod 2018). In terms of the educational platform of this book, degrowth and its principles are a future social underpinning to the pedagogic opportunities presented by the analysis of the four unconscious drives (Nx) and the global thinking matrix (Chapter 7). Further, we need to comprehend differences in consciousness to augment the likelihood that a Green Utopia could be imagined in and through education, especially in instances where the degrowth model of human society as an imagined Green Utopia is not already embedded.

Changes in consciousness that aim towards a greener society, present a move to an updated Buddhism, as the 'best fit' ecological religion (e.g., Batchelor 1994). The practice of Buddhism, involving meditation, deep contemplation of the universe, understanding how to raise one's consciousness so as not be duped by the many levels of 'Maya', self-deceit, or illusion that frequently beset us (e.g., as propagated by marketing), and being able to generally fit into one's ecological situation by living simply, are all worthy and noble aims, that would certainly help in the imagining of a Green Utopia as an underpinning for a differentiated educational practice. However, the history of Buddhism reveals that even though it is still an incredibly influential and well-respected religion, its focus on the production of a pacifist nature, has often meant that it has lost out to more hostile, dominating, and proselytising religions such as Christianity, Islam and in the Indian subcontinent, to Hinduism (cf., Conze 1993). In the current situation of the Anthropocene, one could say that the 'enemy' is the fossil fuel empire, and its perpetuation at the heart of global capitalism, that has taken human civilisation over the edge of the Holocene, and into a new, uncertain epoch of global warming, and a myriad of climate disruptions, called the Anthropocene. Buddhism gives the practitioner a spiritual discipline, that helps them to think about a Green Utopia, and provides mental strategies and tactics to understand and work through the labyrinth of missteps, false starts and illusions that inevitably leads back to enhanced profit for fossil fuel capitalism, and the lining of the pockets of already capitalised classes (cf., Wallin 2017, 2020). This is why a change of consciousness model for thought is an important addition to the notion of degrowth, and as an underpinning to the pedagogy, education (Nx + global thinking matrix) and social change of this chapter, but it is not enough on its own to challenge the domination of capitalism

There has been an effort to link Buddhism with Deleuze, as a concentrated and focused rethinking of western philosophy (e.g., See and Bradley 2016). Certainly, there are parallels between the many-layered thought levels and practises in Buddhism and Deleuze's rewriting of western thought, through key philosophers such as Nietzsche, Spinoza, Bergson, Kant, Leibniz and Hume. However, whether or not we get to the level of a Buddhist practice through Deleuze, is debatable. His aim as a philosopher is to rethink the assumptions, privileges, and power-control factors in western thought, and to subtract the transcendent, sedentary and external impositions on thought, to make thought work in reality, with all its infuriating/contradictory complications. As such, Deleuze on his own, does not consider the idealism of Utopia, or the underlying material Green Utopia of this section through the imagination, to shift away from the catastrophe of the Anthropocene as education (Nx) and social change. However, there are shades of a (re)constructed Utopia in the dual works with the militant anti-psychiatrist, Félix Guattari (1996b), who was arguably a utopian thinker, in that he spent the whole of his life trying to change society for the better (as he saw it). *1000 Plateaus* was inspired by Gregory Bateson's (2000) *Ecology of the Mind*, and hence it does bring us closer to the strategy of imagining a Green Utopia as a motor for social change, as immanent thought patterns about the world, history and life, that could be merged with Buddhist practice. Furthermore, the thought of an imagined Green Utopia that emerges from Deleuze/Guattari's (1984, 1988) dual earlier work, is strengthened by the third aspect of social change, and the task of an immanent critique of capitalism, with respect to the freedom of thought to rethink exploitation, domination, and to tackle the schizophrenia produced by the double think of capitalism (as profit).

It is possible to understand that in the Anthropocene, the major institutions under which we live, that are connected to state and national governments, can be reformed from being responsible for perpetuating one world capitalist system, with large corporations competing for market share and increased capital flows, to being recalibrated to deal with climate change (cf., Byrne and James 2019). Could this seemingly obvious move create the Green Utopia imaginary that we seek? Green Marxian critiques of capitalism have become increasingly common, as climate change has augmented, and one could position Guattari's influence on the Deleuze/Guattari writing team along these lines (e.g., Guattari 1996b). However, other than a mention of immanent, eco-revolution as utopia in *What is Philosophy?* and as a counter to the domination of the ideal of the Greek polis in thought Deleuze/Guattari (1994: 99–100), Deleuze/Guattari (1984, 1988), do not work out a program for a Green Utopia, or what it might look like as a transitional ecological society, or that we could apply to the Anthropocene as an object. Rather, their attention is focused on providing conceptual tools for an immanent critique of capitalism, in which they specifically state that utopia is a bad concept (Deleuze and Guattari 1994: 99), hence their critique includes, for example, working out the effects of capitalism on the psyche, and, pointedly, how capital flows can make one become schizophrenic as a practice of thought. This book does not posit utopia as a bad concept, but deploys the Green Utopia as a prompt for the imaginary, and the resulting synthesis of degrowth, consciousness raising and immanent critique. With these points in mind, the rest of the chapter is devoted to figuring out what the immanent-critical thoughts might look like, in terms of changing society for the better in the Anthropocene, keeping the Green Utopia imaginary as an important motor for change in conjunction with immanent critique and consciousness raising, as they lend themselves to circumventing capitalist exploitation via the analysis of the drives (and not making a profit out of green desires). This focus for the rest of the chapter on the immanent critique of capitalism, resolves itself in educational practice as the opportunities for pedagogy supplied by the four unconscious drives of the Anthropocene (Nx), in the global thinking matrix, and as an overall propensity to social change.

3 Changing Society at the Micro-Level

This chapter follows the structure of Chapter 6 on education, by analysing societal change at the micro and macro levels. The combination of the 'degrowth', raising consciousness, and immanent-critical theory, potentially treads a path to a better future (a Green Utopia imaginary), that would result in changes to society at the micro-level, or as has been seen in the previous chapter on teaching and learning differently in the Anthropocene, as a redirecting and manipulation of the drives that have produced the Anthropocene (Nx). This combined work is a continuous, ongoing, differentiation of now (N) through education, that could result in profound societal changes over the long-term, in a staggered, incremental, and non-linear fashion, as the resistances and inbuilt ways in which the capitalist fossil fuel status quo is maintained are prevalent and deep set (Malm and Hornberg 2015).

Firstly, the drive of tool-enhancement can be operationalised as a means to achieve desired micro-societal changes that move us towards a better future or imagined Green Utopia, and that mesh with the pedagogic opportunities of tool-enhancement (tNx). In terms of the degrowth path to a better society, the drive of tool-enhancement is already shaped and reshaped in a plethora of manners to enhance tools for a liveable future. For example, tools that help with small scale, self-sufficient living need to be favoured over mega-machines, and tools that can become part of enhanced ecological living can be sought out, rather than being used for systematic environmental destruction (cf., Meyer 2004). The drive of tool-enhancement could be resolved to attend to nomadic societal norms, rather than sedentary value systems, as sedentary life directs tools to function on behalf of capturing, exploiting and controlling the (human and non-human) world around us (cf., Chapter 2). Nomads use tools as parts of their bodies, to work with, feel, and comprehend the forces of nature, rather than capturing and repeatedly destroying them in the names of industry, efficiency, profit and progress (cf., Khazanov 1994). Similarly, consciousness raising with respect to tool-enhancement is about making the tools that one uses fit in with environmental conditions through contemplation, rather than working against prevalent conditions in thought (e.g., as dialectic/agency). The tools that enhance the human form could be congruent with how nature works, and not extend to the monstrous otherness that has beset human tool extension over the past few centuries (e.g., by producing nuclear bombs). We cannot reverse the trend to produce monstrous tools and technologies that have unleashed many of the forces that are negatively impacting on and as the Anthropocene, but we can redirect and modify them through conscious practice as an expanded now (education/N), to make sure that we are not merely fitting into mega-machines, as just one more cog in an engine. Further, the critical-immanent Deleuze/Guattari (1984, 1988) philosophy that has been used to analyse the four unconscious drives of the Anthropocene, makes us cognisant that many 'green tools' that we can seize to change the situation, are clever marketing inventions/mechanisms of green capitalism (Smith 2016). One can speculate that many of the 'green products' that are created to make a profit by appealing to the green consumers, are inculcated with capital markets and entrepreneurship, because green solutions to environmental problems are presently seen to be attractive future investment options (e.g., buying Tesla shares). Hence, we can apply the immanent, critical approach to social change with respect to researching and understanding what 'green tools' we are using, in order to make the incremental switch to a better society, and to not become part of a 'green scam' which in reality perpetuates the domination of fossil fuel energy consumption, by predominantly increasing returns for capital (fossil) markets with a few interspersed green options, and this analysis is an aspect of the educational plan put forward by this book.

Next, the micro alterations required to change society in conjunction with pedagogic strategies (ctNx), could deal with the carbon trails that flow through and beyond us. As was argued previously, the drive of the carbon trail is deeply set and closely aligned with tool-enhancement, and hence to change it is not in any way straightforward, but involves an unravelling of both drives. For example, the path to an imagined Green Utopia that follows a 'degrowth' model involves living a low consumption, low carbon emissions life, which many populations already currently follow in poorer countries (cf., Ritchie and Roser 2017). Hence, societal changes with respect to the carbon trails, will be primarily implemented in highly industrialised countries, rather than in developing countries, where the desire to emulate a luxurious and consumptive, first world life will be powerful, but the infrastructure is not as destructive in terms of the carbon trails. One can surmise that some industrialised countries could alter their carbon trails, as they possess extended middle and civil classes, and who can be persuaded to change their habits, and embrace the degrowth strategies for living, given the climate emergency, and their ethical standpoint. For example, countries such as those in the Scandinavian peninsula, might well-prove to be hotbeds for the kind of consciousness raising required to move to low carbon emissions, as fossil fuel market forces and profits may be genuinely seen as secondary to making a difference with respect to climate change by these populations (cf., Houser 2009).

Similarly, the carbon trail can be subject to widespread and penetrating critical thought, to comprehend how deeply inter-twined fossil fuel production and consumption has become in everyday life. Again, if one lives merely to survive, as many do all across the world, this type of thinking might be entirely alien, as the majority of the Earth's population are only worried about how to earn the next dollar to keep themselves alive. As such, the diversion of the carbon trail through immanent, critical thought, and the pedagogic opportunities that this action affords (ctNx), will only happen in places where it is possible to be able to step back from the enforced strictures on labour and time, and henceforth have the ability to analyse, and to understand how and to what extent the carbon trails are present in one's life. Further, it takes bravery and courage to critically address such entanglements, and to disentwine them, for example, with respect to understanding how doing well in one's career is still heavily bound up in enhanced fossil fuel consumption (cf., Galaz 2014). Furthermore, the contemporary fossil fuel/capitalist elite conspire to shut down dissenting voices by funding so called 'green activism', which in reality does nothing to challenge the status quo, but often perpetuates change mythologies that go nowhere but dead ends and more fossil fuel domination. In reality, the critical-immanent thought necessary to dislodge the carbon trail from our lives might be the most momentous and complex to fully conceive of and act upon as social change and education (ctNx).

In terms of the phallocene, micro changes in society and pedagogy (pNx) closely mirror the types of modifications based in the move to a degrowth model of society (e.g., Bauhardt 2014). This is because addressing the phallocene concerns working in terms of the relations through which we live and exist. By inviting large scale relations into our lives, that frequently promote the type of runaway profit-driven growth that accompanies capitalist accumulation, and its cyclic rebound that we find in economic collapses (Cole 2012), we give the ecology of our lives over to the phallocene (or the self-same). As was seen in Chapter 4, the phallocene has been redirecting our drives since approximately 3200 BC, when the drive direction was formalised by the ancient Egyptians and others as multiple 'God-heads'. Hence, it is not straightforward to question the phallocene 'head on', and to effectively avert the effects of this drive. Yet the enhanced communal, egalitarian, and practical assertions of life that the degrowth path to a Green Utopia imaginary can present (e.g., Brossmann and Islar 2020, Hickel 2020), offer a means to begin such a process. Many of the negative assumptions that are currently written into our lives (e.g., over work and its necessary stress), come from the patterns and forces that attempt to keep the possibility of high economic growth open, with its accompanying losses of control, balance and direction.

Degrowth is about resolving the multiple ways in which we can become slaves to the forces of the self-same, for example, wholly dependent on capital flows that reduces life to a quest for money, and this can be questioned through enhanced education about the phallocene (pNx). Similarly, the type of consciousness raising required to question the phallocene begins with understanding the relations, and the quality of relations that we find ourselves embedded within (a type of pedagogy). For example, if we feel powerless, alienated, not connected to anyone or anything, we can sink into a black hole of depression and vulnerability, wherein any negative effects directed against us, and that we might perceive and encounter in our everyday lives, can be exaggerated and augmented (Cole 2017a). Whilst this black hole can be a creative space, it is simultaneously dangerous in terms of trying to escape the lines of unconscious attack taken by the phallocene through an expanded now/education (pNx), as one can sink deeper into non-relation and potentially become weaker as a result. Questioning the phallocene is a critical task that has been started in earnest by feminist writers and thinkers over many years (e.g., Konior and Granata 2018). To initiate the types of micro societal changes necessary to address the Anthropocene, the immanent, critical thought that can be derived from feminism cannot be solely antagonistic or dismissive of what it means to be a male. Rather, feminism can initiate a mode of critical thinking about human relations, and attempt to heal the modes in which these inter-relations have been damaged over millennia through the tactics and strategies of the phallic-same, and that can manifest in and as education (pNx). The application of feminist thinking is not a 'magic solution' in this context, that will immediately resolve the often burnt and torn relationships that many find themselves inextricably buried within through contemporary capitalism, but can help to redirect the forces of the Anthropocene at the relational and matter levels as learning (Ibid.).

Lastly, the micro changes in society that can work towards the imaginary of a Green Utopia can attend to the forces of time embedded in our drives as 'atomic-time'(aNx). As was described in Chapter 5, atomic-time can be understood as a 'dead time', as a result of the stasis produced by and in the standoff of the nuclear détente, and the modes in which we have been separated and atomised in the current one world capitalist situation (e.g., Anievas 2008). Simultaneously, paradoxically, the atomic-time of the Anthropocene is an accelerated time (cf., Sellar and Cole 2017), in which global flows of capital have made time speed up, and commerce sits within these tramlines of capital, that have increasingly connected everything in the world, human and non-human, through the desire and necessity to make money through profit. Hence, we are simultaneously separated and accelerated in time, which produces a disembodying and disorientating effect, both of which are attended to by the degrowth path to an imagined Green Utopia. The degrowth model is about introducing slow time into one's life, not on the back on capitalist accumulation, but by purposefully slowing down, and consciously taking control of the flows of time as they pass through one's mind as learning (aNx). Degrowth is about re-experiencing the natural flows of time, and not choosing to be caught up in the time of consumerism, consumption, money and debt as flows (cf., Cole 2019b). Again, as we live in a capitalist society, this choice can be extremely hard to follow through and achieve, yet as a thinking practice of raising consciousness, it is a life goal, that creates the conditions through which one's quality of life is improved (aNx). The enhanced consciousness model to take us towards an imagined Green Utopia, includes the sense that all thought, belief and feeling happens in time, and hence to change these factors in one's life and how they can affect us, one must firstly change one's perception of time.

Further, the critical thinking model to shift thought and human focus away from the destructive path of environmental damage due to unmitigated capitalism, and in the direction of an imagined Green Utopia, one also has to rethink time as and through education (aNx). At the moment, time is variously connected by capitalist endeavour in terms of labour, working efficiently, the creation of surplus and profit, debt and repayment, and with respect to increasing these connections as relating to capital flows in education. Critical thinking immanently in the Anthropocene is hence about disconnecting these mechanisms with respect to time, to allow for and to encourage thought of time itself, and not to become trapped by time as enslaved by the need for money (Smith 2019, Deleuze 1989). In the end, the purpose of attending to atomic-time with respect to micro-changes in society, is to reconnect time with the body, and to find a natural time, through and by which human flourishing can recommence as learning (aNx). In the contemporary moment, when one's time is most usually laid out in advance by work, and with battling the onslaught of impending debt and money arrangements, such a thought of time might indeed seem to be 'escapist'. This conundrum is why the invention of a malleable drive of 'atomic-time' through the philosophical analysis of Deleuze/Guattari (1984, 1988) serves as a means to encapsulate the thought of a better time, in and of the Anthropocene through education (aNx) and social change.

4 How Can the Minor Societal Changes Be Augmented?

The aim and purpose of this chapter (and book) is not to remain on the micro level in terms of societal and educational change, as many schemas in environmental education (e.g., Payne 2019) and Education for Sustainable Development (ESD) can do, but entreats us that this is the best (and only) place to start. We make a difference at this level, and even though large institutions and the global forces that are powering climate change have to alter course, the argument presented here is that the greatest effect that the philosophy of Deleuze/Guattari (1984, 1988) can make is primarily on the micro (bottom up) level as a mutated, educative now (N). On this immanent plane, four strategies are examined below, to augment these micro changes beyond remaining as minor and potentially ignored in the Anthropocene:

1. *Digital Technology*: Tool-enhancement is one of the fundamental drives which this book deals with in terms of the Anthropocene and education (tNx). However, one could make the case that the proliferation of technology, and especially digital technology has exceeded the bounds and scope of such a direct characterisation as tools and learning (cf., Nowviskie 2015). In many ways, digital technology has become something other than its primary human drive might suggest, and, more pertinently, is pivotal to augmenting the micro societal and educational changes as presented in this book (N). The fundamental problem with digital technology in the contemporary world, is that it has become ubiquitous, and in this ubiquity, it is entirely integrated with the functioning of one world capitalism. For example, one may think that it is still possible to advocate for a move to a degrowth model of human society, and to advocate for environmental issues in an open, progressive, and fair debate on the Net. However, the underlying commercial and algorithmic interests that are present online, frequently dictate and influence the ways in which posts are read, and even though one can upload worthwhile data and approaches to positive changes for the better in the Anthropocene, the chances are that without substantial backing from capital, or coming from an organisation with capital, these digital messages will inevitably go unheeded (cf., Stokols 2018). Of course, there are successful groups that use digital media to advertise their pro-environmental messages online, the problem here is that without substantial funding and backing, these messages are not likely to be acted upon in the maelstrom of available online and mediated material. By seeking funding, and by being successful, online environmental groups may attract the attention of fossil fuel capital or related interests, who offer funding, but with the inbuilt caveat that the group does not threaten the fossil fuel status quo. Thus, we are stuck in a double bind (cf., Chapter 8), in that messages are now transmitted and relayed via digital media (semiotics), but in so doing, they run the threat of fossil fuel capital control. For example, the current series of 'Earth Days' that have taken place every year on April 22nd since 1970, are now funded by major companies and donors such as Toyota and Bloomberg (Rome 2013). The reality is that organisations such as 'Earth Days' must seek funding from large companies, many of which do not have exemplary environmental records, but without such backing, their voices cannot be heard, and their outreach would be compromised, ignored and diminished. In sum, digital means of augmentation are sought for the semiotics that avoids capital control and integration.[2]

2. *Research:* The micro changes in society and education as suggested above can be purposefully researched. At the moment, the degrowth model (e.g., Paulson 2017), change of consciousness model, and the critical/political immanent model, are an open, inter-twined, and potential means to head towards a Green Utopia imaginary, but require a research and evidence base for them to be recognised and acted upon (cf., Cole and Mirzaei Rafe 2017). The fundamental question that is at hand is: Can these three themes work as effective mechanisms for social change in the Anthropocene? And, how do these mechanisms relate to specific educational practices? The proposal is that these motors of social change may be operationalised in unison with the educative parameters as expressed through the analysis of Chapters 2–5, and in Chapter 6 (Nx + global thinking matrix), to enhance modification in the Anthropocene. One way to do this is to feedback the research into the implementation of degrowth, consciousness raising, and critical/political schemas for immanent analysis in education, as teaching and learning episodes, and to henceforth move us towards progressively integrated and augmented educative practice in the Anthropocene. Research in this context has to reflexively address the modes in which degrowth, consciousness raising, and immanent-critical theory translate into new forms, to organise and sustain society through education (cf., Cole 2011). However, there are many false paths for these inter-related nexuses so that they could prove to be ineffective in the current situation, especially as global cities are organised through hierarchies of capital and status, wherein these plans for ecological change might be too impracticable to take hold. For example, the degrowth complex of social and educative change could be novel in affluent zones, for example, amounting to increases in gardening activity, the sharing of already surplus resources, and decarbonisation. In less affluent situations, degrowth strategies amount to survival, especially in light of how future (and present) climate change will disrupt and impede widespread food supplies (cf., Hamilton 2017). In short, nuanced, detailed, and open-minded research is required into the means to produce social and educative change in the Anthropocene (N). This research is multi-site, and not bounded by contextual requirements, as the situation is too perilous for a minority of societies to change in the face of the existential threat of climate change (Ibid.). The research carried out on models of social and educative change in the Anthropocene (Nx), has to be accessible and actioned, and not locked up in highly specialised firewalled journals, that allow little opportunity for inspection, uptake, and/or debate.

3. *Collectivity*: It is incumbent on the micro social changes that embrace the imaginary of a Green Utopia, that 'collectivity' is resolved. In the contemporary, globalised world of total capitalism, the most ubiquitous and dominant value system that we face encourages us to become entrepreneurial, profit-making, self-sufficient, money-making machines, with little care for anything else, let alone saving the environment, and dealing with the sixth great extinction event (Ceballos, Ehrlich and Barnosky 2015). Hence, the breaking with the neoliberal, capitalist ego, based on fossil fuel assisted accumulation, is the priority for breakout in light of these suggested micro societal changes, embodied by degrowth, consciousness raising, and immanent-critical theory. As the survey of non-linear history of the drives and its pedagogic opportunities (Nx) has shown (Chapters 2–5), small scale, collective societies have thrived and succeeded throughout history, and hence the move to individualism through neoliberal capitalism is not an evolutionary or necessary step for survival, though it may prove to be the case that unavoidable survivalism is produced, if climate change is not addressed, and worldwide civilisational breakdown occurs (Clarke 2014). Until this human calamity takes place (even though we have perhaps moved closer to it in 2020/1), it is worth thinking through the type of collectivity that this chapter on social change and this book on education, Deleuze/Guattari and the Anthropocene, is advocating and encouraging:

Firstly, there is a mode of 'herd mentality' that is promulgated through contemporary, neoliberal democracy, and that involves being subjected to the constant pressure to be financially independent in the environment created by universal capitalism. Clearly, this type of fake collectivity has to be circumvented, and it is one of the functions of the combination of degrowth, consciousness raising and immanent-critical theory, that the generalised herd mentality under capitalism will be surpassed Deleuze/Guattari (1984). Further, the mode of collectivity promoted here is not a matter of repeating the tendency to (re)produce large scale societies, wherein local matters are ignored or dealt with as secondary to climbing to the top of global governance, for example, by becoming the CEO of a large enterprise. The collectivity at stake in this book is embodied by local co-operation, and not only that which reacts to threats from global corporations, or companies exploiting surplus value at the local level, and in so doing ignoring environmental concerns (cf., Barbier 2010).

Rather, the collectivity sought here is a reconstruction of the local, based on the micro changes as explained above; i.e., degrowth, consciousness raising, and immanent-critical theory as applied to the contemporary global situation. It is the contention of this book that this type of collectivity is rare in the contemporary world, as it is assailed at every turn by the pressures of survival and individualism in the competitive, capitalised environment. Hence, the move to collectivity that will make a difference in the Anthropocene as pedagogy (Nx) is a convoluted road, and one that avoids short-term, opportunistic ideas for making money out of the situation based on 'green solutions' to community needs and shortfalls in natural wellbeing. This book is not about faux team building with respect to 'green solutions' for local environmental problems, but about tackling the modes in which we have become isolated and dislocated in our attempts to work with difference and change in the Anthropocene (cf., Fox, Pope and Ellis 2017). As a result, collectivity is about more than marching for climate change action, but concerns finding anthropocenic differentials, amidst the ways in which our lives our bundled up and carried away from us, in and as, so many capital flows (-N +1).

4. *Art*. Finally, it is worth considering the role of art in the augmentation of the micro changes in society and education that are being presented in this chapter. The situation is critical, the consequences of inaction are dire, and have been researched and presented by many in the scientific and environmental communities (e.g., Steffen et al. 2015). The Anthropocene recognises the telluric force of humans, as a planet changing species, that is now able to dominate the environment and nature, in short, humans are changing the ecology of the Earth. However, moral and reactive calls for humanity to alter course go unheeded, because they do not address the unconscious drives in the Anthropocene or offer escape routes through education (Nx), as was described in Chapters 2–6. Rather, well-founded calls to change behaviour and society by environmental and ecological groups are diverted and subsumed through the tactics and strategies of capitalist power, and turned into 'more of the same', money-making, alienation, and increasing, accumulative, environmental degradation (e.g., Angus 2016). In short, this book claims that pedagogic art has the power to avert such a calamity, because it is able to uncover the unconscious drives, and automatic, pre-designated ways in which we stride unwittingly down the path of the Anthropocene as an unchanging, continuous now. Further, the assessment of teachers and other educators as artists, is in line with the autonomy that this Deleuze/Guattari (1984, 1988) book gives those involved with education as philosophers.

Pedagogic art, whether it is in the form of teaching about language and ideas, such as novels, poems, short stories or imaginative commentary, or if it is visual/sonic as in the modes of video production, painting, installation, music or cinema, can be provocative, surprising, experimental and raw (cf., jagodzinski 2019). Pedagogic art does not have to follow any pre-set course, or narrow guidance in terms of its range of expression, and means to penetrate consciousness. Pedagogic art does not have to concern itself with 'fake news' or factual truth claims on either side of the environmental and/or climate change deniers debate. Rather, pedagogic art functions in this context to make us think more deeply in the now (N). Pedagogic art is fundamentally philosophical in nature and with respect to the Anthropocene and the images/text that can be created about it (cf., Cole and Bradley 2016). Pedagogic artists need to have a full range of conceptual tools at their disposal to make aesthetic interventions in the current situation that could make a difference, and will not be dismissed or ignored. The chapters on tool-enhancement, the carbon trail, the phallocene and atomic-time in this book, present a non-linear history of the drives of the Anthropocene, that are conceptual tools, ready to be played with by pedagogic artists. Further, these tools are educative in terms of what to do now (Nx), in that they are simultaneously ready to be incorporated into the art of teaching and learning differently in the Anthropocene (Chapter 6). This book recognises teachers as artists/philosophers, and suggests that their work will make a positive contribution to altering the unconscious drives of the Anthropocene, to help produce a better future. This desired result of this book will happen when the connections between a teacher's work and art are established, and teachers are empowered to play, experiment and share the concepts and ideas as laid out here,[3] including that of the environmental double bind (Chapter 8).

Notes

[1] Educators are invited to further comment on their understanding of social change with respect to the Anthropocene on https://iiraorg.com/inducing-social-change/
[2] See https://iiraorg.com/
[3] See https://iiraorg.com/education-the-anthropocene-and-deleuze-guattari/

CHAPTER 8

Conclusion: The Double Bind

1   Introduction

This book presents a formidable challenge, to fully think through the drives that are creating the Anthropocene, and to do something about them through education as an expanded now (Nx), that does not fall back into the machine processing of one world capitalism, and the sophisticated, inter-connected mechanisms that keep this machine running, such as the global media, and the multiple ways in which messages, codes and instructions about how to tackle climate change are presently transmitted (cf., Hornsey and Fielding 2016). In the introduction to this book (Chapter 1), this challenge was characterised by the singularity of the Anthropocene, a literal black hole, that we are ironically being drawn into through societal progress, and that can be intensely convoluted to arrest. For example, as I write these words, the human world is experiencing a global pandemic, caused by the COVID-19 virus. Along with the health risk associated with the spread of this virus, there has been a widespread economic slowdown, as quarantine measures have meant that many of the 'normal' activities that people engage in to earn a living have been shut down to, due to social/physical distancing laws. Now that the threat of the pandemic seems to be easing in some parts of the world such as Australia (in fact, as I revise these words, Australia is experiencing a new wave of infection), the social distancing laws are being relaxed, and the economy is gradually restarting. Even though Australia suffered from catastrophic bush fires at the beginning of the year (2020), and that have been attributed to the effects of climate change (e.g., Yu et al. 2020), nobody appears to be explicitly talking about restarting the economy with heightened environmental safeguards in place, we have (perhaps modestly and with oscillations) resumed our collective path into and because of the singularity of the Anthropocene as analysed above (Chapters 2–5).

Hence, the suggested changes in education and society, as presented by the analysis of Chapters 2 to 5 (Nx), and augmented in Chapters 6 and 7, are construed with the caveat that they are in constant danger of being over-ridden by the powerhouse of the universal general economy. Even though hardly anyone would argue for the wilful destruction of the environment (cf., Clark and York 2005), the silence about environmental matters post-pandemic is extraordinary. Part of the reason for this omission is due to the increased concern for saving human life that the pandemic has unleashed, and the fact that capital would have to be diverted away from restarting the economy, and spent on natural ecological matters (and not, for example, on vaccines). In sum, it is easier, and politically ameliorating for governments to restart the economy through already known economic boosting schemes, that are largely built on the history and infrastructure of fossil fuel consumption, rather than imaging (and enacting) a new, renewable, ecological, future economy, that would be costly and politically risky (Keys et al. 2019); as it would be hard to fully explain and sell to the public post-pandemic, given the present economic turbulence and decimation. As such, we are left with an unenviable 'fork in the road', one path where we forage along the route of enhanced, runaway climate change, the other through which the economy will not recover so obviously, in that it ushers in the unknown future(s) of reliance on renewables and new scenarios of (un)sustainability, for example, predominantly using electric cars might cause other shortages, produced by the cost and supply of lithium. This fork in the road for global humanity (and this book) is here named as the 'double bind'. The double bind is an important conceptual figure to consider with respect to the analysis of the unconscious drives of the Anthropocene and its escape routes through education (Nx), as it adds to the realism and multi-levelled thought of learning on offer here.

2 What Is the Double Bind?

Gregory Bateson was one of the first to theorise the expression 'double bind' through his extensive work in anthropology and other fields (Visser 2003). The most straightforward manner to understand the double bind is when two undesirable options present themselves as the only ways forward, as I have described the current 'fork in the road' above with respect to either increased climate change or compromised economic activity, post-pandemic. However, Bateson, who was dissatisfied with the prevailing behaviourist theories of how we learn, used the 'double bind' as a concept to realise and understand the different levels of learning (cf., Tognetti 1999), and how they are manipulated. As applied to the 'fork in the road' metaphor, it may seem like we are being given two simple choices, both of which in the case of the 'double bind' are undesirable. Yet in the instance of either increased economic activity and worsening climate change, or potential economic uncertainty, but positive measures to address climate change, it is clear that this is not a simple choice, that we can consciously make, and such segmentation in the problematics of the Anthropocene in thinking and life, can lead to idealistic and unrealizable 'solutions' to climate change, such as the notion of a sudden and easy 'switch' to a green economy, or the idea of green capitalism being straightforward to implement in general, and not continuing to reproduce the environmental destruction of the past (e.g., Barbier 2010). In contrast, Bateson (1979) described our situation in the Anthropocene quite beautifully, when he said:

> There is a quasi-scientific fable that if you can get a frog to sit quietly in a saucepan of cold water, and if you then raise the temperature of the water very slowly and smoothly so that there is no moment marked to be the moment at which the frog should jump, he will never jump. He will get boiled. Is the human species changing its own environment with slowly increasing pollution and rotting its mind with slowly deteriorating religion and education in such a saucepan? (98)

Put directly, we are the frogs in the saucepan, but the saucepan is the atmosphere, which we are heating up through carbon dioxide emissions and the action of sunlight. We know the facts of climate change, that have been repeatedly proven through science (e.g., Hall 2020), yet the problem remains with respect to how to do anything worthwhile about it. The situation is not helped by the last two points from Bateson (1979) in the quote above, which denote the other side of the moment in history and singularity in which we find ourselves enwrapped. One might assert that the learning required to extract ourselves from the singularity of the Anthropocene is extraordinary, especially as it is not simply a 'techno-knowledge-problem', but a behavioural, pedagogic and thinking problem, that will not be solved by the application of behaviourist principles to life, as the learning required for extraction from the Anthropocene goes against the implicit positivist logic contained in and by behaviourism (cf., Adams 2020a). Rather, we need to expand the double bind from a simple, exclusionary, linguistic and logical 'either-or', exemplified, for example, by a mother telling her child "to be spontaneous", thus condemning the child to either following her instructions and thus not being spontaneous because she is merely obeying, or just not being spontaneous at all, to the extensive, exaggerated, dyadic thinking as learning, that we find in Deleuze/Guattari's (1988) *1000 Plateaus* through their continuous call to 'double'.

The notion of the 'double bind' proliferates in *1000 Plateaus*. The double is mentioned 151 times throughout the plateaux. In effect, the doubling is produced by the plateaux, and it is implicitly in them, and is part of the immanent functioning of the plateaux. The plateaux in *1000 Plateaus* are constructed through conjoining intensities in space/time, and hence the doubling results from this lateral construction, it is an essential aspect of the logic of *1000*

CONCLUSION: THE DOUBLE BIND

Plateaus that looks to explain the ways in which capitalism takes over the psyche and produces schizophrenia. In this book on climate change, the plateaux and their doubling are the pedagogic opportunities opened up by the analyses of the four unconscious drives of the Anthropocene in Chapters 2–5, (Nx), and as presented by the web site.[1] *1000 Plateaus* followed on in a non-conventional, heterodox manner from *Anti-Oedipus* that examined the possibility of 'schizoanalysis' as a practice, and as an escape from the 'schizophrenising' effects of capitalism through history, Deleuze/Guattari (1984). Schizoanalysis in *Anti-Oedipus* is a reverse of psychoanalysis, and deliberately opens up and breaks free from the 'schizo' effects of capitalism on the psyche, but assumes a common history through and by which this can happened (cf., Guattari 2013). *1000 Plateaus* does not assume a universal history through and by which capitalism has become operant (on desire), but constructs the different plateaux as a non-linear mode of historical and contextual thought, and as such, the double binds are historical, and possible to locate in situational and postqualitative (non-orthodox qualitative research) analysis, yet operant in a multiplicity of ways, such as 'becoming-animal' (Deleuze and Guattari 1988: 232–310). This doubling methodology is here translated to education, and the production of pedagogic resources and episodes *in situ* and as contextual time elongations (Nx). Similarly, the 'becoming-animal' feature of the plateaus introduces a different vista on learning and becoming, as expressed by the anthropological double bind from Bateson (2000), and by David Abram (2010):

> To our indigenous ancestors, and to the many aboriginal peoples who still hold fast to their oral traditions, language is less a human possession than it is a property of the animate earth itself, an expressive, telluric power in which we, along with the coyotes and the crickets, all participate. Each creature enacts this expressive magic in its own manner, the honeybee with its waggle dance no less than a bellicose, harrumphing sea lion... Nor is this power restricted solely to animals. The whispered hush of the uncut grasses at dawn, the plaintive moan of trunks rubbing against one another in the deep woods, or the laughter of birch leaves as the wind gusts through their branches all bear a thicket of many-layered meanings for those who listen carefully. (168)

The type of learning as expressed in the quote above from David Abram (2010), demonstrates the double bind extension from a simple 'either-or', and as contained by and in *1000 Plateaus* through animism and becoming-other. Similarly, the pedagogy opened up by this book (Nx) follows a path to expanded ontological and epistemological realms for educators wishing to make a difference in the Anthropocene. In contrast, *Anti-Oedipus*, Deleuze/Guattari (1984) is a darker text, because the accelerating, schizophrenising forces of capitalism are not resolved in history as multiple escape routes (here as Nx), but are extended/expanded, and treated like a panpsychic, reciprocating, natural system, that can only run its course and leads to the practice of schizoanalysis as singular. In *1000 Plateaus*, the double binds appear elliptically, haphazardly, are akin to chaotic forces, rather than something machinic, predetermined, and that is determined to dominate the world (Ibid.). Thus, the different elements of the 'double bind' are opened up and expounded throughout *1000 Plateaus*, such as 'becoming-animal', as treated by David Abram (2010) above, and as potential escape routes from now through education (N). Becoming-animal suggests an animist approach to the double bind, that circumvents the becomings of capitalism through its engagement with and in nature (animism may be considered to be a pre-capitalist practice). Animism is immanent, and stands in contrast to the possible (human) transcendence of Buddhism mentioned in Chapter 7, which has been put forward in this book as a non-Christian religion, capable of being a component with degrowth and immanent critique, and the imaginary of a Green Utopia, and that could augment social change through consciousness raising (i.e., Buddhism is not being deployed here in terms of its transcendence). However, capitalism can be figured as a machine that exploits nature and consciousness for profit (e.g., Malm 2016), and thus we are again caught in a double bind. This double bind is strengthened when we consider how the surplus value of being able to relate, talk to, and commune with animals and plants may be exploited (I am thinking, for example, about horse whisperers (Farmer-Dougan and Dougan 1999)). Thus, even though the expanded, animist, non-human, relational becoming of the double bind in *1000 Plateaus* (also called a rhizome), gives us a clue as to how to escape the nullifying forces of capitalism, alone, it is not enough to effect the emergence that we seek though this book (Nx), which is the analysis of the unconscious forces of the Anthropocene (Chapters 2–5), and their resolution through and in education and social change, due to the (re)combinatory powers of capitalism. In short, we need to go back to the analysis of time to strengthen the concept of the double bind suitable for this final chapter on education, the Anthropocene, and Deleuze/Guattari.

3 The Double Bind of the Future

The general problem of what to do about climate change in the Anthropocene, is the most profound, multi-levelled, and complex problem that we have ever faced. As such, the double bind that we may derive from Bateson (2000)

CONCLUSION: THE DOUBLE BIND 143

is extended and expanded through the philosophy of Deleuze/Guattari (1984, 1988), and reaches its zenith with respect to climate change. Further, the double bind at the zenith or singularity of the Anthropocene, is not only about how to escape through education by deploying learning, language, and understanding coercion, power, capitalism, the non-human, animism, chaos and affect: *it is also about time*. In effect, the double bind of the singularity of the Anthropocene works in two ways: 1) As an example of a thought experiment about and in time, that functions backwards to open up paradoxes similar to that of time travel, wherein the past is changed by future travellers. In the case of climate change, everything that we can do now to arrest climate change sets up the possibility of cascading events and feedback loops in the future, as we become 'future-actors', but functioning in the expanded and transformed present (N); 2) As a mode of 'ethical-augmentation'. In this mode, we posit the future as redolent of a failed past (cf., Cole, Dolphijn and Bradley 2016). Thus, we cast ourselves as saving the future through present actions, cumulatively, and through subsidiary means to stop climate change (Nx + global thinking matrix). Hence, the double bind of the future and this book works as (de)subjectification as and about climate change, as Guattari (1996b) has expressed with respect to his three ecologies thesis:

> Vectors of subjectification do not necessarily pass through the individual, which in reality appears to be something like a 'terminal' for processes that involve human groups, socio-economic ensembles, data-processing machines, [and the like]. Therefore, interiority establishes itself at the crossroads of multiple components, each relatively autonomous in relation to the other and, if need be, in open conflict. (25)

Climate change subjectivity functions as a double bind in time, as it passes through the wormhole in the singularity of the Anthropocene. In the apex of the singularity that is dragging us towards the future, is a space in which time will mutate further, similar to going down the famous rabbit hole of Lewis Carroll (1865/2008). Unpredictability becomes the norm in the wormhole, non-normative functioning takes over, and can dominate the subjectivity produced, as time is warped, and takes on new and surprising forms. In the present augmented day (N), past environmental and ecological work (cf., Collins and Barkdull 1995), wherein the effects of climate change were a 'future-present', could be seen as noble quests to alter the future path of humanity towards a better, more ecological life on Earth. Now, as we enter the wormhole of the Anthropocene, we are in a situation of the 'future-future', whereby the predictions, extrapolations, and dire warnings about climate change are no longer a science fiction novel that could be set on a different planet. We are, as a result, actors in a science fiction novel, wherein the subjectivity of environmentalism and desiring to change the atmosphere to return to Holocene levels of carbon dioxide is a failed thought endeavour (cf., Wallin 2020) which will not happen (perhaps for 100,000+ years (Ulph and Ulph 1997)). Rather, the only subjectivity that is possible to unravel the many levels of the double bind of the Anthropocene is a thought experiment, for example, as presented by this book, as education in a transformed context of now (Nx + global thinking matrix).[2]

As such, the chapters of this book are set in time, and correspond to the double bind of the future as the Anthropocene, as we engage with the effects of climate change as an everyday reality (the future now), and try and do something about it (Nx + global thinking matrix). Hence, tool-enhancement is not only about the tools we have at present to arrest climate change, but about the imaginative (re)creation of future-tools in (tNx) that could have an effect on climate change (cf., Schneider, Kuntz-Duriseti and Azar 2000). Further, the carbon trail is not just about dealing with the current state of fossil fuel consumption, and how to have got there, but it is about imagining the future of fossil fuels now, not as a magically post-fossil fuel future, but as a real means to divert the drive of the carbon trail today (ctNx). The phallocene as a deeply embedded drive in everything that we do has to be reconsidered as a future-future, and how phallic-same functioning may be averted (pNx); and lastly, atomic-time itself is subject to the dynamics of the future-future, as its formulation is specifically designed to deal with the time-based drives of the Anthropocene (Head 2014), and is projected into the future, to be seriously considered (aNx). In sum, the open thought experiments of teaching and learning differently (Nx + global thinking matrix in Chapter 6) and social change (Chapter 7) also involve resuscitation as the 'future-future' to deal with the time warping life emanating from the singularity of the black hole of the Anthropocene. If this theorisation is not to be in vain, and the singularity of the Anthropocene is not to degenerate into an absolute, painful, disintegrative and prolonged global extinction level event (which has perhaps already started), the most horrific projections of this event have to be dealt with (N) in education, and as the double bind of the Anthropocene in time. This double bind includes politics.

4   The Role of Politics in the Double Bind

Perhaps the most famous example of the use of the double bind as a literary motif comes in George Orwell's *1984*. Winston Smith worked in the Ministry of Truth, falsifying historical records, as the ruling Party manipulated the masses through the brainwashing technique of Doublethink, and by propagating slogans such as 'War is Peace' (Orwell 1949/2008). Orwell wrote *1984* in post-war Britain, as a reflection on the power of totalitarian governments to subjugate the masses by any means possible, including the ubiquitous use of the double bind as a weapon of mind control. Now, with the proliferation in social media and potential for ambiguous communication, the means to execute and distribute double binds has grown exponentially (Duffy and Pruchniewska 2017). Hence, the role of politics in the double bind has changed from the directionality of the authoritarian state, deploying the double bind as a means to divide, obfuscate and confuse, to being caught up in a multi-directional, electronically mediated 'free-for-all', in which messages are transmitted and received (including various double binds), with little purpose or meaning other than to create an audience, or as a means to sell products, including the agendas of ill-equipped politicians. This change has happened because in many developed economies, global, financial, neoliberal capitalism has infiltrated and replaced the strong nation states of the past (cf., Giroux 2005), that were possible to be turned into dictatorships, and this take over has been accompanied by the development of the global media. Yet even though in reality the takeover of nation states by global capitalism is virtually complete, governments still do retain vestiges of pre-Anthropocene decision-making processes, which they apply to the problematics of climate change, frequently unsuccessfully (Galaz 2014).

In liberal democracies, political parties have to aim their policy settings at the majority of the population to succeed, or at least sell and spin them in that direction to gain and maintain power. Political systems in these democracies have largely devolved into oscillatory two-party systems, with little choice between parties, other than one marginally favouring social or pro-business policies. Hence, one may say that the duality of two-party political systems in liberal democracies is itself a double bind. Markedly, political parties with wholly green agendas become side-lined, as and in the periphery of political life, because they may be perceived to not appeal to the majoritarian needs of job security, money, economic growth and increased enterprise, or augmented capital flows (Peters 2017). Further, the election cycle in democratic countries makes long term planning for significant green initiatives impossible. Moves to a new green economy are most often swallowed up and dissolved by overriding business and financial concerns, as such, fundamental shifts in the economy and consumer behaviours, for example, using solar panels for power or driving electric cars, become wrapped up in notions of marketing for consumer choice, and are hence unlikely to be implemented, other than by relatively wealthy pro-environmentalists. In sum, the transition to a green economy is stymied by the very dynamics of capitalism, in which it is conceived and produced, because cost, and problems such as producing enough baseload power, frequently override the benefits to the environment that, for example, using renewable energy sources would produce (e.g., Şener, Sharp and Anctil 2018). The politics of the Anthropocene therefore rests on two axes that have to be considered if any meaningful changes are to be made to deal with climate change, as is being suggested here through education (Nx + global thinking matrix): (1) Diverting politics away from and around the double bind of the current liberal democratic two-party model, that only succeeds in producing 'more of the same' in terms of policies that have little or no effect on averting the climate crisis; (2) Divesting environmental politics of monetary control, so that solutions to the climate crisis in the Anthropocene are not reduced to a 'cost-benefit-analysis'.

The first point in terms of the politics of the Anthropocene has been seen by some as a call to return to large governments, in order to fundamentally reformulate state control over human affairs, and to address the looming environmental crisis of global warming in terms of state intervention (e.g., McCright, Dunlap and Xiao 2013). This move takes away the oscillation in liberal democracies between the 'left-right', and shifts thinking about environmental governance to the left, whereby strong governments could issue binding environmental protective laws, and, for example, substantially funnel investment into renewable energy sources. Others, inspired by free market ideology, look to divest from government, and create a stronger entrepreneurial environment, wherein green solutions to the environmental breakdown will be created through market forces, for example, as could be seen in individual households investing in solar roof panels ubiquitously (e.g., Alexander and Gleeson 2019). This book suggests that a thoroughgoing analysis of the drives which have made up the Anthropocene (Chapters 2–5), followed by their treatment through education and social change (Chapters 6 and 7), as a differentiated educative now Nx + global thinking matrix, could lead to the stabilisation of politics, neither as further to the left or to the right, but as a flourishing of and in thought as learning how to exit the failed political landscape of the past, that has been created and maintained by fossil fuel capitalism through history (Malm 2016). If this stabilisation in politics away from the left-right oscillation (the political double bind) can be achieved, the second point above, that concerns the detachment of environmental politics from capitalism, will also be more likely to happen. However, it has to be mentioned that the fossil fuel interests that currently back the world capitalist and market-based order are powerful, and, as has been mentioned, still largely control the capital flows around the world (cf., Braungardt, Bergh and Dunlop 2019). Thus, for these educational suggestions about how to move forward in terms of a new politics

CONCLUSION: THE DOUBLE BIND

for the Anthropocene to be enacted, beyond the double bind of the right-left oscillation and capital manipulation, power has to be concentrated in the means to achieve this goal. The next two sections are dedicated to examining this 'bridge to the future' and the circumvention of the double bind as a differentiated educative now (N).

5   Realism and 'Fabulation'…

It is self-evident that the double bind is a barrier to effective action on climate change, as it narrows one's options down to dyadic thinking, the 'either-or' of logical propositions, thinking as language and logic, and simple, dualistic, ethical choices. The main reduction that the double bind configures is the either-or between economy and environment, which this book has worked against in terms of looking for non-linear escape routes through education (Nx), via a nonlinear analysis of the drives of the Anthropocene. Further, as has been described above, the double bind is embedded in the future, and as the politics of the present moment, because the Anthropocene makes action on climate change necessary (Lewis and Maslin 2015), yet less likely to be imagined and enacted, as time passes, and we pass further into the new reality of climate change. Hence, to build a bridge around the double bind of the Anthropocene requires thinking of an unprecedented and unimagined scale, thinking that literally takes us beyond the contemporary moment as an expanded now (N), and as learning. Deleuze (1995: 174), in an interview late in his career, named this type of thinking as 'fabulation' after Bergson. Yet Deleuze almost entirely inverts Bergson's use of the term, and instead of a closed aspect of a community's reimagining of themselves, Deleuze suggests that 'fabulation' could be an open part of a politics of the concept, that would use the delirium of artistic hallucination and the production of multiple futures as a way forward for thought (cf., Bogue 2006). Specifically, Deleuze's political and artistic take on fabulation reverses:

> The fabulation function as a particular function of the imagination that creates "voluntary hallucinations." The fabulation function takes our sense that there is a presence watching over us and invents images of gods. These images then insure strict obedience to the closed morality. In short, they insure social cohesion. (Lawlor and Moulard 2020)

As has been suggested, Deleuze's specific take on fabulation heads in the opposite direction to the quote above, and coincides with the notion of an open society reinventing itself through the imagination, and producing "a people-yet-to-come" (Deleuze 1991). In the focused Anthropocene terms of this book, i.e., as tool-enhancement, carbon trail, the phallocene, atomic-time, (Nx + global thinking matrix), this reinvention is in relation to climate change and what to do about it, and henceforth to enable the production of narratives about climate change through education, to be able to reimagine the future, beyond the double bind of the Anthropocene, and in line with the imaginary of a Green Utopia (degrowth). Deleuze suggests that the notion of fabulation could replace that of utopia, which he describes as a weak concept (cf., Holland 2006), and in this book, the Green Utopia is aligned with fabulation in terms of being productive of multiple green futures through the imagination. Fabulation is a concentration of all the imagined futures that we can muster in relation to climate change, not as a mode of social control and obedience, but as a means to set thought free with respect to 'what can be done', initially as a mode of delirium. However, as has been the case at the junctions of this book on the Anthropocene and education, the type of zealous over-production of thought can simultaneously lead to unlikely and unrealizable dream-fictions, such as an unattainable, homogenised, social fictions, wherein cooperation and harmony are assumed givens to reinforce and produce an ecological status quo, rather than as material and immanent aspects of social change, as has been presented by Chapter 7. Pointedly, even though Deleuze specifically advocates fabulation as a mode of artistic creativity and the renewal of thought, he is also cautious about its actual social consequences, and he is in many ways a realist (cf., Lundy 2013), at the same time as being an expansive, imaginative, creative thinker of future open systems. Deleuze's realism contrasts with Guattari's (1996b) faith in revolutionary action being able to overturn the ecological destruction that we see today through and as capitalism, and his continued thought of a possible, green, ecological utopia as a militant starting point for the imaginary.

In sum, the base Deleuze/Guattari (1984, 1988) strategy for educational philosophy being proffered here, is to over-run the double bind of the Anthropocene, through the augmented production of the creative (unconscious) imagination and multiple potential narratives about global warming through fabulation (cf., Woodrow 2019), as, education (Nx + global thinking matrix). At the same time, a parallel realist approach is advocated, one that I have dealt with in terms of 'immanent materialism' (Cole 2013, 2014). Hence, the fundamental problematic is revealed with respect to applying Deleuze/Guattari's philosophy to the Anthropocene and the resolution through education and social change, as (Nx + global thinking matrix), in that 'we' are being asked to imagine and reimagine potential ways through the impasse of the Anthropocene as education, for example, through the creation of a 'people-yet-to-come', who will figure out a way to live in the Anthropocene without making things worse, yet 'we' are at the same time being challenged to attend to our inherent assumptions, prejudices and generalisations with respect to global warming in the now (N), a process I have called: critical-thinking-practice (Cole 2017b). Pertinently, as was seen in Chapter 7, the application of critical-thinking-practice induces scepticism about market-based solutions to climate change, because of the mode in which they have become corrupted, and are, in fact, an essential component part of the capitalist system that is producing the problem, and still reliant on fossil fuels (e.g., Angus 2016). Deleuzian realism is in this context a mode of 'thought-inquiry', that demands that one asks fundamental questions about solutions to climate change, and requires that we do not put faith in the latest fade for techno-change.

Realism is in this context a clearing away of the climate change solutions that feed into and extend capitalist endeavour and fossil fuel power in the world (i.e., are primarily designed for profit and do not, in reality, arrest climate change). Deleuzian realism as a thinking practice applied to the Anthropocene, has to circumvent the many ways in which thinking, language, technology and subjectivity are co-opted and funnelled by capitalism to present an image of thought that appears to be green and likely to help, but is in fact a money-making, fossil fuel extending, and capital inducing exercise (Bauhardt 2014). An expression that has been used for this process is 'greenwashing' wherein companies proudly signal their green credentials as a marketing and public relations strategy (Delmas and Burbano 2011). Greenwashing goes along with companies and businesses claiming to be organic, environmentally friendly, carbon-neutral, and helping with climate change, for example, through carbon offset strategies. These measures are held to account via a Deleuzian critical-thinking-practice, as so much 'foam-on-a-wave', when the underlying processes and forces that the company may present are analysed; i.e., by applying the concepts of Chapters 2–5 as escape routes from the Anthropocene in education (Nx + the global thinking matrix), to the companies' activities, and hence arriving at their environmental impacts and dynamics through learning. In sum, the approach of this book is to suggest that the best way to avert catastrophic climate change is to (re)formulate thinking as learning (education, Nx + global thinking matrix), and henceforth via the combination of realism and fabulation with respect to the contemporary double bind, and that leads to a recursive analysis of the drives of the Anthropocene (Chapters 2–5, Nx + 1), and the augmentation of this practice in and through pedagogy and social change (Chapters 6 and 7, n(Nx + 1 + global thinking matrix)). These recursive and combined actions make the conditions by which the climate change narrative of the last fifty+ years may be attended to (the great acceleration) and the double bind of the Anthropocene brought to the fore in education, thought and (ethical) action.

6   This Is the End of the 'End-Times'

The singularity of the Anthropocene induces notions of the 'end of times', apocalyptic thinking (e.g., Ginn 2015), and a consideration as to the finitude of human endeavour (extinction). As a species, if we continue on the path that we currently tread, this will be the case. Beyond hope, or the construction of an artificial rescue plan that will not work, this book looks to circumvent the double bind of the end of times through an excavation of its drives (Pichler, Schaffartzik, Haberl and Görg 2017), and their escape routes through and in education (Nx). Further, this book is not specifically 'post'- anything (for example, post-structural, post-modern or post-human), but looks to produce a questioning of an image of thought that sits behind previous success in civilisation and life, and that was derived from the fossil fuel era, reminiscent of U.S.A. urban sprawl in the 1970s, with large, gasoline-guzzling cars, dominating a suburban, commuter world of 'nowheres' (cf., Cole 2019c), and all the emptiness that this life contains. This book produces new learning and thinking about (an)other world, a different future, and an achievable, non-idealistic way forward, amidst the hubris and bluff of the present political, economic and social situation.

Certainly, the present situation with respect to the Anthropocene is bad enough is produce nihilism, hopelessness, and a sense that there is no obvious way to avoid the cliff of climate change destruction, towards which we are heading as a society (e.g., Smith and Zeder 2013). This book suggests that it is precisely in these feelings of nihilism, hopelessness, and the idea that humanity is on a false path, that new thought about the Anthropocene may emerge as education. Elsewhere (Cole 2017a), I have termed this shift in philosophical speculation as 'dark thinking', that takes as given the worst consequences of the Anthropocene, and looks for a means to escape them in the very drives of their production as a reinvigorated now (Nx). Dark thinking is cold, planetary, expansive and fully cognisant of the dangers and perils of the Anthropocene (realism), yet able to imagine multiple escape routes from human-produced geology (fabulation), not to create more hopeless dreams that will not come true, but to establish a pivot and means to counter-attack the domination of thought, action and power by fossil fuel capitalism, and its creation of the world in which we live today (Nx + global thinking matrix). As I write these words in the COVID-19 pandemic crisis of 2020/1, some think that a true rupturing may have already occurred in the fossil fuel empire by the social and economic lockdown that has been enforced by the spread of the virus (e.g., Adams 2020b). However, as I see it, without imagination, leadership and new thought, the same forces of capitalist control will snap back into place once the virus threat has passed, in fact, humanity will probably accelerate down the fossil fuel capitalist path post-pandemic, in a bid to re-establish previous economic activity, and to fix temporarily broken global economic systems to re-establish financial growth.

As a general counter and resistance to the momentum of (re)fossilisation, to finish off this chapter on the double bind, and to summarise this book on 'Education, the Anthropocene, and Deleuze/Guattari', I would like to take inspiration from Bogna M. Konior's (2016) 13 propositions for the Anthropocene as a mode for reinventing teaching and learning:

1. The narratives that we communally produce to counter the domination of the fossil fuel empire, could embrace and be connected to the human-induced changes in planetary systems as they unfold due to their drives and its escape through education (Nx). Further, the 'within-ness' of these changes has to be demonstrated; i.e., a going beyond the story of human agency causing climate change, but encouraging the changes in the climate and all other connected systems on Earth to speak for themselves.
2. Research needs to be rethought and reimagined beyond limiting factors to establish a genuine interdisciplinary basis for comprehending the Anthropocene (e.g., Wright 2017). Capital influences on research that depend on fossil fuel sources in any way could be curtailed. Research and pedagogy will emerge around the material and historical facts and tendencies in the Anthropocene (Nx), that proves the inter-dependence of all life on Earth, and that shows how it is changing synchronously and asynchronously.
3. The time dimension is of incredible significance in the Anthropocene, in order to understand how to work through education with the global forces that are in the process of subsuming us (Nx + global thinking matrix). Time is becoming stranger and more subject to warping in the Anthropocene, hence a new critical discipline has to emerge to be able to read the time dimension of the Anthropocene, and that is fundamentally beyond the measurement of time as was described in Chapter 1.
4. Human identity is compromised in the Anthropocene. All indications as to exceptionalism of human-kind need to be rethought. The thesis of the Anthropocene proves that humans are as thoroughly implicated in every earthly process and force, and as such need to consider their relations with other living and non-living creatures and things. In fact, as the only

other species to have induced its own extinction through climate change, we share much in common with bacteria, *apropos*, we are bacteria.

5. As the creators of the sixth great extinction event, we are impelled to search for evidence of this extinction at every level. As such, we are in the process of examining our psyches, as well as our emotional proclivities for anything inter-connected with the progress of extinction (Ceballos, Ehrlich and Barnosky 2015). In effect, we are carrying the germ of the extinction event in our everyday behaviours and lives, which henceforth can be excavated, meaning, the interiors of our bodies and psyches have to be mapped for the death machine of extinction.

6. What does decisive action consist of in the Anthropocene? Millions have already demonstrated against climate change, yet governments still resist acting, as a result, binding agreements on emissions are elusive or are lied about. This book suggests that an extension of the realist position from Deleuzian philosophy into and combined with the realm of creative fabulation as a relay n(Nx + global thinking matrix), would be able to cut through the power concerns that fossil fuel interests have overlaid on the situation, to obscure the path on which we need to tread, as and through education (Nx + global thinking matrix). What will this path look like? This is the task of the 'people-yet-to-come.'[3]

7. In the Anthropocene, there is nowhere to hide. The Holocene may be seen as a positive environmental epoch that engendered the enabling conditions for humans to thrive and augment their drives (Chapters 2–5), yet this thriving has been premised on the ability of humans to move once resources were depleted (nomadism). In the Anthropocene, this is no longer possible, as nomadism today only produces movement between sedentary and globally connected nodes of human inhabitation, all engaged with resource depletion. Hence, humans need to recreate the conditions wherein movement was possible again as learning (Nx).

8. At the end of the book *What is Philosophy?* Deleuze/Guattari (1994) call for a non-philosophy. This non-philosophy is thinking as a practice of understanding the real, whilst at the same time attending to and deleting the human as the thinker of those thoughts. Hence, as applied to this book, we are not proposing a set of normative instructions or guidelines for ecological life in the Anthropocene (Nx), rather, we look to induce the absence of negative human impact on planet Earth starting now.

9. Buried within the codes and practices of human collectivity, are the means to comprehend how to live properly, and to be at one with nature. Of course, these meticulous insights and living forces have been driven to the peripheries of sedentary human communities, and named as witch-

craft, shamanism, sorcery, and demonic possession (cf., Duerr 1978/1985). Hence, a great reversal has to occur in the Anthropocene through an education of the drives (Nx), to re-establish disguised, camouflaged and underground human practises as mainstream life in the Anthropocene. A possible survival and counter to the global warming death of capital and economics, demands that we re-found these rituals.

10. Following on from the last proposition, is the notion that we can remake vital relations with everything around us, and that we can become part of these processes, as they culminate and fulminate through time as an expanded now (N) as learning. This relationship-building is the very opposite of the capitalist profit-drive, that looks to make relations only in order to profit and exploit that relation. Hence, we need to re-establish and maintain relations with all things as partners and kin, and not to co-opt them in and as capital/profit flows.

11. The human species is playing a type of 'necropolitics' (Mbembé and Meintjes 2003) with the planet Earth. Every day that we continue on the path of fossil fuel capitalist expansion, we exterminate more species and biodiversity. Thus, we are gambling with possible ecological future(s), as well as death, and our power over life on Earth, as an intimate aspect of our creative expressions. In summary, we need to rethink our role as a species through (re)education of the drives (Nx), and rename ourselves as a collective tribe of mourners-in-grief for what we have killed.

12. One of the most important aspects of the collective rethinking as a species that is required is to reconsider mammalian reproduction (cf., the phallocene, Chapter 4). The question of human population, though controversial, is pivotal to embracing and working with our continued existence in the Anthropocene (e.g., Adamo and Izazola 2010). It is too easy to move to moral reaction with respect to questions about human population. Rather, it is posited that genuine thinking with respect to the Anthropocene (Nx) can emerge through education, that incorporates the notion that an exponentially growing human population, augmented by a capitalist growth model, and equipped with the current fossil fuel lifestyle as a means to extenuate global warming, is unsustainable. Thus, action needs to be taken with respect to human reproduction.

13. Finally, one may state that the systems and ways of living in the past may seem flagrant and extravagant at this juncture (e.g., as presented by history). However, the Anthropocene does not necessitate a great levelling of distances and power, that attempts to make us equal under the laws of nature, or to live ecologically sensitive lives that tends to nullified equilibrium (cf., Lent 2018). Rather, if we closely examine, for exam-

ple, the modes of nomadism still accessible to us, we might understand that becoming closer to nature, and potentially surviving in the Anthropocene, is not about diminishing the drives as described by the book, but about their full comprehension and resolution. Once the drives have been set free through education (Nx + global thinking matrix), we may be able to live again, as so many flows, and not be perturbed or contained by the forces of extinction that currently bind us…

Notes

1. See https://iiraorg.com/education-the-anthropocene-and-deleuze-guattari/
2. See https://iiraorg.com/education-the-anthropocene-and-deleuze-guattari/
3. Imagined on https://iiraorg.com/education-the-anthropocene-and-deleuze-guattari/

References

Abel, T., & McQueen, D. (2020). The COVID-19 pandemic calls for spatial distancing and social closeness: Not for social distancing. *International Journal of Public Health*, *65*, 231.

Aberg, F. A. (1957). The early plough in Europe. *Gwerin: A Half-Yearly Journal of Folk Life*, *1*(4), 171–181.

Abram, D. (2010). *Becoming animal: An earthly cosmology*. Pantheon Books.

Abrams, H. L. Jr. (1982). Anthropological research reveals human dietary requirements for optimal health. *Journal of Applied Nutrition*, *34*(1), 38–45.

Achinstein, P. (2001). Who really discovered the electron? In J. Z. Buchwald & A. Wawick (Eds.), *Histories of the electron: The birth of microphysics* (pp. 403–424). MIT Press.

Adamo, S. B., & Izazola, H. (2010). Human migration and the environment. *Population and Environment*, *32*(2–3), 105–108.

Adams, M. (2020a). *Anthropocene psychology: Being human in a more-than-human world*. Routledge.

Adams, M. (2020b). *Disasters and capitalism... and COVID-19*. http://somatosphere.net/2020/disaster-capitalism-covid19.html/

Alexander, S., & Gleeson, B. (2019). *The suburbs are the spiritual home of overconsumption. But they also hold the key to a better future*. https://iiraorg.com/2019/11/12/the-suburbs-are-the-spiritual-home-of-overconsumption-but-they-also-hold-the-key-to-a-better-future/

Allen, J. (1989). The natural philosophy of Akhenaten. In K. Simpson (Ed.), *Religion and philosophy in ancient Egypt* (pp. 81–102). Yale University Press.

Amzallag, N. (2009). From metallurgy to Bronze Age civilizations: The synthetic theory. *American Journal of Archaeology*, *113*(4), 497–519.

Anderson, A. (2012). Climate change education for mitigation and adaptation. *Journal of Education for Sustainable Development*, *6*(2), 191–206.

Anderson, M. K. (1994). Prehistoric anthropogenic wildland burning by hunter-gatherer societies in the temperate regions: A net source, sink, or neutral to the global carbon budget? *Chemosphere*, *29*(5), 913–934.

Anderson, P. C. (1999). *Prehistory of agriculture: New experimental and ethnographic approaches*. ISD LLC.

Angus, I. (2016). *Facing the Anthropocene: Fossil capitalism and the crisis of the earth system*. NYU Press.

Anievas, A. (2008). Theory of the global state: Globality as an unfinished revolution. A theory of global capitalism: Production, class, and the state in a transnational world. *Historical Materialism*, *16*(2), 190–206.

Anton S., Potts, R., & Aiello, L. C. (2014). Evolution of early Homo: An integrated biological perspective. *Science, 345*, 128–142.

Arrighi, G. (2001). Braudel, capitalism, and the new economic sociology. *Review* (Fernand Braudel Center), *24*(1), 107–123.

Asfaw, B., White, T., Lovejoy, O., Latimer, B., Simpson, S., & Suwa, G. (1999). Australopithecus garhi: A new species of early hominid from Ethiopia. *Science, 284*(5414), 629–635.

Assmann, J. (2003). *The mind of Egypt: History and meaning in the time of the Pharaohs.* Harvard University Press.

Au, W. (Ed.). (2009). *Rethinking multicultural education: Teaching for racial and cultural justice.* Rethinking Schools Ltd.

Bader, R. F. W., & Nguyen-Dang, T. T. (1981). Quantum theory of atoms in molecules – Dalton revisited. *Advances in Quantum Chemistry, 14*, 63–124.

Badry, M., Hassan, H., Bayomi, H., & Oakasha, H. (2018). QTID: Quran Text Image Dataset. *International Journal of Advanced Computer Science and Applications, 9*(3), 385–391.

Barbier, E. B. (2010). *A global green new deal: Rethinking the economic recovery*, Cambridge University Press.

Barkai, R., & Yerkes, R. W. (2008). Stone axes as cultural markers: Technological, functional and symbolic changes in bifacial tools during the transition from hunter-gatherers to sedentary agriculturalists in the Southern Levant. *Prehistoric Technology, 40*, 159–167.

Barker, E. (1995). The scientific study of religion? You must be joking! *Journal for the Scientific Study of Religion, 34*(63), 287–310.

Batchelor, M. (1994). *Buddhism and ecology.* Motilal Banarsidass Publisher.

Bateson, G. (2000). *Steps to an ecology of mind: Collected essays in anthropology, psychiatry, evolution, and epistemology.* University of Chicago Press. (Original work published 1972)

Bateson, G. (1979). *Mind and nature: A necessary unity* (Vol. 255). Bantam Books.

Batnitzky, L. (2013). *How Judaism became a religion: An introduction to modern Jewish thought.* Princeton University Press.

Bauhardt, C. (2014). Solutions to the crisis? The green new deal, degrowth, and the solidarity economy: Alternatives to the capitalist growth economy from an ecofeminist economics perspective. *Ecological Economics, 102*, 60–68.

Becking, B. (Ed.). (2001). *Only one god? Monotheism in ancient Israel and the veneration of the goddess Asherah.* A&C Black.

Bennett, J. (2010). *Vibrant matter: A political ecology of things.* Duke University Press.

Bergendorff, S. (2020). *The social and cultural order of ancient Egypt: An ethnographic and regional analysis.* Lexington Books.

Berryman, S. (2016). Democritus. In E. N. Zalta (Ed.), *The Stanford encyclopedia of philosophy* (Winter 2016 ed.). https://plato.stanford.edu/archives/win2016/entries/democritus/

Bikhazi, R. J., & Gervers, M. (1990). *Conversion and continuity: Indigenous Christian communities in Islamic lands; Eighth to eighteenth centuries.* Pontifical Institute of Mediaeval Studies.

Bogue, R. (2006). Fabulation, narration and the people to come. In C. V. Boundas (Ed.), *Deleuze and philosophy* (pp. 202–227). Edinburgh University Press.

Bonneuil, C., & Fressoz, J.-B. (2016). *The shock of the Anthropocene: The earth, history and us* (D. Fernbach, Trans.). Verso.

Boot, H. M. (1998). Government and the colonial economies. *Australian Economic History Review, 38*(1), 74–101.

Boot, M. (2006). *War made new: technology, warfare, and the course of history, 1500 to today.* Penguin.

Boyd, H. H. (1999). Christianity and the environment in the American public. *Journal for the Scientific Study of Religion, 38*(1), 36–44.

Boyd, J. R. (1996). Unpublished briefings. Defence and the National Interest. http://tinyurl.com/4ly3eg5

Bradley, J. P. N., & Cole, D. R. (2018). Afterword: Zhibo, existential territory, inter-media-mundia. In D. R. Cole & J. P.N. Bradley (Eds.), *Principles of transversality in globalization and education* (pp. 227–245). Springer.

Brain, C. K. (1989). The evidence of bone modification by early hominids in southern Africa. In R. Bonnichsen & M. H. Sorg (Eds.), *Bone modification* (pp. 291–297). University of Maine, Orono.

Braungardt, S., van den Bergh, J., & Dunlop, T. (2019). Fossil fuel divestment and climate change: Reviewing contested arguments. *Energy Research and Social Science, 50*, 191–200.

Brossmann, J., & Islar, M. (2020). Living degrowth? Investigating degrowth practices through performative methods. *Sustainability Science, 15*, 917–930.

Bryant, J. M. (2006). The West and the rest revisited: Debating capitalist origins, European colonialism, and the advent of modernity. *The Canadian Journal of Sociology, 31*(4), 403–444.

Bullough, V. L. (1976). *Sexual variance in society and history.* John Wiley & Sons.

Byrne, D., & James, P. (2019). Thinking anthropocenically. https://iiraorg.com/2019/08/25/thinking-anthropocenically/

Cain, P. (2016, September 12). Empty skies after 9/11 set the stage for an unlikely climate change experiment. *Global News.* https://globalnews.ca/news/2934513/empty-skies-after-911-set-the-stage-for-an-unlikely-climate-change-experiment/

Cameron, A., Nesvetailova, A., & Palan, R. (2011). Wages of sin? Crisis and the libidinal economy. *Journal of Cultural Economy, 4*(2), 117–135.

Carroll, L. (2008). *Alice's adventure in Wonderland*. Gutenberg Project. https://www.gutenberg.org/files/11/11-h/11-h.htm (Original work published 1865)

C.C.R.U. (Cybernetic Culture Research Unit). (2018). *CCRU writings 1997–2003*. Urbanomic.

Ceballos, G., Ehrlich, P. R., & Barnosky, A. D. (2015). Accelerated modern human-induced species losses: Entering the sixth mass extinction. *Science Advances*, *1*(5), e1400253

Chadwick, R. (1984). The origins of astronomy and astrology in Mesopotamia. *Archaeoastronomy*, *7*(1–4), 89–95.

Chakrabarty, D. (2009). The climate of history: Four theses. *Critical Inquiry*, *35*, 197–222.

Chazan, M. (2017). Toward a long prehistory of fire. *Current Anthropology*, *58*(S16), S351–S359.

Christensen, J. (2004). Warfare in the European neolithic. *Acta Archaeologica*, *75*(2), 129–156.

Chwałczyk, F. (2020). Around the Anthropocene in eighty names – Considering the urbanocene proposition. *Sustainability*, *12*(4458), 1–33. https://iiraorg.com/2020/06/22/around-the-anthropocene-in-eighty-names-considering-the-urbanocene-proposition/

Clark, B., & York, R. (2005). Carbon metabolism: Global capitalism, climate change, and the biospheric rift. *Theory and Society*, *34*(4), 391–428.

Clark, T. (2015). *Ecocriticism on the edge: The Anthropocene as a threshold concept*. Bloomsbury Publishing.

Clarke, N. (2014). Geo-politics and the Disaster of the Anthropocene. *Sociological Review*, *62*, 19–37.

Cline, E. H., & Graham, M. W. (2011). *Ancient empires: From Mesopotamia to the rise of Islam*. Cambridge University Press.

Cochrane, G. W. G. (2008). A comparison of middle stone age and later stone age blades from South Africa. *Journal of Field Archaeology*, *33*(4), 429–448.

Cohen, T., Hillis Miller, J., & Colebrook, C. (2016). *Twilight of the Anthropocene idols*. Open Humanities Press.

Cole, D. R. (2007). Techno-shamanism and educational research. Ashe! *Journal of Experimental Spirituality*, *6*(1), 1–16.

Cole, D. R. (2011). *Educational life-forms: Deleuzian teaching and learning practice*. Sense Publishers.

Cole, D. R. (2012). *Surviving economic crises through education*. Peter Lang.

Cole, D. R. (2013). *Traffic jams: Analysing everyday life using the immanent materialism of Deleuze & Guattari*. Punctum Books.

Cole, D. R. (2014). *Capitalised education: An immanent materialist account of Kate Middleton*. Zero Books.

REFERENCES

Cole, D. R. (2017a). *Black Sun: The singularity at the heart of the Anthropocene.* https://iiraorg.com/2017/07/31/first-blog-post/

Cole, D. R. (2017b). Deleuze and learning. In M. Peters (Ed.), *Encyclopaedia of philosophy of education and theory* (pp. 1–6). Springer. https://link.springer.com/referenceworkentry/10.1007/978-981-287-532-7_68-1

Cole, D. R. (2019a). Analysing the matter flows in schools using Deleuze's method. *Studies in Philosophy and Education, 38*(30), 229–240.

Cole, D. R. (2019b). The designation of a Deleuzian philosophy for environmental education and its consequences.... *Australian Journal of Environmental Education, 35*(3), 173–182.

Cole, D. R. (2019c). Nowhere ‖ Erewhon. *Educational Philosophy and Theory, 51*(3), 255–264.

Cole, D. R. (2020). Learning to think in the Anthropocene: What can Deleuze-Guattari teach us? In K. Maiti & S. Chakraborty (Eds.), *Global perspectives on eco-aesthetics and eco-ethics: A green critique* (pp. 31–47). Lexington Books.

Cole, D. R., & Bradley, J. P. N. (2016). *A pedagogy of cinema.* Sense Publishers.

Cole, D. R., & Bradley, J. P. N. (Eds.). (2018). *Principles of transversality in globalization and education.* Springer.

Cole, D. R., Dolphijn, R., & Bradley, J. P. N. (2016). Fukushima: The geotrauma of a futural wave. *Trans-Humanities Journal, 9*(3), 211–233.

Cole, D. R., & Hager, P. (2010). Learning-practice: The ghosts in the education machine. *Education Inquiry, 1*(1), 21–40.

Cole, D. R., &Mirzaei Rafe, M. (2017). Conceptual ecologies for educational research through Deleuze, Guattari and Whitehead. *International Journal of Qualitative Studies in Education, 30*(9), 849–862.

Cole, D. R., & Mirzaei Rafe, M. (2018). Positioning whitehead as a mean to enhance social justice in education. *Interchange, 49*(3), 377–391.

Cole, D. R., & Pullen, D. L. (Eds.). (2010). *Multiliteracies in motion: Current theory and practice.* Routledge.

Cole, D. R., & Somerville, M. (2018). Thinking school curriculum through country with Deleuze and Whitehead: A process-based synthesis. In C. Naughton, G. Biesta, & D. R. Cole (Eds.). *Art, artists and pedagogy: Philosophy and the arts in education* (pp. 71–83). Routledge.

Cole, D. R., & Woodrow, C. (Eds.). (2016). *Super dimensions in globalisation and education.* Springer.

Collins, D., & Barkdull, J. (1995). Capitalism, environmentalism, and mediating structures. *Environmental Ethics, 17*(3), 227–244.

Comaroff, J., & Comaroff, J. L. (2008). *Of revelation and revolution, Volume 1: Christianity, colonialism, and consciousness in South Africa.* University of Chicago Press.

Conty, A. F. (2019). *Religion in the age of the Anthropocene.* The White Horse Press.

Conze, E. (1993). *A short history of Buddhism*. Oneworld Publications.

Corning P. A. (1987). Evolution and political control a synopsis of a general theory of politics. In M. Schmid & F. M. Wuketits (Eds.), *Evolutionary theory in social science* (Theory and Decision Library, Vol. 4, pp. 127–169). Springer.

Cowell, F. R. (1976). *Life in ancient Rome* (Vol. 421). Penguin.

Cox, G. W. (2004). *Alien species and evolution: The evolutionary ecology of exotic plants, animals, microbes, and interacting native species*. Island Press.

Crary, J. (2013). *24/7: Late capitalism and the ends of sleep*. Verso.

Crawshaw, P. (2013). Public health policy and the behavioural turn: The case of social marketing. *Critical Social Policy, 33*(4), 616–637.

Crutzen, P. J. (2002). Geology of mankind. *Nature, 415*, 23.

Dayanandan, A., & Donker, H. (2011). Oil prices and accounting profits of oil and gas companies. *International Review of Financial Analysis, 20*(5), 252–257.

Deleuze, G. (1989). *Cinema 2: The time-image* (H. Tomlinson & R. Galeta, Trans.). University of Minnesota Press. (Original work published 1985)

Deleuze, G. (1991). *Bergsonism* (H. Tomlinson & B. Habberjam, Trans.). Zone Books. (Original work published 1966)

Deleuze, G. (1994). *Difference & repetition* (P. Patton, Trans.). Columbia University Press. (Original work published 1968)

Deleuze, G. (1995). *Negotiations* (M. Joughin, Trans.). Columbia University Press. (Original work published 1990)

Deleuze, G. (1998). *Spinoza: Practical philosophy* (R. Hurley, Trans.). City Lights Publishers. (Original work published 1970)

Deleuze, G. (2006). *Nietzsche and philosophy* (H. Tomlinson, Trans.). Columbia University Press. (Original work published 1962)

Deleuze, G., & Guattari, F. (1984). *Anti-oedipus: Capitalism & schizophrenia* (R. Hurley, M. Steen, & H. R. Lane, Trans.). The Athlone Press. (Original work published 1972)

Deleuze, G., & Guattari, F. (1986). *Kafka: Toward a minor literature* (D. Polan, Trans.). University of Minnesota Press. (Original work published 1975)

Deleuze, G., & Guattari, F. (1988). *A thousand plateaus: Capitalism and schizophrenia II* (B. Massumi, Trans.). The Athlone Press. (Original work published 1980)

Deleuze, G., & Guattari, F. (1994). *What is philosophy?* (H. Tomlinson & G. Burchell, Trans.). Columbia University Press. (Original work published 1991)

Delmas, M. A., & Burbano, V. C. (2011). The drivers of greenwashing. *California Management Review, 54*(1), 64–87.

Deming, D. (2014). *Science and technology in world history, Volume 1: The ancient world and classical civilization*. McFarland.

Demos, T. J. (2018). To save a world: Geoengineering, conflictual futurisms, and the unthinkable. *e-flux Journal, 94*. https://www.e-flux.com/journal/94/221148/to-save-a-world-geoengineering-conflictual-futurisms-and-the-unthinkable/

d'Errico, F., & Backwell, L. (2009). Assessing the function of early hominin bone tools. *Journal of Archaeological Science, 36*(8), 1764–1773.

Devine-Wright, P. (2013). Think global, act local? The relevance of place attachments and place identities in a climate changed world. *Global Environmental Change, 23*(1), 61–69.

Diepart, J. C., & Schoenberger, L. (2017). Governing profits, extending state power and enclosing resources from the colonial era to the present. In S. Springer & K. Brickell (Eds.), *The handbook of contemporary Cambodia* (pp. 157–168). Routledge.

Dietrich, O., Heun, M., Notroff, J., Schmidt, K., & Zarnkow, M. (2012). The role of cult and feasting in the emergence of Neolithic communities. New evidence from Göbekli Tepe, south-eastern Turkey. *Antiquity, 86*(333), 674–695.

Dodson, J., Li, X., Sun, N., Atahan, P., Zhou, X., Liu, H., ... Yang, Z. (2014). Use of coal in the Bronze Age in China. *The Holocene, 24*(5), 525–530.

Dryzek, J. S. (1997). *The politics of the earth*. Oxford University Press.

Duerr, H. P. (1985). *Dreamtime: Concerning the boundary between wilderness and civilization* (F. Goodman, Trans.). Basil Blackwell. (Original work published 1978)

Duffy, B. E., & Pruchniewska, U. (2017). Gender and self-enterprise in the social media age: A digital double bind. *Information Communication & Society, 20*(6), 843–859.

Dunstan, W. E. (2010). *Ancient Rome*. Rowman & Littlefield Publishers.

Ellis, E. C., & Ramankutty, N. (2008). Putting people in the map: Anthropogenic biomes of the world. *Frontiers in Ecology and the Environment, 6*(8), 439–447.

Engels, F. (1987). *The condition of the working class in England* (V. Kiernan, Ed.). Penguin Classics. (Original work published 1845)

Engzell, P., Frey, A., & Verhagen, M. D. (2021). Learning loss due to school closures during the COVID-19 pandemic. *Proceedings of the National Academy of Sciences, 118*(17), 1–7.

Erlichson, H. (1999). Sadi Carnot, 'Founder of the Second Law of Thermodynamics'. *European Journal of Physics, 20*(3), 183–192.

Falb, D. (2020). Defossilization and refossilization: Deleuze/Guattari to the Anthropocene. In M. Ziółkowska (Ed.), *Plasticity of the planet. On environmental challenge for art and its institutions* (pp. 253–270). Mousse Publishing.

Farmer-Dougan, V. A., & Dougan, J. D. (1999). The man who listens to behavior: Folk wisdom and behavior analysis from a real horse whisperer. *Journal of the Experimental Analysis of Behavior, 72*(1), 139–149.

Fedosejeva, J., Bočē, A., Romanova, M., Iliško, D., & Ivanova, O. (2018). Education for sustainable development: The choice of pedagogical approaches and methods for the implementation of pedagogical tasks in the Anthropocene age. *Journal of Teacher Education for Sustainability, 20*(1), 157–179.

Feynman, R. P. (2005). Space-time approach to non-relativistic quantum mechanics. In L. M. Brown (Ed.), *Feynman's thesis – A new approach to quantum theory* (pp. 71–109). World Scientific. (Original work published 1942)

Foster, J. B. (1994). *The vulnerable planet: A short economic history of the environment.* Cornerstone Books.

Foucault, M. (1990). *The history of sexuality, Volume 2: The use of pleasure* (R. Hurley, Trans.). Vintage Books. (Original work published 1983)

Fox, T., Pope, M., & Ellis, E. C. (2017). Engineering the Anthropocene: Scalable social networks and resilience building in human evolutionary timescales. *The Anthropocene Review, 4*(3), 199–215.

Freire, P. (1996). *Pedagogy of the oppressed* (Rev. ed.). Continuum.

Freud, S. (1905). Three essays on the theory of sexuality. In J. Strachey (Ed.), *The standard edition of the complete psychological works of Sigmund Freud* (Vol. 7, pp. 125–245). The Hogarth Press.

Frye, R. N. (1984). *The history of ancient Iran.* Verlag C.H. Beck.

Furley, D. F. (1987). *The Greek cosmologists, Volume 1: The formation of the atomic theory and its earliest critics.* Cambridge University Press.

Galaz, V. (Ed.). (2014). *Global environmental governance, technology and politics: The Anthropocene gap.* Edward Elgar Publishing.

Galbraith, J. K. (1993). *American capitalism: The concept of countervailing power* (Vol. 619). Routledge. (Original work published 1952)

Gilgen, A., Wilkenskjeld, S., Kaplan, J., Kühn, O. T., & Lohmann, U. (2019). Did the Roman Empire affect European climate? A new look at the effects of land use and anthropogenic aerosol emissions. *Climate of the Past Discussions.* https://doi.org/10.5194/cp-2019-56

Ginn, F. (2015). When horses won't eat: Apocalypse and the Anthropocene. *Annals of the Association of American Geographers, 105*(2), 351–359.

Giroux, H. A. (2005). The terror of neoliberalism: Rethinking the significance of cultural politics. *College Literature, 32*(1), 1–19.

Glynn, I. M. (1990). Consciousness and time. *Nature, 348*(6301), 477–479.

Goddard, H. (2003). *Christians and Muslims: From double standards to mutual understanding.* Routledge.

Goldwasser, O. (2010). The aten is the 'Energy of light': New evidence from the script. *Journal of the American Research Center in Egypt, 46*, 159–165.

Gough, N. (2006). Shaking the tree, making a rhizome: Towards a nomadic geophilosophy of science education. *Educational Philosophy and Theory, 38*(5), 625–645.

Gowlett, J. A., & Wrangham, R. W. (2013). Earliest fire in Africa: Towards the convergence of archaeological evidence and the cooking hypothesis. *Azania: Archaeological Research in Africa, 48*(1), 5–30.

Grassby, R. (1999). *The idea of capitalism before the industrial revolution.* Rowman & Littlefield.

Greco, M. (2005). On the vitality of vitalism. *Theory, Culture & Society, 22*(1), 15–27.

Grimes, R. (2014). Performance is currency in the deep world's gift economy: An incantatory riff for a global medicine show. In G. Harvey (Ed.), *The handbook of contemporary animism* (pp. 501–512). Routledge.

Grodin, D., & Lindlof, T. R. (Eds.). (1996). *Constructing the self in a mediated world*. Sage Publications.

Guattari, F. (1995). *Chaosmosis: An ethico-aesthetic paradigm* (P. Bains & J. Pefanis, Trans.). Indiana University Press. (Original work published 1992)

Guattari, F. (1996a). *The Guattari reader* (G. Genosko, Ed.). Blackwell.

Guattari, F. (1996b). *The three ecologies* (I. Pindar & P. Sutton, Trans.). Athlone Press. (Original work published 1989)

Guattari, F. (2009). La Borde: A clinic unlike any other. In F. Guattari, *Chaosophy: Texts and interviews 1972–1977* (D. L. Sweet, J. Becker, & T. Adkins, Trans.; pp. 176–194). Semiotext(e). (Original work published 1995)

Guattari, F. (2013). *Schizoanalytic cartographies* (A. Goffey, Trans.). Bloomsbury. (Original work published 1989)

Gupta, A. K. (2004). Origin of agriculture and domestication of plants and animals linked to early Holocene climate amelioration. *Current Science-Bangalore, 87*, 54–59.

Hall, H. R. (2015). *The ancient history of the Near East: From the earliest times to the battle of Salamis*. Routledge.

Hall, K. R. (2016). Commodity flows, diaspora networking, and contested agency in the Eastern Indian Ocean c. 1000–1500. *TRaNS: Trans-Regional and-National Studies of Southeast Asia, 4*(2), 387–417.

Hall, W. P. (2011). Physical basis for the emergence of autopoiesis, cognition and knowledge. *Kororoit Institute Working Papers, 2*, 1–63.

Hall, W. P. (2020). *Is this the start of runaway global warming?* https://iiraorg.com/2020/07/04/is-this-the-start-of-runaway-global-warming/

Hall, W. P., Dalmaris, P., Else, S., Martin, C. P., & Philp, W. R. (2007, December 9–11). *Time value of knowledge: Time-based frameworks for valuing knowledge*. Paper presented at the 10th Australian conference for knowledge management and intelligent decision support.

Hamilton, C. (2010). Consumerism, self-creation and prospects for a new ecological consciousness. *Journal of Cleaner Production, 18*(6), 571–575.

Hamilton, C. (2017). *Defiant earth: The fate of humans in the Anthropocene*. John Wiley & Sons.

Hamilton, C., & Grinevald, J. (2015). Was the Anthropocene anticipated? *The Anthropocene Review, 2*, 59–72.

Hamilton, L. C. (2011). Education, politics and opinions about climate change evidence for interaction effects. *Climatic Change, 104*(2), 231–242.

Haraway, D. (2015). Anthropocene, Capitalocene, Plantationocene, Chthulucene: Making kin. *Environmental Humanities, 6*, 159–165.

Harvey, G. (2005). *Animism: Respecting the living world.* Wakefield Press.

Hawkesworth, M. E. (2006). *Feminist inquiry: From political conviction to methodological innovation.* Rutgers University Press.

Hawthorne, N. (2010). Fire worship. *The New Atlantis.* https://www.thenewatlantis.com/docLib/20110406_HawthorneFireWorship.pdf (Original work published 1843)

Head, L. (2014). Contingencies of the Anthropocene: Lessons from the 'Neolithic'. *The Anthropocene Review, 1*(2), 113–125.

Heidegger, M. (2010). *Being and time* (J. Stambaugh, Trans.). SUNY Press.

Hennessy, R. (Ed.). (2012). *Materialist feminism and the politics of discourse (RLE Feminist Theory).* Routledge.

Hickel, J. (2020). What does degrowth mean? A few points of clarification. *Globalizations.* doi:10.1080/14747731.2020.1812222

Hillel, D. (1992). *Out of the earth: Civilization and the life of the soil.* University of California Press.

Hills, R. L., & Pacey, A. J. (1972). The measurement of power in early steam-driven textile mills. *Technology and Culture, 13*(1), 25–43.

Hobbs, A., & Angela, H. (2000). *Plato and the hero: Courage, manliness and the impersonal good.* Cambridge University Press.

Hof, A. R., Dymond, C. C., & Mladenoff, D. J. (2017). Climate change mitigation through adaptation: The effectiveness of forest diversification by novel tree planting regimes. *Ecosphere, 8*(11), e01981.

Hoffman, A. J. (2005). Climate change strategy: The business logic behind voluntary greenhouse gas reductions. *California Management Review, 47*(3), 21–46.

Holland, E. W. (2006). The utopian dimension of thought in Deleuze and Guattari. *Arena Journal, 25/26,* 217–242.

Hopkins, E. (1982). Working hours and conditions during the industrial revolution: A re-appraisal. *Economic History Review, 35*(1), 52–66.

Hornsey, M. J., & Fielding, K. S. (2016). A cautionary note about messages of hope: Focusing on progress in reducing carbon emissions weakens mitigation motivation. *Global Environmental Change, 39,* 26–34.

Houser, N. O. (2009). Ecological democracy: An environmental approach to citizenship education. *Theory & Research in Social Education, 37*(2), 192–214.

Hroch, P., & Stoddart, M. C. (2015). Mediating environments. *Canadian Journal of Sociology, 40*(3), 295–308.

Huby, P. M. (1978). Epicurus' attitude to Democritus. *Phronesis, 23*(1), 80–86.

Hughes, J. D. (2014). *Environmental problems of the Greeks and Romans: Ecology in the ancient Mediterranean.* JHU Press.

Hughes, T. P., Barnes, M. L., Bellwood, D. R., Cinner, J. E., Cumming, G. S., Jackson, J. B., … Palumbi, S. R. (2017). Coral reefs in the Anthropocene. *Nature, 546*(7656), 82–90.

Humphrey, J. W., Oleson, J. P., A.N. Sherwood and M. Nikolic (1998). *Greek and Roman technology: A sourcebook: Annotated translations of Greek and Latin texts and documents*. Psychology Press.

Ingold, T. (2011). *Being alive: Essays on movement, knowledge and description*. Routledge.

jagodzinski, j. (2019). *Schizoanalytic ventures at the end of the world: Film, video, art, and pedagogical challenges*. Palgrave Macmillan.

James, H. (2006). *The Roman predicament: How the rules of international order create the politics of empire*. Princeton University Press.

James, P. (2014). *Urban sustainability in theory and practice: Circles of sustainability*. Routledge.

James, S. R. (1989). Hominid use of fire in the Lower and Middle Pleistocene: A review of the evidence. *Current Anthropology, 30*(1), 1–26.

Jarzabkowski, P., & Kaplan, S. (2015). Strategy tools-in-use: A framework for understanding "technologies of rationality" in practice. *Strategic Management Journal, 36*(4), 537–558.

Jeffries, V., & Tygart, C. E. (1974). The influence of theology, denomination, and values upon the positions of clergy on social issues. *Journal for the Scientific Study of Religion, 15*(1), 309–324.

Jenkins, P. (2007). *God's continent: Christianity, Islam, and Europe's religious crisis*. Oxford University Press.

Jickling, B. (1992). Why I don't want my children to be educated for sustainable development. *The Journal of Environmental Education, 23*(4), 5–8.

Johnson, D., Tyldesley, J., Lowe, T., Withers, P. J., & Grady, M. M. (2013). Analysis of a prehistoric Egyptian iron bead with implications for the use and perception of meteorite iron in ancient Egypt. *Meteoritics & Planetary Science, 48*(6), 997–1006.

Johnston, S. I. (Ed.). (2004). *Religions of the ancient world: A guide*. The Belknap Press of Harvard University Press.

Jonsson, F. A. (2012). The industrial revolution in the Anthropocene. *The Journal of Modern History, 84*(3), 679–696.

Jördens, A. (2012). Government, taxation, and law. In C. Riggs (Ed.), *The Oxford handbook of Roman Egypt* (pp. 65–67). Oxford University Press.

Joshel, S. R., Joshel, S. R., Malamud, M., & McGuire Jr., D. T. (Eds.). (2001). *Imperial projections: Ancient Rome in modern popular culture*. JHU Press.

Kallis, G. (2018). *Degrowth*. Agenda Publishing.

Kanarfogel, E. (2011). Prayer, literacy and literary memory in the Jewish communities of Medieval Europe. In R. S. Boustan et al. (Eds.), *Jewish studies at the crossroads of anthropology and history: Authority, diaspora, tradition* (pp. 250–270). Penn Press.

Kerschner, C., Wächter, P., Nierling, L., & Ehlers, M. H. (2018). Degrowth and technology: Towards feasible, viable, appropriate and convivial imaginaries. *Journal of Cleaner Production, 197*, 1619–1636.

Kertzer, D. I. (1988). *Ritual, politics, and power.* Yale University Press.
Keys, P. W., Galaz, V., Dyer, M., Matthews, N., Folke, C., Nyström, M., & Cornell, S. E. (2019). Anthropocene risk. *Nature Sustainability, 2*(8), 667–673.
Khazanov, A. M. (1994). *Nomads and the outside world* (2nd ed.). University of Wisconsin Press.
Klein, R. (2018). Hominin dispersal in the old world. In C. Scarre (Ed.), *The human past: World prehistory & the development of human societies* (4th ed., pp. 71–107). Thames & Hudson.
Knoppers, G. N. (1995). Images of David in early Judaism: David as repentant sinner in chronicles. *Biblica, 76*(4), 449–470.
Konior, B. M. (2016). *13 propositions for theory in the Anthropocene* [Online manifesto]. https://www.bognamk.com/
Konior, B. M., & Granata, Y. (2018). *Envenoment, an excavation: Towards a feminism-without-example in ten parts.* https://iiraorg.com/2018/06/06/envenoment-an-evacuation-towards-a-feminism-without-example-in-ten-parts/
Kopnina, H. (2014). Education for Sustainable Development (ESD) as if environment really mattered. *Environmental Development, 12*, 37–46.
Kopnina, H. (2020). Education for the future? Critical evaluation of education for sustainable development goals. *The Journal of Environmental Education, 51*(4), 280–291.
Kordela, A. K. (1999). Political metaphysics: God in global capitalism (the slave, the masters, Lacan, and the surplus). *Political Theory, 27*(6), 789–839.
Kuhrt, A. (2013). *The Persian Empire: A corpus of sources from the Achaemenid period.* Routledge.
Kunin, S. D. (2003). *Religion: The modern theories.* Taylor & Francis US.
Læssøe, J., Schnack, K., Breiting, S., Rolls, S., Feinstein, N., & Goh, K. C. (2009). *Climate change and sustainable development: The response from education.* A cross-national report from International Alliance of Leading Education Institutes. The Danish School of Education, Aarhus University.
Lambeck, K., Purcell, A., Flemming, N. C., Vita-Finzi, C., Alsharekh, A. M., & Bailey, G. N. (2011). Sea level and shoreline reconstructions for the Red Sea: Isostatic and tectonic considerations and implications for hominin migration out of Africa. *Quaternary Science Reviews, 30*(25–26), 3542–3574.
Land, N. (1995). Machines and technocultural complexity: The challenge of the Deleuze-Guattari conjunction. *Theory, Culture & Society, 12*(2), 131–140.
Land, N. (2018). *Fanged Noumena: Collected writings 1987–2007* (R. Mackay & R. Brassier, Eds.). Urbanomic.
Lanzetta, B. (2001). *The other side of nothingness: Toward a theology of radical openness.* SUNY Press.
Lappert, M. F., & Murrell, J. N. (2003). John Dalton, the man and his legacy: The bicentenary of his atomic theory. *Dalton Transactions, 20*, 3811–3820.

Latouche, S. (2009). *Farewell to growth*. Polity.

Latour, B. (2017). Anthropology at the time of the Anthropocene: A personal view of what is to be studied. In M. Brightman & J. Lewis (Eds.), *The anthropology of sustainability* (pp. 35–49). Palgrave Macmillan.

Laurence, R. (2009). *Roman passions: A history of pleasure in Imperial Rome*. Bloomsbury.

Lawlor, L., & Moulard, V. L. (2020). Henri Bergson. In E. N. Zalta (Ed.), *The Stanford encyclopedia of philosophy* (Summer 2020 ed.). https://plato.stanford.edu/archives/sum2020/entries/bergson/

Le Grange, L. (2019). The Anthropocene: Becoming-imperceptible of environmental education. *On Education, Journal for Research and Debate*, 2(4). https://doi.org/10.17899/on_ed.20

Lent, J. (2018). *We need an ecological civilization before it's too late*. https://iiraorg.com/2018/10/16/we-need-an-ecological-civilization-before-its-too-late/

Letiche, H. (2000). Phenomenal complexity theory as informed by Bergson. *Journal of Organizational Change Management*, 13(6), 545–557.

Levy, T. E., Adams, R. B., Hauptmann, A., Prange, M., Schmitt-Strecker, S., & Najjar, M. (2002). Early Bronze Age metallurgy: A newly discovered copper manufactory in southern Jordan. *Antiquity-Oxford*, 76(292), 425–437.

Lewis, S. L., & Maslin, M. A. (2015). Defining the anthropocene. *Nature*, 519(7542), 171–180.

Lovecraft, H. P. (1973). *Supernatural horror in literature*. Dover Publications. (Original work published 1921)

Lundy, C. A. (2013). Who are our nomad's today? Deleuze's political ontology and the revolutionary problematic. *Deleuze Studies*, 7(2), 231–249.

Lyotard, J.-F. (1993). *Libidinal economy* (I. H. Grant, Trans.). The Athlone Press. (Original work published 1974)

Macfarlane, R. (2016, April 1). Generation Anthropocene: How humans have altered the planet forever. *The Guardian*. https://www.theguardian.com/books/2016/apr/01/generation-anthropocene-alteredplanet-for-ever

MacGregor, K., & Murray, W. (Eds.). (2001). *The dynamics of military revolution, 1300–2050*. Cambridge University Press.

Maddin, R. (1975). Early iron metallurgy in the Near East. *Transactions of the Iron and Steel Institute of Japan*, 15(2), 59–68.

Maggs, D., & Robinson, J. (2016). Recalibrating the Anthropocene. *Environmental Philosophy*, 13(2), 175–194.

Malm, A. (2016). *Fossil capital: The rise of steam power and the roots of global warming*. Verso Books.

Malm, A., & Hornborg, A. (2015). The geology of mankind? A critique of the Anthropocene narrative. *The Anthropocene Review*, 1, 62–69.

Malone, T. W. (2004). *The future of work.* Harvard Business School.

Manning, R. (2004). *Against the grain: How agriculture has hijacked civilization.* Macmillan.

Mannion, G., Fenwick, A., & Lynch, J. (2013). Place-responsive pedagogy: Learning from teachers' experiences of excursions in nature. *Environmental Education Research, 19*(6), 792–809.

Marks, J. (1998). *Gilles Deleuze: Vitalism and multiplicity.* Pluto Press.

Marshall, Y. (2006). Introduction: Adopting a sedentary lifeway. *World Archaeology, 38*(2), 153–163.

Martin, C. (2016). The aeolipile as experimental model in early modern natural philosophy. *Perspectives on Science, 24*(3), 264–284.

Marzke, M. W. (2013). Tool making, hand morphology and fossil hominins. *Philosophical Transactions of the Royal Society B: Biological Sciences, 368*(1630), 20120414.

Masny, D., & Cole, D. R. (2012). *Mapping multiple literacies: An introduction to Deleuzian literacy studies.* Continuum.

Mathisen, R. (2019). *Ancient Roman civilization: History and sources.* Oxford University Press.

Matsumura, H., Hung, H., & Zhen, L. (Eds.). (2017). *Bio-anthropological studies of early Holocene hunter-gatherer sites at Huiyaotian and Liyupo in Guangxi China.* National Museum of Nature and Science Tokyo.

Mazoyer, M., & Roudart, L. (2006). *A history of world agriculture: From the neolithic age to the current crisis.* NYU Press.

Mbembé, J. A., & Meintjes, L. (2003). Necropolitics. *Public Culture, 15*(1), 11–40.

McClellan, J. E., & Regourd, F. (2011). *The colonial machine: French science and overseas expansion in the old regime.* Brepols.

McCright, A. M., Dunlap, R. E., & Xiao, C. (2013). Perceived scientific agreement and support for government action on climate change in the USA. *Climatic Change, 119*(2), 511–518.

McDonnell, J. J. (1991). *The concept of an atom from Democritus to John Dalton.* Edwin Mellen Press.

McHenry, H. M., & Coffing, K. (2000). Australopithecus to Homo: Transformations in body and mind. *Annual Review of Anthropology, 29*(1), 125–146.

McIntosh, J. R. (2005). *Ancient Mesopotamia: New perspectives.* ABC-CLIO.

McIntosh, S. K., & McIntosh, R. J. (1981). West African prehistory: Archaeological studies in recent decades have illuminated the prehistory of this vast region, revealing unexpected complexity in its development from 10,000 BC to AD 1000. *American Scientist, 69*(6), 602–613.

McLaren, P., Martin, G., Farahmandpur, R., & Jaramillo, N. (2004). Teaching in and against the empire: Critical pedagogy as revolutionary praxis. *Teacher Education Quarterly, 31*(1), 131–153.

McLeod, K. (2018). *Learning to think like a planet.* https://iiraorg.com/2018/10/21/learning-to-think-like-a-planet/

McNeill, J. R. (2001). *Something new under the sun: An environmental history of the twentieth-century world.* WW Norton & Company.

McPherron, S. P., Alemseged, Z., Marean, C. W., Wynn, J. G., Reed, D., Geraads, D., ... Béarat, H. A. (2010). Evidence for stone-tool-assisted consumption of animal tissues before 3.39 million years ago at Dikika, Ethiopia. *Nature, 466*(7308), 857–860.

Mcphie, J., & Clarke, D. A. G. (2015). A walk in the park: Considering practice for outdoor environmental education through an immanent take on the material turn. *The Journal of Environmental Education, 46*(4), 230–250.

Mellaart, J. (1965). *Çatal Hüyük: A neolithic city in Anatolia.* Oxford University Press.

Metzger, E. P., Blockstein, D. E., & Callahan, C. N. (2017). Interdisciplinary teaching and sustainability: An introduction. *Journal of Geoscience Education, 65*(2), 81–85.

Meyer, V. (2004). *The ecological footprint as an environmental education tool for knowledge, attitude and behaviour changes towards sustainable living* [Doctoral dissertation]. University of South Africa.

Michie, R. (2011). *The London and New York stock exchanges 1850–1914.* Routledge Revivals.

Mirzaei Rafe, M., Bagheri Noaparast, K., Sadat Hosseini, A., & Sajadieh, N. (2019). The application of critical realism as a basis for agency in environmental education: The case of Roy Bhaskar. *Australian Journal of Environmental Education, 35*(3), 230–238.

Mitchell, R. (2013). *Experimental life: Vitalism in romantic science and literature.* JHU Press.

Mithen, S. (2007). Creations of pre-modern human minds: Stone tool manufacture and use by Homo habilis, heidelbergensis, and neanderthalensis. In E. Margolis & S. Laurence (Eds.), *Creations of the mind: Theories of artifacts and their representation* (pp. 289–311). Oxford University Press.

Mokyr, J. (2011). The European Enlightenment, the industrial revolution, and modern economic growth. In P. Zumbansen & G.-P. Calliess (Eds.), *Law, economics and evolutionary theory* (pp. 33–53). Edward Elgar Publishing.

Monastersky, R. (2015). Anthropocene: The human age. *Nature News, 519*(7542), 144.

Moore, J. (Ed.). (2016). *Anthropocene or Capitalocene? Nature, history and the crisis of capitalism.* PM Press.

More, T. (1516). *Utopia.* https://www.planetebook.com/free-ebooks/utopia.pdf

Morris, A. (2016). *The challenge of state reliance on revenue from fossil fuel production* [Discussion paper]. Brooking Institution, Climate and Energy Economics.

Motz, L., & Weaver, J. H. (1989). Atomic structure and stellar spectra. In L. Motz & J. H. Weaver (Eds.), *The unfolding universe: A stellar journey* (pp. 193–222). Springer.

Moynihan, T. (2020). *X-risk: How humanity discovered its own extinction.* Urbanomic.

Mumford, L. (1966). The first megamachine. *Diogenes, 14*(55), 1–15.

Murray, M. J. (1992). 'White gold' or 'white blood'?: The rubber plantations of colonial Indochina, 1910–40. *The Journal of Peasant Studies, 19*(3–4), 41–67.

Müller, D. B., Liu, G., Løvik, A. N., Modaresi, R., Pauliuk, S., Steinhoff, F. S., & Brattebø, H. (2013). Carbon emissions of infrastructure development. *Environmental Science & Technology, 47*(20), 11739–11746.

Muraca, B. (2012). Towards a fair degrowth-society: Justice and the right to a 'good life' beyond growth. *Futures, 44*(6), 535–545.

National Research Council (NRC). (2010). *Verifying greenhouse gas emissions: Methods to support international climate agreements.* National Academies Press.

Naughton, C., Biesta, G., & Cole, D. R. (Eds.). (2018). *Art, artists and pedagogy: Philosophy and the arts in education.* Routledge.

Nene, S. R. (2005). Relevance of Kaṇāda's Vaiśeṣika and Upaniṣadic Brahman to modern physics. *Annals of the Bhandarkar Oriental Research Institute, 86*, 135–137.

Neusner, J. (1969). The phenomenon of the rabbi in Late Antiquity. *Numen, 16*(1), 1–20.

Neyrat, F. (2019). *The unconstructable earth: An ecology of separation* (S. Drew Burk, Trans.). Fordham University Press.

Nicholson, P. T., & Shaw, I. (Eds.). (2000). *Ancient Egyptian materials and technology.* Cambridge University Press.

Nietzsche, F. W. (1889). Letter to Jacob Burckhardt (English Trans.). In *Nietzsche's letters.* http://www.thenietzschechannel.com/correspondence/eng/nlett-1889.htm

Nietzsche, F. W. (1989). *On the genealogy of morals* (R. J. Hollingdale, Trans.). Vintage. (Original work published 1887)

Nowviskie, B. (2015). Digital humanities in the Anthropocene. *Digital Scholarship in the Humanities, 30*(s1), 4–15.

Orwell, G. (2008). *Nineteen eighty-four.* Penguin Books. (Original work published 1949)

Pan, Y., Zheng, Y., & Chen, C. (2017). Human ecology of the early Neolithic Kuahuqiao culture in East Asia. In J. Habu, P. V. Lape, & J. W. Olsen (Eds.), *Handbook of East and Southeast Asian archaeology* (pp. 347–377). Springer.

Panofsky, W. K., & Phillips, M. (2005). *Classical electricity and magnetism.* Dover Publications.

Papadopoulos, J. K., & Urton, G. (Eds.). (2012). *Construction of value in the ancient world.* Cotsen Institute of Archaeology.

Parikka, J. (2015). *The anthrobscene.* University of Minnesota Press.

Parker, B. (1997). Garrisoning the empire: Aspects of the construction and maintenance of forts on the Assyrian frontier. *Iraq, 59*, 77–87.

Parkington, J. (2003). Middens and moderns: shellfishing and the Middle Stone Age of the Western Cape, South Africa: Reviews of current issues and research findings: human origins research in South Africa. *South African Journal of Science, 99*(5 & 6), 243–247.

Patton, P. (2000). *Deleuze and the political.* Psychology Press.

Paulson, S. (2017). Degrowth: Culture, power and change. *Journal of Political Ecology*, *24*(1), 425–448.

Payne, P. G. (2019). Performative abstractionism in environmental education: A critical theory of theory. *The Journal of Environmental Education*, *50*(4–6), 289–320.

Peoples, H. C., Duda, P., & Marlowe, F. W. (2016). Hunter-gatherers and the origins of religion. *Human Nature*, *27*(3), 261–282.

Peters, M. A. (2017). *Education for ecological democracy.* https://iiraorg.com/2017/09/07/education-for-ecological-democracy/

Pettman, D. (2016). *Infinite distraction.* Polity Press.

Pettman, D. (2020). *Peak libido: Sex, ecology and the collapse of desire.* Polity.

Phang, S. E. (2008). *Roman military service: Ideologies of discipline in the late Republic and early Principate.* Cambridge University Press.

Philip, G. (1988). *Metal weapons of the Early and Middle Bronze Ages in the Levant* [Doctoral dissertation]. University of Edinburgh.

Phillips, D. J. (2001). *Peoples on the move: Introducing the nomads of the world.* William Carey Library.

Pichler, M., Schaffartzik, A., Haberl, H., & Görg, C. (2017). Drivers of society-nature relations in the Anthropocene and their implications for sustainability transformations. *Current Opinion in Environmental Sustainability*, *26*, 32–36.

Pickrell, J. (2020, March 21). Smoke from Australia's bushfires killed far more people than the fires did, study says. *The Guardian.* https://www.theguardian.com/australia-news/2020/mar/21/smoke-from-australias-bushfires-killed-far-more-people-than-the-fires-did-study-says

Plato (360 BC). *The republic* (B. Jowett, Trans.). http://classics.mit.edu/Plato/republic.html

Pleiner, R., & Bjorkman, J. (1974). The Assyrian Iron Age: The history of iron in the Assyrian civilization. *Proceedings of the American Philosophical Society*, *118*(3), 283–313.

Popkewitz, T. S. (1988). Culture, pedagogy, and power: Issues in the production of values and colonialization. *Journal of Education*, *170*(2), 77–90.

Portelli, A. (1988). Uchronic dreams: Working class memory and possible worlds. *Oral History*, *16*(2), 46–56.

Preston, G. W., Parker, A. G., Walkington, H., Leng, M. J., & Hodson, M. J. (2012). From nomadic herder-hunters to sedentary farmers: The relationship between climate change and ancient subsistence strategies in south-eastern Arabia. *Journal of Arid Environments*, *86*, 122–130.

Punt, J. (2005). Paul, body theology, and morality: Parameters for a discussion. *Neotestamentica*, *39*(2), 359–388.

Raichlen, D. A., Gordon, A. D., Harcourt-Smith, W. E., Foster, A. D., & Haas Jr., W. R. (2010). Laetoli footprints preserve earliest direct evidence of human-like bipedal biomechanics. *PLoS One*, *5*(3), e9769.

Raknes, O. (2004). *Wilhelm Reich and orgonomy.* American College of Orgonomy.

Read, J. (2009). The fetish is always actual, revolution is always virtual: From noology to noopolitics. *Deleuze Studies, 3*(Suppl), 78–101.

Reyes-García, V., Kightley, E., Ruiz-Mallén, I., Fuentes-Peláez, N., Demps, K., Huanca, T., &Martínez-Rodríguez, M. R. (2010). Schooling and local environmental knowledge: Do they complement or substitute each other? *International Journal of Educational Development, 30*(3), 305–313.

Rich, J., & Wallace-Hadrill, A. (Eds.). (2003). *City and country in the ancient world* (Vol. 2). Routledge.

Richet, J.-L. (2020). A loose coupling perspective on Ancient Egypt economy and society. *Business History.* doi:10.1080/00076791.2020.1754802

Rifkin, J. (1995). *The end of work.* Tarcher/Putnam.

Rigby, K. (2009). Writing in the Anthropocene: Idle chatter or ecoprophetic witness? *Australian Humanities Review, 47.* http://australianhumanitiesreview.org/2009/11/01/writing-in-the-anthropocene-idle-chatter-or-ecoprophetic-witness/

Risler, R., Grüebler, W., König, V., & Schmelzbach, P. A. (1974). Investigation of a polarized neutral atomic beam. *Nuclear Instruments and Methods, 121*(3), 425–430.

Ritchie, H., & Roser, M. (2017). *CO_2 and greenhouse gas emissions.* OurWorldInData.org. https://ourworldindata.org/carbon dioxide-and-other-greenhouse-gas-emissions

Roberts, J. M., & Case, D. (1999). *Twentieth century: The history of the world, 1901 to 2000.* Viking.

Rocke, A. J. (2005). In search of El Dorado: John Dalton and the origins of the atomic theory. *Social Research, 72*(1), 125–158.

Rockefeller Brother Fund. (2020). *350.org funding details.* https://www.rbf.org/grantees/350org

Rohr, R. R. (2012). *Sundials: History, theory, and practice.* Courier Corporation.

Rolle, R. (1989). *The world of the Scythians.* University of California Press.

Rome, A. (2013). *The genius of Earth Day: How a 1970 teach-in unexpectedly made the first green generation.* Macmillan.

Rose, K. D. (2006). *The beginning of the age of mammals.* JHU Press.

Rosenbaum, R., & Iwata-Weickgenannt, K. (2014). *Visions of precarity in Japanese popular culture and literature.* Taylor & Francis Ltd.

Rosenberg, E. S. (1985). Foundations of United States international financial power: Gold standard diplomacy, 1900–1905. *Business History Review, 59*(2), 169–202.

Rousell, D. (2021). A map you can walk into: Immersive cartography and the speculative potentials of data. *Qualitative Inquiry, 27*(5), 580–597.

Roux, V., & Bril, B. (2005). *Stone knapping: The necessary preconditions for a uniquely hominin behaviour.* McDonald Institute for Archaeological Research, University of Cambridge.

Rowley-Conwy, P. (2001). Time, change and the archaeology of hunter-gatherers: How original is the 'Original affluent society?' In C. Panter-Brick, R. H. Laton, & P. Rowley-Conwy (Eds.), *Hunter-gatherers: An interdisciplinary perspective* (pp. 39–72). Cambridge University Press.

Ruddiman, W. F. (2013). The anthropocene. *Annual Review of Earth and Planetary Sciences, 41*, 45–68.

Runciman, W. G. (1983). Capitalism without classes: The case of classical Rome. *The British Journal of Sociology, 34*(2), 157–181.

Scherer, F. M. (1965). Invention and innovation in the Watt-Boulton steam-engine venture. *Technology and Culture, 6*(2), 165–187.

Schneider, S. H., Kuntz-Duriseti, K., & Azar, C. (2000). Costing non-linearities, surprises, and irreversible events. *Pacific and Asian Journal of Energy, 10*(1), 81–106.

Scott, A. C., Meyer-Berthaud, B., Galtier, J., Rex, G. M., Brindley, S. A., & Clayton, G. (1986). Studies on a new Lower Carboniferous flora from Kingswood near Pettycur, Scotland: Preliminary report. *Review of Palaeobotany and Palynology, 48*(1–3), 161–180.

Scott, A. J. (1996). Regional motors of the global economy. *Futures, 28*(5), 391–411.

See, T., & Bradley, J. (Eds.). (2016). *Deleuze and Buddhism*. Palgrave Macmillan UK.

Sellar, S., & Cole, D. R. (2017). Accelerationism: A timely provocation for the critical sociology of education. *British Journal of Sociology of Education, 38*(1), 38–48.

Şener, Ş. E. C., Sharp, J. L., & Anctil, A. (2018). Factors impacting diverging paths of renewable energy: A review. *Renewable and Sustainable Energy Reviews, 81*, 2335–2342.

Shahak, I. (1994). *Jewish history, Jewish religion: The weight of three thousand years*. Pluto Press.

Sherby, O. D., & Wadsworth, J. (2001). Ancient blacksmiths, the Iron Age, Damascus steels, and modern metallurgy. *Journal of Materials Processing Technology, 117*(3), 347–353.

Shumaker, R. W., Walkup, K. R., & Beck, B. B. (2011). *Animal tool behavior: The use and manufacture of tools by animals*. JHU Press.

Simpson, L. R. (2004). Strategies for the recovery and maintenance of Indigenous knowledge. *American Indian Quarterly, 28*(3/4), 373–384.

Singh, G. S. (2008). *History of Sikh Gurus retold: 1606–1708*. Atlantic Publishers.

Singh, U. (2008). *A history of ancient and early medieval India: From the Stone Age to the 12th century*. Pearson Education India.

Sissa, G., & Detienne, M. (2000). *The daily life of the Greek gods*. Stanford University Press.

Smil, V. (2017). *Energy and civilization: A history*. MIT Press.

Smith, B. D., & Zeder, M. A. (2013). The onset of the Anthropocene. *Anthropocene, 4*, 8–13.

Smith, D. W. (2003). Mathematics and the theory of multiplicities: Badiou and Deleuze revisited. *The Southern Journal of Philosophy, 41*(3), 411–449.

Smith, D. W. (2019). The pure form of time and the powers of the false. *Tijdschrift voor Filosofie, 81*(1), 29–51.

Smith, R. (2016). *Green capitalism: The god that failed.* College Publications.

Solanas, V. (1968). *S.C.U.M. Manifesto (Society for Cutting up Men).* Phoenix Press. https://www.ccs.neu.edu/home/shivers/rants/scum.html

Sousa, F. W., Sousa, M. J., Oliveira, I. R., Oliveira, A. G., Cavalcante, R. M., Fechine, P. B., ... Nascimento, R. F. (2009). Evaluation of a low-cost adsorbent for removal of toxic metal ions from wastewater of an electroplating factory. *Journal of Environmental Management, 90*(11), 3340–3344.

Sprenger, R., Cherry, C., Healey, A., Payne-Frank, N., & Lamborn, K. (2019, December 3). Inside the mission to create an army of Greta Thunbergs' [Video]. *The Guardian.* https://www.theguardian.com/global/video/2019/dec/02/inside-the-mission-to-create-an-army-of-greta-thunbergs-video

Starr, P. (1995). *Logics of failed revolt: French theory after May'68.* Stanford University Press.

Steffen, W., Broadgate, W., Deutsch, L., Gaffney, O., & Ludwig, C. (2015). The trajectory of the Anthropocene: The great acceleration. *The Anthropocene Review, 2*(1), 81–98.

Steffen, W., Rockström, J., Richardson, K., Lenton, T. M., Folke, C., Liverman, D., ... Donges, J. F. (2018). Trajectories of the earth system in the Anthropocene. *Proceedings of the National Academy of Sciences, 115*(33), 8252–8259.

Steinberger, J. K., & Roberts, J. T. (2010). From constraint to sufficiency: The decoupling of energy and carbon from human needs, 1975–2005. *Ecological Economics, 70*(2), 425–433.

Steinert, M., & Leifer, L. J. (2012). 'Finding one's way': Re-discovering a hunter-gatherer model based on wayfaring. *International Journal of Engineering Education, 28*(2), 251–252.

Stiegler, B. (1998). *Technics and time: The fault of Epimetheus* (Vol. 1; R. Beardsworth & G. Collins, Trans.). Stanford University Press.

Stiegler, B. (2018). *The Neganthropocene* (D. Ross, Trans.). Open Humanities Press.

Stokols, D. (2018). *Social ecology in the digital age: Solving complex problems in a globalized world.* Academic Press.

Stout, D., & Chaminade, T. (2012). Stone tools, language and the brain in human evolution. *Philosophical Transactions of the Royal Society B: Biological Sciences, 367*(1585), 75–87.

Stromquist, N. P., & Monkman, K. (Eds.). (2014). *Globalization and education: Integration and contestation across cultures.* R&L Education.

Tawney, R. H. (1998). *Religion and the rise of capitalism (Vol. 23).* Transaction Publishers. (Original work published 1926)

Teeple, H. M. (1992). *How did Christianity really begin? A historical-archaeological approach.* Religion and Ethics Institute.

Thacker, E. (2011). *In the dust of this planet – Horror of philosophy, Vol. 1.* Zero Books.

Tognetti, S. S. (1999). Science in a double-bind: Gregory Bateson and the origins of post-normal science. *Futures, 31,* 689–703.

Topping, P. (Ed.). (1997). *Neolithic landscapes: Neolithic studies group seminar papers 2.* Oxbow Books.

Torrence, R. (Ed.). (1989). *Time, energy and stone tools.* Cambridge University Press.

Toscano, A. (2017). *Fanaticism: On the uses of an idea.* Verso Books.

Toth, N. (1987). Behavioral inferences from early stone artifact assemblages: An experimental model. *Journal of Human Evolution, 16*(7–8), 763–787.

Travers, T. H. E. (1979). Technology, tactics, and morale: Jean de Bloch, the Boer War, and British military theory, 1900–1914. *The Journal of Modern History, 51*(2), 264–286.

Tremlin, T. (2006). *Minds and gods: The cognitive foundations of religion.* Oxford University Press.

Trigger, B. G. (1993). *Early civilizations: Ancient Egypt in context.* American University in Cairo Press.

Tsing, A. (2015). *The mushroom at the end of the world: On the possibility of life in capitalist ruins.* Princeton University Press.

Ulph, A., & Ulph, D. (1997). Global warming, irreversibility and learning. *The Economic Journal, 107*(442), 636–650.

Valentine, S. C. (2012). Enhancing climate change mitigation efforts through Sino-American collaboration. *The Chinese Journal of International Politics, 6*(2), 159–182.

Van Der Ploeg, F., & Withagen, C. (2012). Too much coal, too little oil. *Journal of Public Economics, 96*(1–2), 62–77.

Van der Toorn, K. (1996). *Family religion in Babylonia, Syria and Israel: Continuity and change in the forms of religious life.* Brill.

Vargo, C. J., Guo, L., & Amazeen, M. A. (2018). The agenda-setting power of fake news: A big data analysis of the online media landscape from 2014 to 2016. *New Media & Society, 20*(5), 2028–2049.

Visser, M. (2003). Gregory Bateson on deutero-learning and double bind: A brief conceptual history. *Journal of the History of the Behavioral Sciences, 39*(3), 269–278.

Vonnegut, K. (2000). *Slaughterhouse-five, or, The children's crusade: A duty-dance with death.* Vintage. (Original work published 1969)

Vries, P. H. (2002). Governing growth: A comparative analysis of the role of the state in the rise of the west. *Journal of World History, 13*(1), 67–138.

Wagner, H. J. (2009). *Energy: The worlds race for resources in the 21st century* (P. Hill, Trans.). Haus Publishing.

Wakefield, S. (2018). Inhabiting the Anthropocene back loop. *Resilience: International Policies, Practices and Discourses, 6*(2), 77–94.

Wakefield, S. (2020). *Anthropocene back loop: Experimentation in unsafe operating space*. Open Humanities Press.

Waldron, J. (2010). *The image of God: Rights, reason, and order*. NYU School of Law, Public Law Research Paper No. 10-85. https://papers.ssrn.com/sol3/papers.cfm?abstract_id=1718054

Walker, D. B. (2003). The displaced self: The experience of atopia and the recollection of place. *Mosaic: A Journal for the Interdisciplinary Study of Literature, 36*(1), 21–33.

Wall, T. F., Gupta, R. P., Gururajan, V. S., & D.K. Zhang, D. K. (1991). The ignition of coal particles. *Fuel, 70*(9), 1011–1016.

Wallerstein, I. (1979). *The capitalist world-economy*. Cambridge University Press.

Wallin, J. J. (2017). Pedagogy at the brink of the post-anthropocene. *Educational Philosophy and Theory, 49*(11), 1099–1111.

Wallin, J. J. (2020). The Holocene simulacrum. *Educational Philosophy and Theory*. doi: 10.1080/00131857.2020.1835644

Wandsnider, L. (1999). Late prehistoric high plains foragers: Sstarving nomads, affluent foragers? *Great Plains Research, 9*(1), 9–39.

Weber, M. (1992). *The Protestant ethic and the spirit of capitalism*. Routledge. (Original work published 1904–5)

West, S., Jamila Haider, L., Stålhammar, S., & Woroniecki, S. (2020). A relational turn for sustainability science? Relational thinking, leverage points and transformations. *Ecosystems and People, 16*(1), 304–325.

Whitehead, M. (2014). *Environmental transformations: A geography of the Anthropocene*. Routledge.

Williams, M. W. (2012). What creates static electricity? *American Scientist, 100*(4), 316–323.

Wills, J. E. Jr. (1993). Maritime Asia, 1500–1800: The interactive emergence of European domination. *The American Historical Review, 98*(1), 83–105.

Wilson Jones, M. (2000). *Principles of Roman architecture*. Yale University Press.

Winterhalder, B. W. (2001). The behavioural ecology of hunter-gatherers. Hunter-gatherers: An interdisciplinary perspective. In C. Panter-Brick, R. H. Laton, & P. Rowley-Conwy (Eds.), *Hunter-gatherers: An interdisciplinary perspective* (pp. 12–38). Cambridge University Press.

Winther, T. (2008). *The impact of electricity: Development, desires and dilemmas*. Berghahn Books.

Wood, B., & Harrison, T. (2011). The evolutionary context of the first hominins. *Nature, 470*(7334), 347–352.

Woodrow, L. (2019). *Climate science communication, storytelling, narrative, Cli-fi* [MA thesis]. Southern Cross University.

Woolf, G. (1992). Imperialism, empire and the integration of the Roman economy. *World Archaeology, 23*(3), 283–293.

REFERENCES

World Nuclear Organization (WNO). (2020). *Where does our electricity come from?* https://www.world-nuclear.org/nuclear-essentials/where-does-our-electricity-come-from.aspx

Wrangham, R. W., & Carmody, R. N. (2010). Human adaptation to the control of fire. *Evolutionary Anthropology, 19*(5), 187–199.

Wright, K. (2017). *Transdisciplinary journeys in the Anthropocene: More-than-human encounters.* Routledge.

Wright, K., & Garrard, A. (2003). Social identities and the expansion of stone bead-making in Neolithic Western Asia: new evidence from Jordan. *Antiquity, 77*(296), 267–284.

Wynn, T. (1993). Two developments in the mind of early Homo. *Journal of Anthropological Archaeology, 12*(3), 299–322.

Yu, P., Xu, R., Abramson, M. J., Li, S., & Guo, Y. (2020). Bushfires in Australia: A serious health emergency under climate change. *The Lancet Planetary Health, 4*(1), e7–e8.

Zayani, M. (2000). Gilles Deleuze, Félix Guattari and the total system. *Philosophy & Social Criticism, 26*(1), 93–114.

Zhu, D., Mortazavi, S. M., Maleki, A., Aslani, A., & Yousefi, H. (2020). Analysis of the robustness of energy supply in Japan: Role of renewable energy. *Energy Reports, 6*, 378–391.

Zimmerman, T. G. (1999). Wireless networked digital devices: A new paradigm for computing and communication. *IBM Systems Journal, 38*(4), 566–574.

Index

1000 Plateaus   7, 10, 18, 126, 140–142
1984   144, 145
9-11   58

Achaemenid Empire   84
Aeolipile   53, 168
Africa   22–25, 31, 34, 42, 43, 46, 50, 51, 84, 157–159, 162, 166, 168–170
agriculture   8, 24–33, 40, 44, 46, 49, 63, 83, 84, 100, 116, 155, 162
Akhenaten   64, 65, 162
Akira   99, 100
Animism   63, 65, 141–143, 163–164
Anthropocene   1–19, 21–37, 103–118, 150–155
Anti-Oedipus   7, 10, 79, 141, 142, 160
art   24, 96, 136, 137, 159, 161, 165, 170
armies   26, 29, 30, 36, 37, 44, 63
astronomy   85, 158
atomic bombs   8, 97–99
atomic theory   85, 87–90, 162, 166, 170
atomic-time   82–96
atopia   17, 176
Australopithecus garhi   22, 156

bacteria   152
Bateson, Gregory   7, 126, 139–142, 156, 175
becoming-animal   141, 142
behaviourism   90, 140
Bergson, Henri   41, 94, 109, 126, 147, 160, 167
Billy Pilgrim   97
Black Sun   86, 93, 159
Blue Mountains   101, 124
bronze   27–30, 40, 47, 63
Bronze Age   155, 161, 167, 171
Buddhism   68, 125, 126, 142, 156, 160

capital   11–19, 34–38, 73–78, 93–100, 128–136, 146–153
capitalism   10–12, 17, 18, 33–39, 56–59, 71–80, 95–99, 110, 126–135, 140–146
capitalocene   9, 163, 169
carbon dioxide (CO_2) emissions   3–6, 48–58, 89–100
Carboniferous   47–49, 173
carbon trails   41–56
cave dwellers   44–46

Cybernetic Culture Research Unit (CCRU)   9, 158
China   25, 29–32, 38, 46–51, 161, 168
Christianity   67–72, 81, 125, 157
cinema   98, 116, 137, 157
citizens   64, 112–114
civil (society)   1, 53, 129
climate change education   13, 15, 104, 155
coal   8, 35–39, 47–59, 91, 92, 161
cockroach   99, 101
collectivity   135, 136, 152
colonialisation   32, 35
colonialism   36, 68, 77, 157
consciousness raising   18, 117, 127–130, 134, 135, 142
computers   37, 40, 75, 100
cooking   28, 43, 162
country   120, 159
COVID-19   1, 89, 116, 138, 150
critical-thinking-practice   149

Dalton, John   87–90, 102, 156, 166, 172
degrowth   18, 122–135, 142, 148, 156–157, 164, 165, 170–171
Deleuze, Gilles   7, 147–150
Deleuze/Guattari   7–12, 118–121
Deleuze's theory of time   94, 95
Democritus   83–88
desire   10–12, 48–54, 66–68, 78, 93, 125–131
deterritorialisation   79–80
Developing world/Third World   115
digital technology   133
double bind   138–150
duality   70, 73, 145
durée   94, 109

ecology   7, 46, 55, 75, 77, 101, 105, 118, 119, 123, 124, 130, 136
economics   17, 34, 38, 71, 72, 78, 113, 124, 153
economy   7, 58, 75, 77, 78, 96, 100, 109–115, 123, 138–140, 145–147
eco-revolution   7, 16–18, 19, 123
education   1, 3, 118
Education for Sustainable Development (ESD)   11, 104, 109, 132, 166
Egypt   3, 29, 30, 46, 49, 63, 64, 155, 156, 172

INDEX

Egyptian   30, 64-5, 130, 165, 170
electric cars   92, 106, 139, 145
end times   150–155
Enlightenment   55, 87, 169
environment   2–5, 8, 12–14, 20–24, 44–50, 78, 79, 106–108, 116–118, 135–137
environmental education   104, 107, 109, 118, 119, 132
electricity   90–93
escape routes   1–10, 12–16, 104–109, 127–132, 150–155
evolution   2, 8, 21–24, 42–49, 55, 64, 77, 105, 135, 160, 162
exchange   14, 28, 34, 49–57, 71, 72, 77, 87, 114

fabulation   147–150
factories   8, 34–38, 74, 75
feedback   3, 16–18, 134, 143
feminism   108, 131, 164, 166
fire   42–47
fire worship   43, 164
fossil fuel capitalism   56–61, 126, 150
fossil fuels   3, 8, 36, 50, 56–61, 92–96, 106–108, 144, 149
Freud, Sigmund   61, 162
furnaces   49–52
future   1–20, 142–144

geoengineering   11, 17, 39, 160
geophilosophy   18, 19, 127, 162
global flow   110, 115, 131
global trade   31–37
global thinking matrix   109–118
globalisation   9, 98, 104, 109–117, 123, 159
Greek mythology   64
green activism   130
green capitalism   39, 128, 140, 174
Green Utopia   123–127
greenwashing   149, 160
Guattari, Felix   14, 118–120
Guattari's 4 zones of the unconscious diagram   14, 107, 118–120, 128
Göbekli Tepe   44, 161
God   64–71
God-heads   62–64

hearth   43, 44, 60
heterodox (methods)   122, 141
Holocene   5, 17–19, 24, 44, 45, 62, 126, 144, 152, 161, 163, 176

hominid   22, 42, 156, 165
hominin   2, 8, 22–24, 27, 28, 38, 42–45, 84, 161, 164, 172
Homo erectus   42, 43
Homo habilis   22, 43, 169
Homo sapiens   22–28, 43–54, 62, 83, 84
hunter/gatherer   45, 62, 63, 73

immanence   19, 76
immanent critique   126, 127, 142
immanent materialism   9, 12, 148, 158
indigenous knowledges   33, 122
industrial   37–40, 52–55, 90–92, 115, 116
Industrial Revolution   50–55, 74, 75, 87, 164, 165
infosphere   75, 76, 78
Ingold, Tim   80, 81, 165
Institute for Interdisciplinary Research into the Anthropocene (IIRA)   19, 40, 60, 81, 102
internet   38, 58, 76, 78, 81, 98, 114–146, 124
iron   30, 31, 40, 50, 54, 165, 171, 173
Islam   67–72, 81, 125, 157, 158, 165

Japan   8, 82, 99–101, 177
Jericho   44
jobs   22, 23, 73, 98, 113
Judaism   65, 81, 156, 165

Kanada   83, 87, 88, 170
Kant, Immanuel   10, 126

Land, Nick   4, 9, 166
libidinal economy   77, 157
literacy   66, 69
Lovecraft, Howard Philips   85, 167
Lyotard, Jean-Francois   76, 77, 167

magic   48, 86, 141
marketing   114, 125, 128, 145, 149, 160
market forces   129, 146
Marx, Karl   79
Marxism   7, 38, 79, 121
May '68   7, 174
measurement of time   2, 3, 151
metallurgy   27–31, 48–52, 155
migration   112, 115, 155, 166
mining   28–31, 47–52, 54, 113
money   11, 28, 33, 34, 38, 49, 52, 57, 59, 71, 73, 76, 78, 93, 95, 105, 115, 122, 123, 130–135, 145

More, Thomas   123, 169
multiculturalism   113

necropolitics   153, 168
neoliberalism   68, 162
Neolithic   25, 27, 28, 31, 44–49, 158, 161, 164
New Green Deal (NGD)   17
Nietzsche, Friedrich   8, 64, 86, 126, 170
nihilism   86, 150
nomads   44, 48, 63, 119, 128, 166, 171, 176
nomadism   52, 54, 119, 152, 154
nonlinear (processes)   2, 3, 14, 24, 34, 36, 38, 41, 49, 54, 82, 135, 147
non-philosophy   152
Now (Nx)   7, 19, 58, 104, 119, 137, 138, 150, 152
nuclear détente   96, 99, 131

OODA cycle   3–5
oil   14, 38, 56, 57, 59, 60, 76, 92, 160, 175
Orwell, George   144, 145, 170

pedagogy   1–3, 19, 40, 56, 57, 60, 62, 67, 81, 85, 102, 103–120, 132–137, 144–147
Persia   51, 87
people-yet-to-come   148, 152
phallocene   61–81
phallus   64–67
phallus-God   67–71
planes of immanence   10, 82, 107
plastics   56, 106, 111
Plato   123, 164, 171
plough   29, 155
politics   5, 6, 14, 78, 79, 115, 144–147, 160–165
polytheism   67
postqualitative   141
pottery   25, 29, 46, 50, 63
power   3–19, 29–31, 37–40, 47–50, 64–74, 87–92, 127–132, 144–147
power stations   53, 57, 92
prehistory   22–24, 42–44
products   54–59, 75, 100, 113–115, 128, 145

quantum mechanics   93–96

Rabbi   66, 170
realism   107, 139, 147–150
research   13–16, 79, 104, 106–118, 129, 134, 135, 151
rhizomatics   10, 59

Rockefeller Brother Fund   59, 172
Rome   50, 54, 60, 160–162, 167
Roman   30, 31, 50–55, 87, 162–167

sales   114
savannah   23
schizoanalysis   10, 141, 142
SCUM manifesto   62, 174
science   4–7, 36, 41, 55, 56, 69, 70, 79, 84, 87–94, 100, 108, 119, 122, 140, 143
Scythians   64, 172
self   10, 70–79, 93, 118, 119, 130, 135
shamanism   43, 67, 73, 81, 84, 118, 153, 158
singularity   9–16, 86, 138–144, 159
situational analysis   105
sixth great extinction event   2, 9, 15–18, 22, 78, 93, 105, 118, 135, 152
skills   22–30, 49–55, 105–108, 113–119
social change   121–137
social ecology   107, 122, 174
society   24–31, 44–52, 121–137, 144–147
solar panels   92, 124, 145
Spinoza   10, 94, 126
state of nature   19, 49, 62
steam engines   8, 52–56, 91
stochastic future   3, 5
stock exchange   36–38, 57, 93, 169
stone age   22–27, 42–47, 158, 170–172
subsistence (survival)   21, 24–29, 44–50, 171
Sumer   30, 63
Sustainable Development Goals (SDGs)   11, 104, 166

tax   49, 51, 57
teaching and learning   12–14, 103–120, 134–136, 151–154
technology   6, 7, 16, 30, 36, 50, 57, 71, 97, 98, 110–122, 133, 149
television   37, 40, 90, 98, 116
Tesla   129
thermodynamics   4, 41, 90, 161
time   1–20, 82–102, 142–144, 150–154
theology   67–71, 165, 166, 171
Thomson, Joseph John   91
Thunberg, Greta   12, 13
tool-enhancement   21–40
Tokyo   100, 101
transport   32, 50–54, 75, 92, 107, 116

unconscious drives   8–10, 18, 54–56, 83, 96, 104, 105, 111, 112, 118, 122, 125, 127, 128, 136–141
United Nations   11, 38, 89, 90
Uruk   63
Utopia   18, 39, 123–137, 142, 148, 169

values   5, 16, 36, 37, 59, 98, 101, 113–116, 125
vitalism   41, 42, 94, 162, 169, 170
Vonnegut, Kurt   96–98, 175

War Machine   55
Watt, James   53, 173
What is Philosophy?   18, 127, 152, 160
World Health Organization (WHO)   89, 90
world machine   4, 37–40
wood (as fuel source)   24, 39, 45–52, 91

yurt   26